MW00695297

Liberation Theology

Liberation
THEOLOGY

by

EMILIO A. NÚÑEZ C.

translated by
Paul E. Sywulka

MOODY PRESS

CHICAGO

Except where indicated otherwise, all Scripture quotations are from
the *New American Standard Bible,* © 1960, 1962, 1963, 1968, 1971,
1972, 1973, 1975, and 1977 by The Lockman Foundation, and are used
by permission.

Orbis Books (Maryknoll, N.Y.) has graciously given permission to use
extended quotations from the following works: Gustavo Gutiérrez, *A
Theology of Liberation: History, Politics and Salvation,* © 1973. Juan Luis
Segundo, *The Liberation of Theology,* © 1976. Jon Sobrino, *Christology at
the Crossroads: A Latin American Approach,* © 1978.

A Theology of Liberation: History, Politics and Salvation and *Christology at the Crossroads: A Latin American Approach* are also used with
permission of SCM Press, London, England. *The Liberation of Theology* is
also used with permission of Gill and Macmillan, Dublin, Ireland.

Library of Congress Cataloging in Publication Data
Núñez C., Emilio Antonio.
   Liberation theology.

   Bibliography: p.
   Includes index.
   1. Liberation theology—Controversial literature.
2. Evangelicalism—Latin America. 3. Latin America—
Church history. I. Title.
BT83.57.N87   1985   230   85-15231
ISBN 0-8024-4893-3

Printed in the United States of America

Contents

CHAPTER   PAGE

Introduction   7

PART ONE
The Historical and Social Context of Liberation Theology
1. Latin America—Yesterday and Today   17

PART TWO
Historical Outline of Liberation Theology
2. European Influence in Liberation Theology   35
3. Church and Society in Latin America: ISAL   53
4. The New Catholicism and Liberation Theology   83
5. The Immediate Origin of Liberation Theology   113

PART THREE
The Method of Liberation Theology
6. A New Way of Doing Theology   131

PART FOUR
Some Fundamental Themes of Liberation Theology
7. Salvation and Liberation   175
8. Jesus the Liberator   207
9. The Ecclesiology of Liberation   241

CONCLUSION
10. Evangelical Theology and Praxis for Latin America   275
    Bibliography   291
    General Index   299
    Scripture Index   303

Acknowledgments

I am deeply grateful to Moody Press for encouraging me to write on the subject of liberation theology; to Paul Sywulka for assuming the responsibililty of translating the work into English; to Manuel Fernández for helping in the translation; and to all those who in one way of another have made this book possible.

I am especially thankful to my wife, Sara, who continually encouraged me to complete the task, even though she was going through a time of serious illness.

May the praise, the honor, and the glory be to Him who having died, risen, and ascended, gives us authentic liberation.

Introduction

Thousands of pages have been written during the past ten years on Latin American liberation theology. Why, then, another book on the same subject? If there is anything special about the present work it is simply that I have written it as a Latin American evangelical who not only was born and raised in a proletarian home in the republic of El Salvador, but also was a member of the working class in my adolescent years, before becoming an elementary school teacher. In addition, I have had a ministry for forty years of preaching the gospel especially among the poor of Central America. I have, therefore, personally experienced the sad economic and social reality that faces the great majority of Latin American people. I know firsthand the anguish, frustrations, and hopes of those people, of whom I feel a part and on whom I have not wanted to turn my back in the theological and ideological controversy that surrounds liberation theology.

I have written the following pages in an attitude of loyalty to the gospel and commitment to my people. In this book liberation theology is approached from the perspective of an evangelical who is Latin American. The order in which those last two terms are expressed is of vital importance to me: that which is evangelical must be placed before that which is merely racial, geographic, cultural, and social.

THE IMPORTANCE OF THE SUBJECT

Contrary to what North American and European observers once believed, the theology of liberation in its various forms has not been a passing fad on the contemporary theological scene. This theology appears to have come to stay with us, whether as a system of thought that carries within itself the seed of its own transformation, or as an aggregate of ideas or questions that are already exercising a profound influence on the theological movements of our time.

Proof of that influence may be seen in the interest that the international theological community has shown in the study of the different theologies of liberation, including, of course, black liberation theology, the theology of women's liberation, and Latin American liberation theology—not to mention the different shades that the last one has acquired through the years.

That liberation theology is also exercising an influence, one way or another, in evangelical circles of the so-called Third World, cannot be denied. Among Latin American evangelical thinkers there has been a renewed interest to seriously study the social implications of the gospel in answer, directly or indirectly, to the challenge of liberation theology. A number of essays have been published in which Latin American evangelical authors evaluate this theological system from a serious academic point of view.[1]

The importance of liberation theology lies not only in its influence in different parts of the world, but also in the characteristics that its representatives attribute to it.

For example, liberationist writers are convinced that their work is eminently theological, notwithstanding their extensive use of the social sciences in their analysis of Latin American reality and in their teaching on the nature and mission of the church. They speak of "a new way of doing theology," not of "a new way of

1. For example, Samuel Escobar, "Beyond Liberation Theology"; the writings of C. René Padilla, especially: "Mensaje bíblico y revolución," "Iglesia y Sociedad en América Latina," "Una nueva manera de hacer teología," "La teología de la liberación," "¿Un nuevo Gustavo Gutiérrez?", and his contribution to the Third International Conference of Institutions for Christian Higher Education, Dordt College, Sioux Center, Iowa, August 13-20, 1981 entitled *The Theology of Liberation* (mimeographed); and Orlando Costas, *Theology of the Crossroads in Contemporary Latin America*. Costas gives a general description and evaluation of the Protestant liberation movement known as Iglesia y Sociedad en la América Latina (ISAL).

doing sociology," even though they admit that their current of thought goes from the social context to the biblical text, from sociology to theology.

They lead us to believe as well that their reflection is biblical, inasmuch as they discover in the Scriptures paradigms of liberation, such as the event of the Exodus in the Pentateuch and the political nature of the kingdom that Jesus and His apostles announced.

They insist, furthermore, on the Christian character of their theology. Liberation theology, they say, addresses the matter of being authentic Christians in a situation of economic dependence and therefore of underdevelopment and social injustice. It deals with what it means to be the true church of Jesus Christ in the context of misery, and concludes that to be the true church is to be in favor of the oppressed.

The theologians of liberation emphasize time after time the Latin American nature of their theological reflection. They affirm that theirs is a theology forged in a social context of extreme poverty and abandonment, a theology for the masses who suffer the tragic results of their economic and political dependence under the domination of neocolonialist powers on the national and international scene. They point out at the same time the "scientific" character of their analysis of the Latin American context, which means that they have also made use of Marxist tools for the description and transformation of society. Those and other characteristics suggested by the liberationists make their system of thought worthy of careful study, especially on the part of evangelicals.

Latin American theology of liberation is much more than an academic exercise for professors and students of theology who enjoy the comforts of an opulent society. It is true that liberationism runs the risk of becoming another bourgeois consumer product in the market of ideas, but its content comes from outside the classroom and carries a message of disquieting social significance.

Because of its bold reference to the situation of extreme poverty in which millions of Latin Americans live, and because of its valiant exhortation for the church to assume its Christian responsibility in that context of spiritual, moral, and material destitution, liberation theology has captured the attention of many Christians around the world. This new way of doing theology cannot be brushed

aside. If it is easy to refute the methodology of liberation theologians, it is not easy to overlook the painful social and ecclesiastical
reality it points out.

The humanitarianism of liberation theology has stirred up great
interest among First World theologians who are sensitive to the
social problems of the underdeveloped nations and who view with
nonpaternalistic eyes the emergence of indigenous theologians in
other latitudes. There seems to be a strong current of sympathy
toward liberation theology in conciliar (ecumenical) Protestantism around the world. Even among Protestant theologians outside
the ecumenical circle there are those who are more ready to point
out the positive features of liberation theology than to denounce
its negative aspects.

In certain Protestant circles it is easy to become popular and
even to obtain academic prestige by speaking only in terms that
favor the theology of liberation. To adopt a critical attitude—even
in the most objective way possible—toward liberationism is to
become known as someone who "is out of contact with social
reality" or who "has not been liberated from North American
fundamentalist Protestantism." The fear of being classified in that
way and of being excluded from the international theological
community may intimidate us Latin American evangelicals, compelling us to maintain a non-critical posture—which in itself is not
academic—or to keep a guilty silence. On the other hand, it may
be expected that the majority of theological professionals will be
ready to listen with due respect to other ideas, including those
that we may offer, regarding a theology that has emerged on our
Latin American soil.

Something should be said about the acceptance of liberation
theology in Latin America. As far as the evangelical church in
general is concerned, it is evident that the theology of liberation,
even its Protestant variety, has not yet reached the ordinary church
members or the great majority of evangelical pastors and other
church leaders in the rural and urban areas of most Latin American
countries. But it is a topic of study in theological seminaries, and
it is not out of the realm of possibility that in the near future the
Protestant liberation movement might grow, especially in those
countries that are experiencing profound social transformations.

At present, the influence of Protestant liberation theologians has
not reached the vast majority of Latin American evangelicals. That

is due in part to the fact that Protestant liberationists have not expressed their ideas in popular language. Their books are not easy reading, and no one has attempted to make them readable for people who read very little, particularly when it comes to works with heavy doctrinal content.

The opposite has occurred in Latin American Catholicism, which finds itself divided over liberation theology. There this theology has been able to descend to the level of the people, in some countries more than in others, and it already has its heroes and martyrs. Some priests have made an effort to teach the basic content of liberation theology on a popular level.[2]

Among the clergy as well as the laity one may find Catholics who favor liberationism and at the same time others who reject it and even condemn it as heretical. Until recently the Vatican had not declared itself officially against the theology of liberation. Pope John Paul II had only tried to limit the political activism of the Catholic priests in Latin America. The Latin American Episcopal Conference (CELAM), when it met in Puebla, Mexico, in 1979, did not step back from the liberating process begun officially in Medellin, Colombia, in 1968; it did not repudiate liberation theology, but rather made an effort to show how it fit within the official teaching of the Roman Catholic church.[3] But a document opposing liberation theology produced by the Vatican in September of 1984 has accentuated the antagonism of the pope toward this Latin American theological system.

Liberation theology may continue to refine itself, or to evolve, or to diversify; but it is also possible that its methodology will continue to influence the development of Latin American theology for a long time to come. At least it will not be possible to return to the days when theology in Latin America was simply a copy of a theology forged in a different social context. Although from a conservative evangelical point of view the liberationist hermeneutic is questionable, it has pointed out dramatically the importance for our theological reflection of taking into account the social reality of which we are a part.

2. See for example the book *Vamos caminando,* published by the Pastoral Team of Bambamarca, Peru, to teach the rural people "a liberating theology in the broadest sense of the word, following the lines drawn by Vatican II, Medellín and the document "Evangelization of the Peruvian Episcopate" (p. 10).
3. Francisco Interdonato, *Teología Latinoaméricana,* pp. 153-65.

We Latin American evangelicals can no longer withdraw from our responsibility to think and speak theologically on the basis of the Scriptures in answer to the vital needs of our own people.

THE APPROACH TO THE SUBJECT

There is more than one way to treat the theology of liberation. In this book the focus is primarily biblical and theological, although the sociological foundations and implications of Latin American liberationism are not overlooked.

Special attention is given to Roman Catholic liberation theology, in view of the fact that it is the best-known type of liberation theology both in and outside of Latin America. But reference is also made to what can be called Latin American Protestant liberationism, although it is not my purpose to analyze each and every one of the liberationist theologians. That would be a project too ambitious for the limits and objectives of this introductory work.

It should be obvious that it is impossible to evaluate liberation theology without entering the area of politics. Liberation theologians affirm that their hermeneutic is political and that the gospel has a political dimension. To evangelize is to "politicize." Furthermore, they have opted for socialism,[4] as over against capitalism, explaining, of course, that the socialism they advocate does not necessarily have to be the same as that which is practiced in other latitudes. That political option creates a serious problem for the Christian who wants to evaluate liberation theology, because he cannot make any negative comments about it without running the risk of being called a "defender of the capitalists, or imperialists." That accusation can be very dangerous in an atmosphere charged with political passions, just as the tag of "leftist" is dangerous for the theologian who, without having opted for any leftist political system, speaks out on behalf of the integral liberation of men and women.

I have the profound conviction that the written revelation of God is far above all political ideologies as the final word of authority for the faith and conduct of the Christian, and that every political system, far from being absolute, is relative, imperfect, and temporary, and therefore is always subject to change, whereas the Word of the Lord abides forever.

4. Gustavo Gutierrez, *A Theology of Liberation,* pp. 111-14.

Within the scope of those human matters that are relative, political systems have their place in society; but the Christian is not called to confer on any of those systems the quality of the absolute, because that which is absolute is found only in God. Furthermore, without pretending to have a false political neutrality, the Christian should always reserve the right to criticize any political system, whether of the left or of the right, in the light of the Word of God. It should not be forgotten that even the theologians of liberation have their "eschatological reservation" in order to deny finality to all political systems.

Those observations have been made because in the discussions about liberation theology there seem to be those who are more interested in defending a political system, whether of the left or of the right, than in rendering unconditional obedience to the Scriptures.

It is also necessary to clarify that I do not direct myself to specialists in the more intricate themes of theology and philosophy, nor to experts in the social sciences, but rather to pastors and seminary students and to other evangelical Christians who desire to obtain basic information on the origin, nature, and objectives of Latin American liberation theology. Those topics are discussed here from the point of view of a Latin American evangelical who desires to be faithful to the Scriptures and at the same time listen to the cry for freedom that comes from his people.

If this book promotes within the Christian community the study of liberation theology under the authority of the Word and of the Spirit, and if it stimulates other evangelicals to express themselves freely on this important subject, I will consider myself amply rewarded for my efforts. And may the honor, the glory, and the praise be to the Lord of the church and of history, now and forever. Amen.

Part One

The Historical and Social
Context of
Liberation Theology

1

Latin America: Yesterday and Today

The theology of liberation treated in this book is a theological system developed in the context of Latin America with the special purpose of answering the social and economic problems of those countries. One of the major distinctives of theological liberationism is its great emphasis on the social context. Other theologies focus on contemporary social problems, but they do so in an atmosphere of economic affluence, in which it is difficult to understand the anguish of the underdeveloped countries. Such is the case with European political theology, of which the best known representatives are the Roman Catholic theologian J. B. Metz and the Protestant theologian Jürgen Moltmann.[1] In contrast, liberation theology has as its social frame of reference the reality of poverty in Latin America.

Furthermore, liberation theologians say that theological reflection should be a product of the social situation and praxis, rooted in the struggle to free those who are oppressed under unjust economic structures. These theologians move from society to theology and give preeminence to the social context, so in order to understand liberation theology it is essential at least to give an

---

1. Johannes B. Metz, *Theology of the World;* Jürgen Moltmann, *Theology of Hope;* Moltmann, *The Crucified God.*

overview of Latin American social reality, emphasizing the way in which theological liberationism analyzes that reality.

HISTORICAL PERSPECTIVE

COLONIAL RULE: A HIERARCHY OF OPPRESSION

Sociologically speaking, the problems of Latin America have their roots in the period of the Iberian conquest and colonization. To be sure, in the pre-Colombian epoch there was also violence, oppression, and even imperialism among the American Indians, as can be seen, for example, in the history of the Aztecs in Mexico and the Incas in Peru.[2] But we are especially interested in the social situation that resulted from the European conquest and colonization, because many aspects of the new order implanted by the Iberians are still prevalent in Latin American culture. That new order annulled or at least repressed that of the American Indians, who were subjected in one way or another to the culture of their conquerors. In addition, ethnic fusion has helped to give Latin America its distinctive character. The racial result of the union between American Indians and Iberians is one of the most important anthropological and sociological factors in the formation of Latin American culture.[3]

The Spaniards took American Indian concubines and, so to speak, procreated a new race. They had come to America, not with their families to establish a European colony in the territories they hoped to discover, but rather to carry out a commercial, political, and religious exploit. It was hoped that the expedition of Christopher Columbus would confirm the existence of a shorter route to India, increase commerce with the Far East, add territories to the Spanish dominion, and extend the influence of Christianity under the papal banner.

Christopher Columbus was a religious man who seems to have

2. Pablo Pérez, *Misión y liberación*, pp. 1-17.
3. Enrique Dussel, *History and the Theology of Liberation: A Latin American Perspective*, p. 79. "From the very start, for us, means from the start of our history in 1492. Our mother is Amerindia, our father Spain—or vice versa, if you will. But the child of this union is something *new*. It is not the culture of Amerindia, Spain, or Europe; nor is it the culture of the Incas or the Aztecs. It is a new culture, a mixed culture, a creole or mestizo culture" (p. 32).

taken very seriously the responsibility of Christianizing the people in the territories he discovered. But what the Iberians sought to implant in America was Christendom, that is to say the European cultural, social, and political system, of which the church was only a part, at the service of economic and political interests, represented by the king of Spain and the pope.[4] That produced ecclesiastical dependence, along with cultural, economic, and political dependence. The church established in America was truly colonial, governed from the other side of the Atlantic for the benefit of the Spanish crown and the papacy.

The dominant social class during the colonial period was formed by the "peninsulars," that is to say the Spaniards born on the Iberian peninsula. The *criollos* (natives), or Spaniards born in America, occupied a second place on the social scale. They were followed in descending order by the *mestizos* (mixed race), who even after independence suffered a crisis of identity—in some countries more than in others—and found themselves excluded from public office in a system dominated by the classes above them. The indigenous race, the "Amerindians," occupied the lowest level in colonial society. The pattern of Spanish class society has been transferred to America.

It can be said of the Christianization of Latin America that in general there was an imposition of medieval, Spanish, and Roman Christianity, but not an evangelization that would convert people to New Testament Christianity. The missionary effort resulted mainly in what we know as popular Catholic religiosity, and in a syncretism of European Christianity with the religion of the indigenous peoples. Today there are still those who worship their ancient gods as they bow before the images of Roman Catholic saints.

It is only fair, however, to recognize that the missionary effort of the Roman Catholic church in Latin America had its positive side. Some missionaries dedicated themselves with great zeal and a spirit of sacrifice to the communication of their message. They lived among the people, learned their native languages, and were in many respects an example of the doctrine they preached. Some of those missionaries became valiant defenders of the American Indians in the face of the abuses committed by the colonizers.

4. Ibid., pp. 75-80.

Special mention should be made of Bartolomé de las Casas, who is known in American history as "the protector of the Indians."[5]

It should be mentioned as well that we owe to the Roman Catholic missionary enterprise the fact that the name of Christ was announced in these lands centuries before the establishment of the Latin American evangelical church. That there were distortions of the gospel message in the church of the colonial period no one can deny; but it is also true that Christianity was not totally unknown in America when the pioneer evangelical missionaries landed on its shores. The case is quite different in other regions of the world where Protestant missionaries have had to develop their work in a culture dominated by religions that do not profess to be Christian.

At any rate, the Catholic church was part of the Iberian project and gave its backing, directly or indirectly, to the social system imported from the peninsula, a semi-feudal system in which the American Indians became dispossessed of their lands and subjected by force to the service of their conquerors. The voice of the missionaries who defended the aborigines was for all practical purposes a cry in the desert. The laws established by the Spanish court to protect the American Indians were not applied as they should have been. Aborigine, the mestizo, and others on a similar social level were at the base of the pyramid, supporting their oppressors.

The ecclesiastical dignitaries were not at the bottom, but rather at the top of the pyramid, next to the civil and military leaders. The stratification of colonial society was well established. Movement from one social level to another was very difficult, and in a sense even impossible for the great majority of people. The colonizers held the concept of aristocracy, of oligarchy, of civil and ecclesiastical hierarchy, not of democracy. The truth of the matter is that no one spoke of democracy in those days. The populace existed to serve the interests of the large landholders, of the civil and ecclesiastical officials, of the crown and the church.

5. Herbert Herring, *A History of Latin America,* pp. 174-77. Moved by his desire to defend the Amerindians, Las Casas proposed in 1517 that Negroes be brought in as substitutes for them. It is said that some time later he became sorry for having suggested such an atrocity and promoted the reform of the *encomienda* system. See Lewis Hanke, *The Spanish Struggle for Justice in the Conquest of America* (Philadelphia: U. of Pennsylvania, 1949).

INDEPENDENCE: CONTINUED INJUSTICE

The independence movement came especially from those of Spanish ancestry who were born in America, the criollos.[6] There were priests, such as José Matías Delgado in Central America and José María Morelos and Miguel Hidalgo y Costilla in Mexico, who joined this movement in spite of the fact that the pope condemned it.[7] It is possible that some of the criollo priests may have seen in independence from Spain an opportunity to ascend the hierarchical ladder.

The influence of the French Revolution and the independence of the United States was evident in the intellectual circles of Spanish America. Those two expressions of liberty were in some sense a fruit of the Enlightenment, the intellectual current in Europe that in the seventeenth and eighteenth centuries led to rationalism and deism, and on the political level to a denial of divine right of kings. In the French Revolution (1789-1794) the spirit of Enlightenment expressed itself in a worship of the goddess of Reason, a determination to eliminate aristocracy and clericalism, a heightened sense of nationalism and the right of the individual, and a desire to establish a new social order based on the ideals of liberty, equality, and fraternity.

Political liberalism, which had a notable influence on the political life of Latin America, was nourished from the fountains of the Enlightenment. The Spanish court could not keep liberal ideas from coming to America and fomenting desire for freedom. Furthermore, at the beginning of the nineteenth century the political situation became propitious in Europe for the independence of the Spanish colonies in America.

But the liberal ideas imported from Europe did not produce on this side of the Atlantic a truly popular revolution in the nineteenth century. Independence brought a mere change of rulers—not of the social and economic system. The system established by the

6. Severo Martínez Peláez, *La Patria del criollo* (San José, Costa Rica: Editorial Universitaria Centroamericana, 1975). See also Dussel, *History and Theology,* pp. 98-101.
7. Speaking of the attitude of Rome toward the independence of Latin America, Dussel says: "She could not accept Latin American independence, and condemned it in 1816. There is actually an encyclical condemning our revolution, our struggle for independence. San Martín was not only regarded as a traitor by Spain; he was condemned by the Pope" (*History and Theology,* p. 97).

colonizers effectively prevailed, for neither the initiative nor the direction of the independence movement had come from the masses. They do not seem to have been even aware of the possibility of a radical change in social structures. They resigned themselves to remain at the base of the pyramid, supporting all the weight of the privileged classes.

Although the church lost some of its privileges as a result of independence, it kept its place of influence in the religious sphere and also in the political sphere, especially when the new republics were governed by archconservatives. Independence did not bring changes that would significantly affect the relationship between church and state, or between the church and the dominant classes, or between the church and the populace in general. It may be said that independence took place within the general framework of Roman Catholic conservatism. The French Revolution of 1789 was not repeated in Latin America, even on a small scale.

LIBERALISM AND GROWING UNREST

In some countries, however, the influence of political liberalism grew and brought about changes in both the legislation and the culture of Latin America. Among other things, the liberals insisted on respect for the citizen's political rights, the separation of church and state, and an education both free from religious control and available to all. Due to those ideas, which were saturated with a strong anticlericalism, the liberals were seen as great enemies of the church. The church in turn had to depend on popular religiosity in order to maintain its prestige and political power. As an ideology, liberalism especially drew the attention of the intellectuals and in the name of science opened the way for positivism and pantheism.[8]

Of special interest to Latin American evangelicals is the fact that the liberals saw in Protestantism a weapon to undermine the power of the clergy. It was partly for that reason that they showed a favorable attitude toward Anglo-Saxon Protestant missionaries. In Guatemala, for example, President Justo Rufino Barrios, leader of the liberal revolution in 1871, invited Presbyterian missionaries from the United States in 1882 to establish the Protestant church

8. John A. Mackay, *The Other Spanish Christ.*

in that Central American country. But General Barrios, as in the case of many other liberals in Latin America, did not become converted to Protestantism. He remained a Catholic, at least in his public life.[9] It is also worthy of note that in spite of backing from the liberals, Latin American Protestantism continued to represent a small minority of very little social influence throughout the period of its beginning, consolidation, and first expansion—that is, from the middle of the nineteenth century to the end of World War II. Dictators who considered themselves liberals politically and socially, such as Jorge Ubico of Guatemala (1931-1944), looked favorably on the Protestants in some ways, perhaps because they considered them politically harmless.

During the second half of the nineteenth century, while the battle between Latin American liberals and conservatives was becoming more intense, positivism was flowering in Europe, and Darwinism and Marxism were putting down their roots. Under Pope Pius IX (1846-1878) the Roman Catholic church made a desperate effort to maintain its political and religious influence. The pope condemned liberalism, which in those days was his number one enemy, and declared himself infallible; but his efforts were not able to prevent the loss of temporal power for the papacy.

In the face of the onslaught of socialist ideas, Pope Leo XIII wrote in 1891 his famous encyclical *Rerum Novarum,* which deals with the problems of the working class and is known as the first pontifical social document in the modern world. Leo XIII also condemned rationalism and made an effort to revive the philosophy of Thomas Aquinas in the teaching ministry of the Roman Catholic church. Under the sign of *Rerum Novarum* the Catholic Church tried to recuperate what it had lost both politically and socially under the liberal Latin American regimes. In Europe Catholic thinkers such as Jacques Maritain had the vision of a "new Christendom." Catholic Action and the Christian Democratic parties of those days tried to put into practice the social teaching of the Catholic church. But the crusade for reconquest did not have all the success in Latin America that its leaders had hoped for, in spite of the fact that in the period between the two great wars the liberal oligarchy was declining. The "new Christendom" was unable to attract the attention of the Latin American masses. It did not

9. Paul Burgess, *Justo Rufino Barrios,* (Quezaltenango, Guatemala: Tipografía El Noticiero Evangélico, 1946).

provide an answer to the new aspirations for a better future. The Latin American people did not want to look back, but rather wanted to continue in quest for their freedom. The awakening of Hispanic America to a new era of great social transformations had already begun.

International criticism of Facism and Nazism brought discredit to the Latin American dictators. Systematic publicity in favor of democracy in the Western World left its mark in many consciences. During the final years of World War II there was wide circulation in Latin America of well-illustrated magazines that communicated the idea that the armies allied against the Berlin-Rome-Tokyo axis were fighting heroically in the defense of freedom. As they read that literature, Latin Americans living under the weight of dictatorship in their own countries asked themselves whether democracy should not also exist for them. It was ironic that Latin American dictators should declare war against Hitler and Mussolini. The word "democracy" had become dangerous for the oppressors of the Latin American people.

The means of mass communication—the written and spoken press, movies, and television—made known more widely, and in considerable detail, the possibility of another way of life, completely different from that of the underdeveloped countries. Progress in the means of transportation, along with the growth of tourism and international trade, helped to point out the enormous difference between the rich countries and the poor ones.

Marxist propaganda, which had sought to sow the seed of social discontent in Latin America since the triumph of the socialist revolution in Russia, became more intense after World War II in the wake of the military and diplomatic victory of the Soviet Union in that conflict.

After the war a cry for liberty was heard throughout the world. The colonialist structures in Asia and Africa began to crack. New independent nations came into being, free at last from the foreign powers that had ruled them for so long. In Latin America as well people became possessed by a spirit of protest and a desire for social change. Several dictators met their end. It was hoped that the democracy for which many lives had been sacrificed in Europe, Africa, and the Far East would become effective in the Americas.

Many Latin Americans believed with Franklin Delano Roosevelt that "true individual freedom cannot exist without economic security and independence."[10] They demanded, therefore, the same rights set forth by the American President in his annual message to Congress in January, 1944: the right to a useful and well-paid job; the right to earn enough for food, clothing, and recreation; the right of every farmer to cultivate land and sell his produce with enough profit to provide him and his family with a decent living; the right of every businessman to do business in an atmosphere free from unjust competition and the control of national and international monopolies; the right of every family to have good housing; the right to receive proper medical attention and enjoy good health; the right to be protected from financial fears related to sickness, accidents, unemployment, and old age; the right to get a good education. All that, said President Roosevelt, means security.[11]

Latin Americans who were aware of their social problems received favorably the Universal Declaration of Human Rights, adopted by the General Assembly of the United Nations in 1948, and at first viewed that global organization as a promise of the coming of a better era for all peoples. Unfortunately for the great majority of people in Latin America as well as in other regions of the so-called Third World, the pronouncements about human rights were characterized by a great deal of idealism and very few tangible results.

During the decade of the sixties the clamor for social change continued in Latin America. Of special interest for the study of this period is the effect of the Cuban revolution on the Latin American consciousness and on the policy of the United States toward Latin America. There is no doubt that at first the triumph of Fidel Castro created a great expectation of freedom in millions of Latin Americans. Many saw in the struggle against Fulgencio Batista, the dictator of Cuba, a model and a beginning of freedom for all Latin America. For its part, the American government responded to Castro's Marxist revolution with the invasion of the Bay of Pigs and with the Alliance for Progress, an ambitious project of economic and social development for the Latin American countries. The first of those efforts did not succeed in overthrowing the Cuban re-

10. Franklin D. Roosevelt, "A New Bill of Rights," in *The Annals of America* (Chicago: Encyclopedia Britannica, 1968), 16:213-14.
11. Ibid.

gime, nor did the second reach its objective. Meanwhile, social unrest continued in Latin America.

In the religious sphere, the teachings of popes John XXIII and Paul VI and the documents of the Second Vatican Council (1962-1965) encouraged those Catholics who were hoping for an authentic ecclesiastical renovation that would favor the oppressed peoples. A new day seemed to be dawning for Catholicism around the world. In Latin America, the bishops meeting at the conference in Medellín, Colombia, in 1968 had the courage to turn their faces toward the impoverished masses. A movement had even sprung up among South American Protestants under the name "Church and Society in Latin America" (ISAL), which would become a pioneer in liberation theology.

UNDERDEVELOPMENT AND DEPENDENCE

Sociological analysis has pointed out that there are developed nations—some of them highly developed—and underdeveloped nations. Latin America fits in the last category, with a few exceptions. Some Latin American countries have reached very low levels of development. The statistics are alarming, in spite of the effort made in some circles to minimize them. Admittedly there may be a manipulation of the statistics; but apart from the technical reports about economic and social underdevelopment, the ordinary observer is struck with the sad condition in which millions of Latin Americans live. It is not necessary to be an expert in the social sciences to point out at least some of the causes of that situation.

The fact that Latin America's social problems have their origin in the colonial period does not justify their existence; neither is their existence justified by the fact that there are poor people in the developed countries. Regarding the last statement, it is not correct to equate, for example, poverty in North America with the poverty of Latin America; the difference is huge. Also, to say that Latin Americans are lazy by nature is nothing more than a generalization. Millions of Latin Americans work diligently from sunrise to sunset and yet remain all their lives in extreme poverty because they do not receive a fair salary for their efforts. It is also a generalization to say that Latin American workers do not move ahead economically because of alcoholism or because they do not want to or cannot better themselves.

From a biblical standpoint there is no justification for the destitution experienced by many Latin Americans in the false meaning attributed to Jesus' statement to the disciples that the poor would always be with them (John 12:8). Our Lord did not say that there should be poor people economically and socially, but that there always would be. Much less did He want to exempt from guilt those who through selfishness cause or increase the poverty of their fellow men. There will always be poor people because of the evil of the human heart.

The vast majority of Latin American evangelicals do not find it hard to understand the reality of underdevelopment because they themselves experience it every day. No one has to convince them that poverty exists; they are looking straight at it, without the need for statistical charts. For Latin American evangelicals the problem has to do with the causes of poverty and with its cure, not with its reality, which is very evident. The deficiency in housing, health, and education is enormous. In some countries the illiteracy rate is still very high. The number of undernourished children is in the millions. Not all Latin American children will have the opportunity to be fed well, receive medical attention, finish their studies in elementary school, enjoy healthful and instructive recreation, and move ahead in their vocations. According to economic predictions, there is no hope at present that all of them will find work when they get old enough to join the working ranks of their respective countries.

A statistical study made in preparation for the Third General Conference of Latin American Bishops in 1979 states:

> Deficient nutrition in children under five years old has arisen as an alarming and untreatable aspect of the problem especially in the light of its long range consequences for the health level of the population. Sample studies carried out in 13 Latin American countries and three countries of the Caribbean in different years between 1965 and 1970 indicate that the percentage of undernourished children (malnutrition being defined by a weight 10% or more under the theoretical normal weight) oscillated between 37% and 80%. With respect to the countries as a whole, more than half these children were undernourished, and in seven countries two thirds or more were undernourished. Second degree malnutrition (a weight 25% or more under normal) affected 20% or more of the sample population.[12]

12. *Iglesia y América Latina: Cifras* (Bogotá: Consejo Episcopal Latinoamericano [CELAM], 1978), p. 51.

Regarding basic services and housing, the report indicates that "in 1971 less than 50% of the urban population in some countries and less than 50% of the rural population in most countries had a supply of water that was safe to drink. In 15 out of 23 countries for which there are statistics for 1970, less than 50% of the urban population had access to sewage service." It also states that "rising costs and the increase in applications for enrollment indicate that the educational crisis will grow steadily worse in the decade of 1980, unless other priorities and hopes are placed first."[13]

The statistical study quoted here seeks to be objective and optimistic, but six years later overwhelming figures continue to be heard regarding our underdevelopment. It is said, for example, 75 percent of the population of Brazil lives in poverty, and it is estimated that 30 percent of the inhabitants of that country find themselves in an extremely precarious situation.[14]

Those facts are sufficient to give an idea, certainly a very general one, of the reality of poverty that confronts Latin America. It is not necessary to set forth the many details that others have presented from a technical point of view in order to understand the situation from which the theologians of liberation speak to us.

One of the principal characteristics of liberation theology is the effort of its authors to make an in-depth study of the Latin American social problem. To that end they avail themselves of the social sciences. At the same time they take for granted that the best economic and social analysis comes from Karl Marx, although they admit that in a certain sense it is necessary to adapt Marxist thought to the concrete situation of Latin America.

Liberation theologians conclude that underdevelopment is a product of the economic dependence of poor countries on rich countries. The fact that there are underdeveloped countries is due to the existence of highly developed countries, those that have taken advantage of others to reach their high level of development. In other words, the development of the rich countries depends on the underdevelopment of the poor countries. The highly developed countries dominate and direct international commerce. They continue to be colonialist in the sense that they exploit underdeveloped countries, so that they obtain cheap raw materials and labor and have markets where they are able to set the price of

13. Ibid., pp. 51, 53.
14. *Lausanne Communique,* December 1983.

their products. In defense of their economic empire they resort to political manipulation of the underdeveloped countries, and if they believe it necessary they opt for military intervention. In that way neo-colonialism sets forth one of its most odious expressions. It is said, furthermore, that in order to maintain their economic and political supremacy the international colonialist powers count on the full backing of the dominant classes in the underdeveloped countries.

But the theologians of liberation seem deluded by ideology when they suggest that the oppression of some nations by others is an evil only of capitalism. Their silence in regard to oppression in socialist and communist societies is eloquent. If for denouncing such oppression the danger of persecution for the church is greater on one side than on the other, that is another indication of the degree of freedom that the people of God have in different parts of the world. To adapt the concept of freedom to the ideology of the system in power does not solve the problem. God freed Israel from slavery in Egypt because He wanted His people to have full freedom to serve Him in the presence of all nations. That is also the freedom that the church should have in today's world.

DEVELOPMENT OR REVOLUTION

The thesis of dependency is accompanied in liberation theology by a total rejection of developmentalism as an answer to the Latin American problem. They do so even though the Second Vatican Council, the Episcopal Conference in Medellín, Colombia, and the teachings of John XXIII and Paul IV support the concept of global development as a way to deal with social problems of our time.

For their part, liberation theologians prefer to go far beyond the social teaching of Catholicism. For them, developmentalism has a negative connotation: it has become a synonym of reformism and modernization and does not attack the roots of the problem. They see the Alliance for Progress as a complete failure. They reject the idea that capitalist culture is a model of development for Latin America. They point out that developmentalism has widened rather than lessened the breach between the underdeveloped and the highly developed countries, between the dominant and the oppressed classes. The rich have become more rich and the poor more poor.

The failure of developmentalism is due, say the liberation theologians, to the capitalistic system of economic production and to the way in which our society is structured. As a result, what is needed is not development or evolution, but rather *revolution*, the radical change of social structures and the establishment of socialism in Latin America. Gustavo Gutiérrez explains:

> Attempts to bring about changes within the existing order have proven futile. This analysis of the situation is at the level of scientific rationality. Only a radical break from the status quo, that is, a profound transformation of the private property system, access to power of the exploited class, and social revolution that would break this dependence would allow for the change to a new society, a socialist society—or at least allow that such a society might be possible.[15]

That in essence is the answer of liberation theology to the economic, social, moral, and political problems of Latin America. The truth is that both in its purely sociological analysis as well as in its missiological and theological reflection, spiritual and ethical aspects remain in subjection to the economic and social factors within the context of a political ideology. According to liberation theologians, the church ought to identify itself with the cause of the oppressed and fight for their total liberation here and now, thus helping to make history. That is its mission, they contend.

It is not surprising that there are Catholic theologians who oppose the tendency to magnify an ideology above the official and traditional teaching of the Roman Catholic church. Neither is it surprising that conservative evangelical theologians deplore the subjection of the Scriptures to an ideology, although it must be admitted that that problem does not exist only in liberationism. It is also possible to subject theology to a rightist ideology. Both extremes have representatives on the contemporary theological scene.

It is also proper that there should be certain reservations about the revolutionary solution the liberation theologians propose. There is indeed urgent need for profound changes, and it is easy to understand the beginning and the original purposes of a revolution; but no one can say for sure what direction those who take

15. Gustavo Gutiérrez, *A Theology of Liberation*, pp. 26-27.

over will give to the revolutionary movement. No one knows whether it will lead to freedom for the people or whether their chains will be tightened.[16] It is indispensable to keep in mind that we need much more than a change of social structures or a change of those in government. The desire for freedom is inherent in the human being, and no lofty social program has a right to usurp it.[17] Sooner or later comes the moment when the people realize that man shall not live by bread alone, that he has other vital needs which cannot be put off forever.

In the history of Latin America there have been cases of Christians who, having placed their hopes in a revolutionary movement, saw those hopes dashed when the movement, instead of fulfilling its promises of liberation, became one more oppressor of the people who had sincerely and enthusiastically believed its promises. Much caution is needed to avoid giving unconditional, uncritical backing to a revolutionary project, whatever its nature or origin. The evangelical Christian feels the obligation to submit his possible options to the scrutiny of the written revelation of God.

What has been said to this point is more than enough to give at least a general idea of the historical, economic, social, and political context from which Latin American liberation theology emerges.

16. Even Richard Shaull, one of the founders of the revolutionary theological movement Church and Society in Latin America (ISAL), has said: "We are surrounded by evidences that revolution is a very ambiguous phenomenon. It represents passion for justice and for the liberation of the oppressed, but it also sets loose great destructive forces and leads to new forms of injustice. Men and women, in great numbers, have fought and sacrificed their lives to bring about a new society; and far too often the order established after the revolution is not very different from the previous one. Movements which are able to awaken the masses and invite them to participate in the use of public power, frequently lead to a destructive fanaticism and in the end deprive them of power. . . . in a revolutionary situation it is impossible to predict how that power will eventually be used." ("Perspectiva teológica de los cambios revolutionarios," p. 14.)

17. Roberto Oliveros Maqueo says that it is necessary to understand what is meant by "intending to create a society where goods are effectively at the service of the collectivity." And if it is thought that the price for this is "freedom," "freedom from what and for whom?" (*Liberación y teología*, pp. 41-42). For his part, José Míguez Bonino affirms: "Thus, in the last stage of the process, freedom—the liberal freedom of the modernizers—becomes the ideological justification for a repressive police state. When a person shouts liberty in Latin America today, one can immediately suspect him of being a reactionary; and one is seldom wrong" (*Doing Theology in a Revolutionary Situation*, p. 17). The statement of Dr. Míguez is not meant to apply in every case, but it can have an intimidating effect.

Part Two

A Historical Overview
of Liberation Theology

2

European Influence in Liberation Theology

The previous chapter offered an overview of the historical and social context of liberation theology. The seedbed of that theology is Latin America, with its burden of sufferings and hopes.

For the first time in the history of Christianity a theology has arisen that, despite having been written by Latin Americans for Latin Americans, has captured the attention of the international ecclesiastical community. At last Latin America has let its voice be heard in the theological centers of greatest prestige in various parts of the world. No self-respecting theologian can contemptuously ignore a theology that has caused such a stir in biblical theology and, consequently, in aspects of such important doctrines as the nature and mission of the church and the nature of the kingdom of God.

In reality we Latin Americans find ourselves facing a new way of doing theology, in answer to economic, social, and political problems of the Latin American people. That new approach represents an effort to radically change the traditional concept of what it means to be the church of Jesus Christ, or to be Christians, in a society marked by conflict, such as ours. It is much more than a theology of revolution; it is nothing less than a revolution of theology itself.

Many people question how Latin American the theology of

liberation really is in view of the foreign influences on it. Obviously, at this point in the history of Christian thought no one can
be totally original any longer; and perhaps it is those concepts that
liberation theology has borrowed that contribute most to making
it understandable in other latitudes.

Consequently, we would do well to consider the extent to
which Latin American liberation has been influenced by Europe,
which has to a great degree formed Latin American culture and
which continues to dominate us with its thinking. I will say then
something about the European currents of thought that have contributed to Catholic liberation theology, for example the political
theology of Catholic and Protestant thinkers in Europe and the
powerful influence of Karl Marx. However, it should be noted that
liberation theologians adopt a critical attitude toward European
ideas, even when they assimilate those ideas in one way or another.
The theology of liberation may have European sap in its roots, but
it denies that it is European or Europeanized. There is both relation
and rupture between Latin American liberation theologians and
European theologians, whether they are Catholic or Protestant.

EUROPEAN THEOLOGY

Although the effort to trace the development of contemporary
theology belongs outside of the purpose and space of this book, it
is important to keep in mind the change brought about in European theology with the advent of liberalism, the origin of which
may be found in the Enlightenment (seventeenth and eighteenth
centuries).

The Roman Catholic church did not remain totally exempt from
the effects of that theological revolution. The threat of "modernism," as it was called in official Catholic circles, was a cause of
concern for the popes from the end of the nineteenth century on.
Both the decree *Lamentabili* (July 3, 1907) and the papal encyclical *Pascendi dominici gregis* (September 8, 1907) condemned
the errors of modernism. Nevertheless, modernism seems to have
continued to influence the "new theology" until the period of Pius
XII (1939-1958).[1]

1. Alfredo Garland, *Como lobos rapaces,* p. 14.

LIBERALISM: TRUST IN MAN

Liberalism not only tried to undermine faith in the cardinal doctrines of the church; it was also intensely humanistic in the sense that it believed man to be essentially good and fully able to solve his problems and build for himself a better world. The liberals were characterized by their great faith in human progress. They seemed to be incurably optimistic. Their theology gave the impression that God was present in the wonderful world of science and technology, working for the benefit of man. They emphasized the immanence of God, passing over His transcendence. They placed the religion of feeling above the authority of written revelation. They subjected the Bible to the judgment of reason in the way they applied historical and literary criticism to it, denying the possibility that God could reveal Himself in a supernatural way through the Scriptures. Thus the liberals sacrificed the Bible's authority on the altar of human reason.

The First World War (1914-1918) was a severe blow to liberalism because it showed that man was still inclined to evil, that the progress of science and technology could not contain the avalanche of selfishness and ignoble ambition, and that it was imperative to trust in the transcendent God, who is found far above earthly circumstances, and in the free exercise of His sovereign will over all peoples of the earth. Liberal theology was built on sand, on the foundation of a humanism that is anti-biblical because it depends not on God but rather on man.[2]

KARL BARTH: RECOVERY OF THE WORD OF GOD

In that crucial hour for humanity, the theologian Karl Barth lifted up his voice against the excesses of theological liberalism. He spoke of the greatness of God and the destitution of man. He emphasized the transcendence of God and His initiative in revealing Himself to man. The road does not lead from man to God, but rather from God to man. Barth took the Scriptures seriously and expounded them with courage, although his concept of the inspiration of the Scriptures was far from being orthodox. Barthian

---

2. See Friedrich Schleiermacher, *The Christian Faith* (Edinburgh: T. & T. Clark, 1976); Albrecht Ritschl, *The Christian Doctrine of Justification and Reconciliation* (Edinbrugh: T. & T. Clark, 1902).

theology has been called "neo-orthodoxy." It was not Barth's intention to return to the old orthodoxy, but rather to proclaim the
message he deemed necessary for the new generations.

Barth sought to exalt the Word of God above that which is
merely anthropological and sociological. He declared that the
encounter with God does not depend on all those things that the
liberals had magnified. Rubem Alves has claimed that Barth "did
not allow for concern for the creation of a new tomorrow."[3] But
Barth did speak of political preaching as necessary and showed
that he had a civic conscience by opposing National Socialism
from the beginning, with the result that he had to abandon his
teaching post in Bonn for refusing to take the Nazi vow. His
opposition to Hitler's dictatorship never lessened. Furthermore,
he later tried in his theology to make less radical the separation
between the temporal and the eternal, between God and man,
between the Word and its recipients.[4] However, the main emphasis
of his theology was not political and social.

RUDOLPH BULTMANN: EXISTENTIAL INDIVIDUALISM

The existential theology of Rudolph Bultmann has also suffered
criticism from those who see in existentialism an absolute denial
of the world[5] and say that the work of Bultmann is individualized,
removed from social reality. It should not be forgotten, however,
that Bultmann also tried to "demythologize" the New Testament,
that is, to adequately interpret its "myths"—those cultural forms
of expression that can hide a "deeper meaning." For example,
according to Bultmann when the Bible says that God has His
dwelling place in Heaven, it is speaking mythologically, that is, "in
a crude manner it expresses the idea that God is beyond the world,
that He is transcendent." The virgin birth of Christ, His miracles,
His resurrection, His ascension, and the second coming are like-
wise myths, cultural forms for communicating certain religious
ideas, but not information about historical realities or events in
time and space.[6]

3. Rubem Alves, *A Theology of Human Hope,* p. 55.
4. Luis Maldonado, *El menester de la prédicación,* p. 35.
5. Alves, p. 43.
6. Rudolf Bultmann, *Jesus Christ and Mythology* (New York: Scribner's, 1958), pp. 18, 20.

Biblical eschatology is definitely mythological for Bultmann. There is no future eschatological fulfillment. "The present time of preaching the gospel is really the formerly expected time of the Kingdom of the Messiah. Jesus is now the Messiah, the Lord."[7] Luis Maldonado has good reason to criticize Bultmann for having given to the future of God "an atemporal, unworldly, dehistorized, and de-eschatologized meaning."[8]

BULTMANN'S FOLLOWERS: SECULAR AND POLITICAL THEOLOGY

The emphasis Bultmann gave to the present did not remain forgotten. His disciples took it and refined it, opening the way for a theology that would concern itself with contemporary political realities. Existential individualism gave way to secular theology and political theology.

Bultmann's disciples took another step forward in the tendency to magnify the present above the past and the future. Maldonado summarizes the eschatological thinking of Ernst Fuchs, one of Bultmann's disciples:

> Genuine Christian preaching announces the coming of God, the saving love of God, now, in the present, in the moment when the announcement is made. . . . This is alluded to by the "fullness of time" which the gospel announces. We have come to the time when the past has ended. There is no longer a past. . . . there is only a present; therefore, a present without end. We live in an unlimited now, a now of fullness. This is eschatology. We are in the definitive "eschaton." History as a succession of periods has ended. . . . The kingdom becomes a reality there, in the "every day," in the life of every day, in human and family sharing, in the experience we have of love and with love.[9]

Gerhard Ebeling, another of Bultmann's disciples, also emphasized the present moment in his existential theology. Ebeling was a close friend of Dietrich Bonhoeffer who, together with Friedrich Gogarten, stands out as a representative of secular theology. Bonhoeffer, who suffered martyrdom under the Nazis, was concerned

7. Ibid., p. 33.
8. Maldonado, p. 45.
9. Ibid., p. 45.

about the confrontation of the Christian faith with the secularized world, "the world come of age" that no longer accepts the old way of speaking about God because it has reached the autonomy of reason. Commenting on secular theology, the German theologian Heinz Zahrnt says that trends such as those noted by Gogarten and others have

> opened the way to the secularisation of the world and the autonomy of human reason, and so to the domination and manipulation of the world by modern science and technology.... the essence of the modern process of secularization which was beginning at this time is that the freedom of man with regard to the world has broken away from Christian faith and freedom for God [Luther].... Modern man ... pleases himself; he is self-sufficient. He no longer relies upon God, and in fact it seems that God now relies upon him.[10]

Bonhoeffer concentrated his theological reflection on the question of how to reinterpret the gospel for the modern adult and proposed a "non-religious interpretation" of the Scriptures. As Zahrnt explains:

> As Bonhoeffer proceeds with his non-religious interpretation of biblical concepts he gradually builds up an exact anti-type to what he has described as the nature of "religion." The chief distinguishing mark of religion is the acceptance of two worlds, one here below and another above and beyond, which brings with it an individualistic concern for the salvation of one's own soul, and a longing for redemption in a better world to come. The non-religious interpretation of the Bible emphasises instead that in a profound sense Christianity is *of this world*.[11]

Ebeling shows the influence of his friend Bonhoeffer, and moves in his hermeneutic away from the dualistic conception of reality. There are not two kingdoms or two different worlds, but rather a single reality. For Bonhoeffer and Ebeling, "the Christian God requires the abolition of the customary separation between the

10. Heinz Zahrnt, *The Question of God: Protestant Theology in the Twentieth Century*, pp. 146-48.
11. Ibid., p. 160.

sacred and the profane which is the principal dichotomy in all religions."[12]

The emphasis of existential theology on the present and the interest of secular theology in contemporary society prepared the way for political theology, which has had an influence, like it or not, on Latin American liberation theologians. Maldonado says that beginning with Barth the line followed by theology is descendent, "as of a progressive landing on human, worldly, temporal realities."[13] The final leap is taken by the exponents of political theology, of whom the best known representatives are J. B. Metz (Catholic) and Jürgen Moltmann (Protestant).

JÜRGEN MOLTMANN: HOPE FOR THIS WORLD

Moltmann published his now-famous *Theology of Hope* in 1964. Maldonado believes that Moltmann "has resituated all of theology in the eschatological perspective."[14] In contrast to Barth and especially to Bultmann, Moltmann makes an effort to recover the dynamic of the future in the Christian message. He opposes the immobilistic eschatological concept. For him the eschatological promise is dynamic, and progressively creates the future. Each fulfillment of the promise opens a new perspective, a new eschatological horizon. The church should not turn so much to the past as to the future, and contribute to the transformation of the present. Moltmann says:

> To believe means to cross in hope and anticipation the bounds that have been penetrated by the raising of the crucified. If we bear that in mind, then this faith can have nothing to do with fleeing the world, with resignation and with escapism. . . . It sees in the resurrection of Christ not the eternity of heaven, but the future of the very earth on which his cross stands. . . . But on the other hand, all this must inevitably mean that the man who thus hopes will never be able to reconcile himself with the laws and constraints of this earth, neither with the inevitability of death nor with the evil that constantly bears

12. Maldonado, p. 65. See also John A. T. Robinson, *Honest to God* (Philadelphia: Westminster, 1963), and Harvey Cox, *The Secular City* (New York: Macmillan, 1966).
13. Maldonado, p. 69.
14. Ibid., p. 107.

further evil. . . . Hope finds in Christ not only a consolation *in* suffering, but also the protest of the divine promise *against* suffering.[15]

In the last chapter of his work Moltmann reflects on "the calling of Christians in society" and affirms that "mission means not merely propagation of faith and hope, but also historic transformation of life."[16] Moltmann has continued to develop the political dimension of Christianity in later articles. "The social revolution to do away with unjust situations is the immanent side of the transcendent hope of the resurrection."[17] In order for the Scriptures to speak in terms of that transformation, the hermeneutic must be political.

Moltmann has made an interesting statement that seems to echo Karl Marx: "The theologian is not concerned merely to supply a different *interpretation* of the world, of history and of human nature, but to *transform* them in expectation of a divine transformation."[18] Ernst Bloch, author of a work entitled *The Hope Principle* and an adherent, according to Gustavo Gutiérrez, of what some have called "esoteric Marxism," has exerted a certain influence on Moltmann. Gutiérrez states:

> The contemporary theology of hope is passing through the breach unexpectedly opened by Bloch. Moltmann and Pannenberg have found in Bloch's analyses the categories which allow them to think through some of the important Biblical themes: Eschatology, Promise, Hope. In this, they are only following an indication of Bloch himself who said: "Where there is hope, there is also religion."[19]

On the other hand, in his dialogue with Bloch, Moltmann makes a critical evaluation of him.[20]

15. Jürgen Moltmann, *Theology of Hope,* pp. 20-21.
16. Ibid., p. 330.
17. Maldonado, pp. 106-7.
18. Moltmann, *Theology of Hope,* p. 84.
19. Gustavo Gutiérrez, *A Theology of Liberation: History, Politics and Salvation,* pp. 216-17.
20. See the Appendix "El Principio Esperanza y Teología de la Esperanza" in the Spanish edition of Moltmann's *Teología de la esperanza,* pp. 437-66. It does not appear in the English edition quoted in these notes.

EUROPEAN THEOLOGY AND LIBERATION THEOLOGY

CRITICISM OF MOLTMANN FROM LIBERATION THEOLOGIANS

In his commentary on the theology of Moltmann, Zahrnt affirms:

the emphasis laid on the future by many theologians at present is so exaggerated that it becomes suspicious. It almost gives the impression that the future has today taken the place formerly occupied by the Beyond. The vertical has become horizontal: the flight "upwards" from the pressure of reality has now been replaced by a flight "forward." But whether the flight is upwards or forward, the demonstration of the truth of God, whether in space or in time, retreats into an indeterminate distance.[21]

There is a certain similarity between those words and the words of Gustavo Gutiérrez in his criticism of the book *Theology of Hope,* although the purpose is different:

The hope which overcomes death must be rooted in the heart of historical praxis; if this hope does not take shape in the present to lead it forward, it will be only an evasion, a futuristic illusion. One must be extremely careful not to replace a Christianity of the Beyond with a Christianity of the Future; if the former tended to forget the world, the latter runs the risk of neglecting a miserable and unjust present and the struggle for liberation.[22]

Hugo Assmann, another prominent liberation theologian, sees the work of Moltmann as "one of the best movements in contemporary theology." But at the same time he points out that "proclaiming a hope that does not articulate and motivate the actual stages in the struggle . . . runs the risk of leaving man an inactive spectator."[23]

Rubem Alves, a Presbyterian theologian from Brazil and an exponent of Protestant liberation theology, feels that Moltmann futurizes God too much, withdrawing Him from the present, making Him ahistorical. Alves does not agree with Moltmann's idea that the movement toward the future arises as a response to a *promise*

21. Zahrnt, p. 231.
22. Gutiérrez, *Theology of Liberation,* p. 218.
23. Hugo Assmann, *Theology for a Nomad Church,* pp. 94-95.

that comes from outside and makes it possible. The renewing movement must spring from the present reality, from man's present condition, not from a promise that is transcendent. "It is only in the context of the ongoing politics of God that it is possible to speak about the future and hope."[24]

In a footnote, Gutiérrez recognizes that more recent works of Moltmann "show an interesting evolution and a fruitful opening to the historical struggle of man today."[25] José Míguez Bonino does the same when he says that, especially in his work *The Crucified God,* Moltmann "has brilliantly corrected and deepened his earlier insight, meeting at the same time both criticisms [of optimism and vagueness] through a concentration on the cross." However, Míguez Bonino asserts that Moltmann has failed "to grasp the basic challenge of Latin American theological thought," and remains, therefore, "within the circle of European political theology."[26] According to liberation theologians, European political theology—precisely because it is not Latin American and because it has been formulated in a context of affluence—cannot understand the economic and social problems of our people.

J. B. METZ: COMMITMENT TO CHANGE THE WORLD

Liberation theologians apply the same basic criticisms they level against Moltmann to J. B. Metz, a Catholic representative of European political theology. Maldonado explains that the political theme appears in European theology as a result of the dialogue between Metz and Bloch, the "esoteric" Marxist. "At the same time the star of sociology rises on the cultural horizon, another star sets, that of Heidegger and his existentialism, which had given heat and light to Bultmann."[27]

For Metz, political theology is Christian theology returning to its social and temporal dimensions. His emphasis is not on explaining the world but rather on changing it. He notes that the Bible uses political categories in referring to God: kingdom, lordship, power. Furthermore, the God of the Bible promotes liberating

24. Alves, p. 98.
25. Gutiérrez, *Theology of Liberation,* p. 241, n. 33.
26. José Míguez Bonino, *Doing Theology in a Revolutionary Situation,* pp. 145-46.
27. Maldonado, p. 71.

movements. The kingdom of God means the integral liberation of the poor as persons, not only as souls. The eschatological promises of Jesus are not directed only to individuals, but rather to the whole human community, and should not be understood only in a futuristic sense, nor be identified with any concrete social situation or any political system. Those promises have begun to be fulfilled now, but they will reach their total fulfillment at the end of history. Furthermore, they serve as an impulse "to bring the hoped-for future, which God will not cause to fall out of the skies without our help."[28]

That suggests that the Christian must commit himself to the present. There is no political neutrality. Pretended neutrality is actually a type of political involvement in which a position is taken. Silence gives consent. Maldonado concludes his commentary on the political theology of Metz by saying that Christian preaching should denounce sin in the ongoing development of society, and announce the kingdom of which that development is a prelude.[29]

THE EUROPEAN ROOTS OF LIBERATION THEOLOGY

Metz's and Moltmann's ideas are echoed in one way or another in Latin American liberation theology, although sometimes harsh criticism is leveled against the Europeans. The liberationists do remain indebted to the Europeans. Míguez Bonino says that "Moltmann is the theologian to whom the theology of liberation is most indebted and with whom it shows the clearest affinity."[30] The debt to Metz is also evident.

In his "Open Letter to José Míguez Bonino," Moltmann asks where, after all, are the characteristically Latin American elements in liberation theology. "One is first criticized intensely, and then, to one's surprise, finds that in the end the critics confirm with their own words exactly the same thing that one had said oneself." Moltmann feels that Gustavo Gutiérrez has made a valuable contribution to European theology, presenting the process of liberation in Latin America "as the continuation and culmination of the European history of freedom." Moltmann asks whether there does

---

28. Ibid., p. 81. For J. B. Metz, *Antropocentrismo Cristiano,* and *Theology of the World,* see bibliography.
29. Ibid., p. 81.
30. Míguez Bonino, p. 144.

not unconsciously exist, between European theologians and Latin American theologians, the relation of the mother country with its colonies, or of the mother church with its daughter church. He believes that the destruction of European theological imperialism should not lead to theological provincialism. On the contrary, the ideal would be the formulation of a theology for the whole world, at the expense of one-sided Western theology.[31]

Enrique Dussel indicates that Latin American theology began to develop as a result of "study in Europe by many Latin American seminary professors and theological teachers."[32] A biographical study of the principal exponents of liberation theology confirms that statement. Dussel himself studied in Germany.

For Moltmann, "the most decisive difference between the Latin American theology of liberation and political theology in Western Europe lies in the assessment of the various historical situations."[33] The Latin American theologians are speaking from their own historical and social context. Reading the works of Metz, Gutiérrez "gets the impression of a certain inadequacy in his analysis of the contemporary political situation."[34] He concludes his evaluation of the "new political theology" by saying:

> The new political theology represents, nevertheless, a fertile effort to think the faith through. It takes into consideration the political dimension of the faith and is indeed aware of the most pervasive and acute problems which today's man encounters. It also represents an original recasting of the question of the function of the Church in the world today. . . . But the approach of the new political theology must avoid the pitfalls both of "naiveté" regarding the influences of advanced capitalist society as well as of a narrow ecclesiastical framework, if it wishes to reach the arena where the future of society and the Church is being decided.[35]

Undeniably, ideas from Europe gave encouragement to the new Latin American theological effort. But as was pointed out at the

31. Jürgen Moltmann, "An Open Letter to José Míguez Bonino," pp. 58-59, 62. This letter was published originally in *Christianity and Crisis,* 29 March 1976. It circulated privately at that time in Latin America in mimeographed form.
32. Enrique Dussel, *A History of the Church in Latin America,* p. 244.
33. Moltmann, "Open Letter," p. 65.
34. Gutiérrez, *Theology of Liberation,* p. 224.
35. Ibid., p. 225.

beginning of this chapter, both *relation* and *rupture* exist between European theologians and their Latin American counterparts regarding the formulation of a theology that aspires to be liberating.

MARXIST THOUGHT IN LIBERATION THEOLOGY

No one can fail to notice that Marxist thought exerts a powerful influence on liberation theology. And the exponents of liberation theology do not try to hide that influence. On the contrary, they seem to pride themselves on the use they make of Marxism both for social analysis and for the action they propose to transform the structures of Latin American society. Some of the prominent ideas of liberation theology reveal Marxist influence: economics as a determining factor in the historical process, Marxist notions of work and class struggle, the liberating praxis of the oppressed by the oppressed themselves, man as a protagonist of his own history, the new man and the new society resulting from the proletarian revolution, as well as the ideological criticism of capitalism.

It is not my purpose to describe Marxism here, much less refute it, but simply to indicate that the liberation theologians are under a Marxist influence of European origin and that they themselves recognize and appreciate that influence.

Commenting on that phenomenon, Moltmann says, "We hear severe criticism of Western theology and of theology in general—and then we are told something about Karl Marx and Friedrich Engels, as if they were Latin American discoveries." He also comments on the fact that the liberation theologians, with the joy of missionary discovery, try to introduce and interpret Marx and Engels to theologians who live in the home country of those two thinkers.[36]

Latin American liberation theology is clearly European in its Marxist presuppositions. But the liberation theologians hope that the socialism that may develop in those countries will be different from that in other parts of the world, even though it has the same Marxist foundation.

Certainly Marxism has diversified up to a point. There is, for example, the so-called revisionism within Marxist ranks. There are orthodox followers of Marx as well as unorthodox, but fundamen-

36. Moltmann, "Open Letter," pp. 59, 62.

tally all are Marxists. Ernst Bloch and Herbert Marcuse, frequently
quoted in liberationist writings, are classified as "Marxists *sui
generis,*" because they do not fit within strict orthodoxy. We have
seen that, according to Gutiérrez, Bloch belongs to esoteric Marxism, "'the warm current of Marxism'—concerned with achieving
the real through what today is only potential."[37]

With his emphasis on hope, Bloch has contributed significantly
to the Marxist-Christian dialogue. Moltmann, who has been interested in this dialogue, says that "it is difficult to imagine a philosophy other than that of *The Hope Principle* [a work by Bloch]
which could be more useful in helping us to renew and elaborate
the Christian doctrine of hope."[38]

Herbert Marcuse directs his attention especially to the society
dominated by science and technology. He is concerned about the
fact that man in the technopolis becomes dehumanized in the
midst of material abundance. Out of that comes his theme of the
"one dimensional man" and his criticism of both capitalism and
Marxist socialism. He sees in both systems a dehumanizing tendency.[39]

Míguez Bonino asks whether esoteric Marxism is not a product
of the situation in the "developed" countries, where the technological society of well-being can reduce the struggle for human
liberation to the level of intellectual debate. What we need in Latin
America is not simply to be made uniform, to become the one-
dimensional man, but rather to make those social changes that
will guarantee the basic necessities for our people. Nevertheless,
Míguez Bonino does not question the elements he considers positive in the thinking of Marcuse.[40]

Assmann explains that the language of liberation in Christian
circles has not arisen spontaneously within postconciliar refor-

37. Gutiérrez, *Theology of Liberation,* p. 240.
38. Quoted by Gutiérrez, *Theology of Liberation,* p. 240.
39. Herbert Marcuse, *One Dimensional Man,* (Boston: Beacon, 1964). In his work
    Los Orígenes del Marxismo, Carlos Valverde sees both capitalism and Marxism
    as the descendents of the "enlightened" ideologists of the eighteenth century,
    that both systems today have much in common, "especially when they try to
    create a type of man based on economics, empiricist, pragmatic, scientific,
    closed in by the earthly horizon. . . . Marcuse has sharply and penetratingly
    criticized the inhuman aspects of both systems" (pp. 50-51).
40. José Míguez Bonino, Prologue to the Spanish edition of Rubem Alves's, *A
    Theology of Human Hope: Religión: ¿Opio o instrumento de liberación?,* pp.
    vii-ix.

mism, the renewal movement that received its inspiration from Vatican II. It is not the language of the European postconciliar vanguard:

> The various movements of national liberation, for example, have exercised a far more direct influence. The language of the revolutionary movements of the Left, the Marxist vocabulary of Latin American "new Marxism" (which is different from the reformist approach of the Communist parties that follow the Moscow line), the terms used by student movements: all these had a more or less direct influence. So, to a certain extent, did the writings of Herbert Marcuse (though somewhat less in Latin America than elsewhere) and documents from international congresses on "the dialectics of liberation."[41]

Gutiérrez treats Marxism with great respect. He believes, for example, that "Marx created categories which allowed for the elaboration of a science of history," and points out that the analysis of European political theology would gain much "from the contribution of certain aspects of Marxism, which, despite (or because of?) the mediation of Bloch's thought, do not seem to be sufficiently present."[42]

Míguez Bonino explains the way in which Marxism is used in liberation theology: dialectical and historical materialism conceived as "a metaphysical theory, an absolute philosophical formulation," and embraced "with a sort of religious fervor," inevitably enters into conflict with the Christian faith. But at the same time Marxism "has proved, and still proves to be, the best instrument available for an effective and rational realization of human possibilities in historical life. A Marxist praxis is both the verification and the source of possible correction of the hypothesis."[43]

Míguez Bonino also explains that the assumption of Marxism in liberation theology "has nothing to do with a supposedly abstract or eternal theory or with dogmatic formulae . . . but with a scientific analysis and a number of verifiable hypotheses." Without taking into account the criticisms that have been directed against the theoretical foundation of Marxism, Bonino maintains that the

41. Assmann, p. 48.
42. Gutiérrez, *Theology of Liberation*, pp. 30, 224.
43. Míguez Bonino, *Doing Theology*, pp. 96-97.

assumption of analytical or ideological elements having their origin in Marxism does not constitute a "sacralization of an ideology," or a "desire to 'theologize' sociological, economic, or political categories." He recognizes at the same time that "Marxism does not behave as the cool rational entity we have described. It is frequently possessed by an apostolic zeal, a dogmatic certainty and a messianic fervor the causes of which we cannot discuss here." However, he appears to believe that liberation theology will neither fall into that dogmatism nor allow itself to be dominated by the philosophy from which the analytical and ideological elements of Marxism have sprung.[44] Nonetheless, the truth of the matter is that "leftist fundamentalism" is already present on the Latin American ecclesiastical scene, promoted in a way by liberation theology.

For his part, José P. Miranda, in his two principal works *Being and the Messiah* and *Marx and the Bible: A Critique of the Philosophy of Oppression,* responds to the Marxist challenge in the area of biblical interpretation, accepting the dialectical method of Marx as a hermeneutic key. He explains that method by contrasting it with "the epistomology of Western science inherited from the Greeks" which, in its employment in ordinary economics, confines itself "to recording facts as they are given in immediate experience, after the fashion of the empiricists, and then to establish the relationship between them." Quoting Roger Garaudy, Miranda says that the dialectical method "consists in seeking, beyond the supposed 'data' of experience, the human relations hidden beneath the 'appearance' of things."[45]

The conflicts in societal relations, says Miranda, are a direct result of the unjust structures inherited from the past and maintained and strengthened by capitalism for its own profit.[46] Miranda suggests that both Marx and the Bible see social reality in a state of conflict: "Marx and Paul coincide in their intuition of the totality of evil: Sin and injustice form an all-comprehensive and all-pervasive organic structure. Paul calls this totality *kosmos.* Marx calls it 'capitalism.'"[47]

The fact that Marx did not recognize that capitalism had been

44. Ibid., pp. 95-98.
45. José P. Miranda, *Marx and the Bible: A Critique of the Philosophy of Oppression,* pp. 260-61.
46. J. Andrew Kirk, commenting on the dialectic method, in *Liberation Theology: An Evangelical View from the Third World,* p. 82.
47. Miranda, *Marx and the Bible,* p. 250.

inherent in human civilization since biblical times does not signify that there was no oppression then:

> the capitalism denounced by Marx is the consistent development of human civilization and oppression. It is the culture of injustice and of the crushing of men carried to extreme perfection and systematic refinement. . . . Marx and the Bible coincide in this affirmation of incalculable importance: Sin's achievement of an institutional system-atization in a flawless civilizing structure is what was historically needed before mankind could change its epoch. This exacerbation of sin to an extreme . . . is, for both Paul and Marx, the total matura-tion of history, the breaking point which mankind needed to become aware of the infernal machinery which it has assembled and to be definitely delivered from it.

These last words suggest that Marx and the Bible also coincide in presenting the possibility of a definitive liberation on the historical plane. Sin and evil "are not inherent to mankind and history; they began one day through human action and can, therefore, be elimi-nated."[48]

Miranda is an enthusiastic apologist of Karl Marx. For example, he says that when Marx does not treat the problem of death, and therefore does not consider the possibility of resurrection, "it is not precisely his lack of faith in God but rather insufficient dialec-tics for which we must reproach him."[49] Miranda Christianizes Marx, although his book *Marx Against the Marxists,* is not all that convincing. But the theological works of Miranda do represent a serious effort to provide a biblical and exegetical foundation for liberation theology. The degree to which that effort succeeds will depend on the theological and political position of the reader.

The debt of Latin American theological liberationism to Euro-pean political theology is evident; the influence of Karl Marx and his followers on the liberation theologians is also clear. In libera-tion theology Marxism can be the supreme rule for the interpre-tation of the sacred text. I will evaluate the liberationist hermeneutic more fully in a later chapter.

In the opinion of Andrew Kirk, the liberation theologians have fallen into the trap of converting Marx into "a new *magisterium*

48. Ibid., pp. 254-55.
49. Ibid., pp. 279.

in the sense that the revelation of God in our days needs to be understood in light of the interpretation which he [Marx] gave to the signs of the times."[50] But for the conservative evangelical Christian, the use of an ideology as the hermeneutic criterion for the study and exposition of the Scriptures is totally unacceptable.

50. J. Andrew Kirk, "Exégesis técnica y anuncio de la fe," p. 45.

3

Church and Society
in Latin America: ISAL

The preceding chapter established that some European Protestant theologians have been influential in the development of Latin American liberation theology. Now it is necessary to mention that before the Roman Catholic theology of liberation made itself felt at a continental and world level, there was already a liberationist current in South American Protestantism. Orlando Costas, an evangelical missiologist from Latin America, says that although liberation theology was initiated in Catholic circles, "it was not long before it gained the interest and attention of Protestant avantgarde groups like ISAL and theologians like Rubem Alves and José Míguez Bonino."[1]

ISAL (Iglesia y Sociedad en América Latina—Church and Society in Latin America) is a movement whose founders had been concerned with responding theologically to the challenge of the social changes in Latin America long before the Second Vatican Council (1962-1965). Hugo Assmann recognizes that the Brazilian Protestant theologian Rubem Alves, who became one of the leaders of Isaline thought, "has the distinction of making a significant contribution, especially in his broad globalization of the basic questions

1. Orlando Costas, *Theology of the Crossroads in Contemporary Latin America: Missiology in Mainline Protestantism 1969-1974*, p. 73.

of a 'theology of liberation.'"[2] Without a doubt ISAL had a very important part in the interconfessional reflection out of which rose elements that were incorporated in the theology of liberation.

THE ORIGINS OF ISAL

It is not difficult to detect in the writings of ISAL the influence of European theology, the Marxist-Christian dialogue, the pedagogical thought of the Brazilian educator Paulo Freire, the World Council of Churches, and Roman Catholic theologians of liberation. This chapter will cover the first four of those influences, reserving discussion of the ideas of the last group for subsequent chapters.

EUROPEAN THEOLOGY

The Uruguayan Protestant theologian Julio de Santa Ana, who was one of the general secretaries of ISAL, indicates that in the decade of the thirties and after World War II "certain information began to circulate regarding the theological efforts of Barth, Brunner, Tillich, Niebuhr, Aulén and others in Europe and the United States." Santa Ana also mentions that ISAL conducted studies concerning the work of the theologians of secularization, Dietrich Bonhoeffer and John A. T. Robinson.[3] The Uruguayan Methodist pastor and theologian Emilio Castro outlines the evolution of biblical hermeneutics in Latin America referring to the thought of Barth, Bonhoeffer, Moltmann, and others:

> Through their theology, Barth and Bonhoeffer have encouraged us to actively participate in the history of our Latin America, even though they begin with different theoretical points of reference. Barth, in his emphasis on that which has been done once for all in Jesus Christ, gives us inner security, the courage to open ourselves to the outside world—in particular the Marxist world—without fear, preconceptions or proselytizing interests, since both they and we were conditioned beginning with Jesus Christ by the "yes" of God to humanity and consequently, freed to work together. In the same way, beginning with Bonhoeffer we had an acceptance of secularity as the field of

2. Hugo Assmann, *Opresión-Liberación: Desafío a los Cristianos*, p. 79.
3. Julio de Santa Ana, *Protestantismo, cultura y sociedad*, pp. 29, 114.

struggle for us Christians, independent of any need for religious approval or sanction. . . . later Moltmann produces for us a total implication in history.[4]

What Castro has said can be applied extensively to the theologians of ISAL.

MARXIST THOUGHT

In the sociological analysis of the Latin American situation carried out by the theologians of ISAL, the esoteric Marxism of Bloch and Marcuse discussed in the previous chapter is quite evident. From sociological analysis and theological reflection, within the framework of secularization, the Isaline theologians go on to assert that the dialogue between the Christian faith and revolutionary ideologies is possible and necessary "because ideology was the proper ambient for the political, for 'praxis,' that is to say, the means for assuming commitment and action for the transformation of society in the sense which is determined by the theological interpretation of history."[5] As South American evangelical theologian C. René Padilla affirms, "the point of reference taken for theology is the Latin American situation, seen, however, through the lens of Marxist analysis."[6]

Paul Lehmann, one of the representatives of situational ethics in North America, has influenced Isaline thought, especially due to his participation and commitment in the dialogue between Marxism and Christianity. According to Julio Santa Ana, Lehmann Marxism "is not a demonic movement, but rather a Christian heresy in

4. Emilio Castro, "La creciente de criterios de interpretación histórica en la evolución de le hermenéutica bíblica." In the first part of his article Castro declares, "Karl Barth invites us to enter a world of biblical history in which God is the principal actor. . . . Barth continues working, and starting from the centrality of his historical affirmation, God in Christ, he draws conclusions which will lead him years later to open the way for an emphasis on historical man and on the importance of all human activity, since beginning with the incarnation God and man are one. No longer is there God and man; God is human" (p. 214).
5. ISAL, *América hoy*, p. 17. This book contains a compilation of the topics and reports presented at the Second Latin American Consultation on Church and Society at El Tabo, Chile, 12-21 January 1966.
6. C. René Padilla, "Iglesia y Sociedad en América Latina", p. 125.

an advanced state of secularization."[7] Due to the fact that Christianity and Marxism propose to reach the same goal (although by different methods), they can enter into dialogue:

> The purpose of the Christian's action is the same as the purpose of the action of God in Christ: the humanization of man. Due to this fact it is possible to dialogue with those other movements or philosophies which, without being Christian and by different and even conflicting ways, are also committed to the humanization of the individual. God also uses them, since they are subject to his will.[8]

On the Marxist side one of the thinkers most interested in the dialogue with Catholicism is Roger Garaudy, who finds elements of convergence between Marxism and Christianity. For example, in Garaudy's opinion both Catholic thought and Marxist thought are making an effort to understand the total man, and in that sense Marxism is also true humanism.[9]

In April of 1972 the first encounter of Christians for Socialism was held in Santiago, Chile. *Cristianismo y Sociedad* (Christianity and Society), a magazine that promotes Isaline thought, reported that the idea of the encounter "took a concrete form in a meeting of people who participate in the Third World Movement of Argentina, ONIS of Peru, Golconda of Colombia, ISAL, and the Secretariat 'Christians for Socialism' of Chile."[10]

The Final Document of the encounter in Santiago is based on the Marxist analysis of society. It criticizes capitalism using Marxist

7. Paul Lehman, *Ethics in a Christian Context* (New York: Harper & Row, 1963); *La etica en el contexto Cristiano* (Montevideo: Editorial Alfa, 1968). See also *Christian Faith and Social Action,* edited by J. A. Hutchison (New York: Scribner's, 1953).
8. Julio de Santa Ana, "Algunas referencias teológicas actuales al sentido de la acción social," pp. 40-42.
9. Raymond Domerge, "¿Es el Marxismo un humanismo?" *Testimonium* (Buenos Aires) vol. 12, no. 3 (1968). *Testimonium* is a publication sponsored by the Christian Student Movement in Latin America. Domerge quotes especially two works by Roger Garaudy: *Humanismo Marxista* (1957) and *Perspectivas del hombre* (1959). In 1965 Garaudy published his book *Del anatema al diálogo* (*From Anathema to Dialogue* [New York: Herder & Herder]).
10. "Primer Encuentro Latinoamericano de Cristianos por el Socialismo," *Cristianismo y Sociedad* (Montevideo, Uruguay) 29-30 (1972). Two movements of "Third World" priests are mentioned here: The Golconda group of Colombia, which is referred to by the sensationalist press as "the revolution of the cassocks," and from Perú the ONIS group (National Office of Social Information).

categories, and accepts class struggle as the key to the process of liberation.[11] Those who defend the document say that it is dealing with "a critically assumed Marxism."[12] José Míguez Bonino states that the document is not a capitulation to Marxism, that it contains no materialistic reductionism, and that the Christian critique is admitted—as long as it comes from within the revolutionary struggle.[13] But even a superficial reading of the document reveals that it contains a criticism of the church and of capitalism, but not of socialism. The ideological commitment to Marxism is quite evident.

The "strategic alliance" that the document suggests between "revolutionary Christians" and "Marxists in the process of the liberation of the continent"[14] will continue to be a controversial issue. That controversy comes not only from those who criticize Christian socialists because of their own political ideology, but also from Christians who are seeking sincerely and seriously to escape any kind of ideological slavery and, at the same time, to maintain their loyalty to the Word of God in the proclamation of the liberating message our people need. For the evangelical Christian there is a natural fear of unconditional ideological commitment, both in social analysis and in political action.

THE THOUGHT OF PAULO FREIRE

The Isaline movement has also been motivated in its reflection and practice by the ideas of the Brazilian Catholic educator Paulo Freire. Orlando Costas mentions that between the years 1967 and 1971 ISAL became involved in the application of the popular pedagogy of Paulo Freire in urban missionary projects, in the training and development of leaders, and in the analysis of the changing situation in Latin America.[15]

Paulo Freire has become particularly known for his method of

11. ["First Encounter of Christians for Socialism, Final Document,"], *Cristianismo y Sociedad,* 31-32 (1972).
12. Hugo Assmann, José Blanes, and Luis Bach, "Exigencias de una opción." *Cristianismo y Sociedad* no. especial (1972).
13. José Míguez Bonino, "¿Partidismo o solidaridad?" *Cristianismo y Sociedad* no. especial (1972).
14. [Final Document of the First Encounter of Christians for Socialism], *Cristianismo y Sociedad* no. especial (1972).
15. Costas, p. 200.

teaching adults to read, which he formally developed in 1961. Freire created "circles of culture" and "centers of popular culture" in all of Brazil. He was in charge of the Department of Adult Literacy of the Ministry of Education and Culture of Brazil before the military coup of 1964, when he was forced to emigrate to Chile.[16]

In 1963 Freire published an article in *Revista de Cultura* of the University of Recife, Pernambuco, in which he joins the concept of "conscientization" to that of literacy. His book *The Pedagogy of the Oppressed* appeared in Portuguese in 1967. Its first Spanish edition was published in 1970. The thought and work of Freire were well known by the theologians of ISAL in the decade of the sixties.

The Jesuit theologian José I. González Faus sees that the ethical, anthropological, and philosophical principles upon which Freire's pedagogy rests "have a very close relationship with theology."[17] That in spite of the fact that Freire himself does not pretend to be a theologian. He makes incursions into the field of theology when he offers counsel to a young theologian and says:

> Since the Word became flesh, it is only possible to approach it through man, so therefore the starting point for theology should be anthropology. In this way, a *utopian* theology must be associated with cultural action for liberation, by means of which men should substitute for their naive conception of God as an alienating myth a new concept: God as a Presence in history which does not impede man in any way from making the history of his liberation.[18]

In an interview published in *Cristianismo y Sociedad* in 1972 Freire explains:

> As I see it, the role of the church is that of the liberator, the humanizer, of man. . . . I believe that theology today has many things to do, which means that from my point of view theology is not something superfluous, but rather the opposite. But it is obvious that I am not referring to false theology or the theology of bla, bla, bla, idealistic theology, but a theology which is part of anthropology,

16. Hugo Assmann, "Bibliografía de y sobre Paulo Freire," Appendix to Paulo Freire, *Pedagogía del oprimido*, pp. 244-50.
17. José I. González-Faus, "La Teología Latinoamericana de la liberación," p. 429.
18. Laulo Freire, "Carta a un joven teólogo," p. 180.

which is historically involved to discuss by example the word GOD and our relationship with the word of God. I believe that my attitude cannot be the attitude of an empty man waiting to be filled with the word of God. I believe that if we want to hear it, it is necessary for me to be involved in the process of the liberation of man. For that reason I believe that theology should be actively involved with liberating education, and liberating education with theology.[19]

Without a doubt, the method and message of Freire fit very well with the aspirations of the revolutionary movements of the Latin American continent.

Freire also writes from the basis of his thinking and experience as an educator of adults. His motto might be "education as the practice of freedom." His method is that of educating by "conscientizing" and "problem-posing." According to Freire, society is divided into *oppressors* and *oppressed*. The latter have within themselves the image of the oppressor, and it is not strange that they should see liberation as the possibility of becoming like their oppressors, of living as the oppressors of today live and becoming themselves tomorrow's oppressors.

At the same time, "the oppressed, who have adapted to the structure of domination in which they are immersed, and have become resigned to it, are inhibited from waging the struggle for freedom so long as they feel incapable of running the risks it requires."[20] The problem becomes more acute due to the fear of freedom that the oppressed feel, the fear of losing their sense of oppression and of having to assume full responsibility for themselves. The oppressed are the only ones responsible for and capable of liberating themselves and of liberating the oppressor.

What can be done for the oppressed to liberate themselves? It is imperative to assume a radical attitude in order to transform the oppressive reality. The oppressed must give themselves to a praxis that is "reflection and action upon the world in order to transform it."[21] Without that praxis it is impossible to overcome the oppressor-oppressed dichotomy.

How can the oppressed be brought to that liberating praxis?

19. "Educación para un despertar de la conciencia: Una charla con Paulo Freire," *Cristianismo y Sociedad* 29-30 (1972).
20. Freire, *Pedagogy of the Oppressed*, p. 32.
21. Ibid., p. 36.

The answer is found in "the pedagogy of the oppressed, which is the pedagogy of men engaged in the fight for their own liberation." According to Freire, there are two types of education: the first is "banking," which consists in the mere depositing of knowledge in the mind of the one that is being educated, leaving him in his state of oppression. The other is "problem-posing," which "conscientizes" the one being educated regarding the "myths" he has received from the oppressor. Liberating education seeks to transform the oppressive situation and not only to transform the mentality of the oppressed.[22]

The initial purpose of that education is to overcome the educator-educated dichotomy, so that both may become, simultaneously, educators and educated. That could be called an educational fellowship, in which he who educates is at the same time being educated, in a liberating pedagogical process. Problem-posing education is "dialogical" and liberating, in contrast to banking education, which is "antidialogical" and serves the interests of oppression.

Authentic liberating action does not seek to conquer the common man but rather to cooperate with him in his liberation; it does not divide people, it unites them; it does not manipulate them, it organizes them; it is not cultural invasion, it is a cultural "dialogical" action that leads to "cultural revolution" and "the participation of the people in power."[23] It is little wonder, therefore, that González-Faus says that the work of Freire, more than a "pedagogy of the oppressed," is a pedagogy of the revolutionary leader.[24] Friere does not believe that there can be a profound and radical transformation in the educational system unless society itself also becomes radically transformed.[25]

A concrete proposal for action is Freire's method of adult literacy. Ivan Illich explains that "the effectiveness of this program is built around key words which are loaded with political meaning."[26] The adults who become interested in the political problems of their community can learn to read and write in six weeks of night

22. Ibid., pp. 39, 60.
23. Ibid., p. 158.
24. González-Faus, p. 434.
25. *Diálogo Paulo Friere-Ivan Illich* (Buenos Aires: Ediciones Búsqueda, 1975), p. 47.
26. Iván Illich, *En América Latina, ¿Para qué sirve la escuela?* (Buenos Aires: Ediciones Búsqueda, 1974), p. 30.

classes. But Illich is quick to point out that the program has its difficulties also. More important than the method of dialogue and "conscientization" is the goal that Freire pursues: social revolution. His major interest is found in humanization. He has great confidence and hope in the human being; he believes that man can change himself and change the world; he accepts the Marxist analysis of society and history. His optimism sometimes sounds exaggerated.

The evangelical Christian is concerned when he sees that Freirean anthropology assigns no proper place to the Scriptures and that man does not appear as a sinner. Dehumanization is, according to Freire, only the result of an unjust social order. In Freire's program, "the point of departure of theology has to be anthropology" and "the theologian has to take as a point of departure his reflection on the history of mankind."[27]

THE WORLD COUNCIL OF CHURCHES

ISAL had its origin under the influence of the World Council of Churches and was promoted especially by that organization's Department of Church and Society. During the Second World War (1939-1945) the Universal Federation of Christian Student Movements (FUMEC) promoted in almost all of the countries of Latin America the creation of small national groups that, under the name Christian Student Movement (MEC), awakened among Protestant university students an interest in Latin American social problems. FUMEC had, of course, a decidedly ecumenical orientation.

Marcelo Pérez Rivas says: "There are few of the great names of Latin American ecumenism who have not participated, at some time in their personal history, in the activities of some MEC."[28] It would not be strange, therefore, if at least some of the leaders of ISAL began their reflection regarding Christian social responsibility in the MEC groups. ISAL had close relationships with ecumenical organisms such as the Latin American Evangelical Commission of Christian Education (CELADEC) and the Provisional Committee for Latin American Evangelical Unity (UNELAM). Under the spon-

---

27. Freire, "Carta a un joven teólogo," p. 180.
28. Marcelo Pérez Rivas, "El Ecumenismo en América Latina," Appendix II in *El movimiento ecuménico,* by Norman Goodall (Buenos Aires: Editorial La Aurora, 1970), p. 221.

sorship of the World Council of Churches several meetings were held in 1957 to which, according to Julio de Santa Ana, "the origin of the Church and Society movement in Latin America can be traced."[29]

ISAL was developed as a group of Protestants and Catholics interested in reflecting upon the problems of Latin American society. Hugo Assmann, the Brazilian Catholic theologian, came to occupy the position of Secretary of Studies of ISAL.

There was a reciprocal influence between ISAL and the World Council of Churches. Richard Shaull, who has been called "the father of ISAL," participated in the preparation of documents for the World Conference of Church and Society, held in Geneva in July of 1966 under the auspices of the World Council of Churches.[30] Among the forty-two Latin American delegates in that conference were people directly or indirectly involved in the theological activities of ISAL. The results of what happened in Geneva in 1966 were felt in the Fourth Assembly of the World Council of Churches, Uppsala, 1968. There was a shift within the ecumenical movement towards a major emphasis on the direct action of the church for social change. In the Uppsala report on the *Renovation of Mission,* Dr. John R. W. Stott "does not find . . . any concern for the spiritual hunger of man; no concern which could be compared to that which has been expressed with respect to physical hunger and poverty."[31]

The 1966 conference took for granted that the church should become involved in contemporary revolutionary movements. The theme of the participation of the church in revolution was discussed freely and at length. Commenting on the Geneva conference, Robert McAffee Brown, a prominent ecumenical leader, says: "For the first time, serious attention was given to the possibility of Christian participation in *violent* revolution and the conference, while clearly not 'advocating violence,' made clear that the use of violence in unseating unjust regimes could not be ruled out *a priori*."[32]

29. Julio de Santa Ana, *Protestantismo, cultura y sociedad,* pp. 125-26.
30. Adam F. Sosa, "Prefacio," in *Hacia una revolución responsable* (Buenos Aires: Editorial La Aurora, 1970), pp. 7-9.
31. John R. W. Stott, in the discussion of the report on "Renewal of Mission," *Upsala, 1968* (Salamanca: Ediciones Sígueme, 1969), p. 64.
32. Robert McAffe Brown, *The Ecumenical Movement* (Garden City, N.Y.: Doubleday, 1967), p. 320. See also *Los Cristianos en las revoluciones técnicas y sociales de nuestro tiempo,* Documents of the World Conference on Church and Society, Geneva, 12-26 July 1966 (Santander, Spain: Sal Terrae, 1971).

In 1970 the World Council of Churches carried out a series of consultations in Latin America with regard to projects for ecumenical action there. Henryanne de Chaponay, who was in charge of organizing the consultations, indicates that the impulse came from Latin American theologians and from the present situation in Latin America. Naturally, it was unanimously recognized in the consultations that there was a need for a profound, radical change in society; emphasis was given to "the need for Christians to commit themselves to the struggle against this unjust situation, and all the theological reflections sanctioned a concrete support of this as a duty to be carried out through the structures."[33] That report was received with enthusiasm by the theologians of ISAL.

In the opinion of Theo Tschuy, the creation of ISAL in 1961 helped to improve the image of the World Council of Churches in Latin America, because it brought the debate over Latin American social conditions to the ecclesiastical level. Due to its solid bond with ISAL, the WCC saw itself suddenly involved in the controversy, although it did not participate directly in it. But from that point on the WCC came to be known especially for its relationship with ISAL. Why? Tschuy answers:

> Because by affirming that the duty of all Christians is to support social justice—which in Latin America cannot mean anything else than to commit oneself to revolution—I.S.A.L. exposed *that ecumenical question* which is vital for Latin America. This question has to do with the very existence of the continent; it is, therefore, *polemical.* Each ecumenical dimension . . . cannot be separated any more from the basic issue, which is social revolution.[34]

ISAL and the WCC were walking hand in hand on the road to revolution to change the structures of society in Latin America.

THE ECUMENICAL MOVEMENT

Through the sixties and at the beginning of the following decade, the dialogue between Catholics and Protestants with regard to theology and liberation was in its heyday. Opportunity was great

33. Henryanne de Chaponay, "¿A dónde va la acción ecuménica en América Latina?" *Cristianismo y Sociedad* 24-25 (1970).
34. Theo Tschuy, "El Consejo Mundial de Iglesias y América Latina," p. 278.

for both groups to contribute to each other in their theological activity. Emilio Castro perceives ISAL as:

> a community which has transcended the limits of the Protestant confessions, to become a whole where evangelicals and Catholics merge; at the same time, both are deeply interested in giving a responsible testimony of their faith before the challenges which the social problems of Latin America present to them.[35]

Catholic-Protestant dialogue was another element that helped shape Isaline thought. At the same time, that dialogue allowed for a Protestant contribution to the development of the Latin American theology of liberation.

As in the history of any movement, some names come to the fore: for example, Richard Shaull, professor at Princeton and ex-missionary to Brazil and Colombia, who has been called "the father of ISAL"; and Luis E. Odell, a prominent ecumenical leader from Uruguay. One of the Isaline volumes has been dedicated to Odell, and in the prologue Pastor Castro underlines that homage is due to the ecumenical vocation of Odell and his efforts toward the creation of ISAL.[36]

Richard Shaull can be considered one of the pioneers of Latin American revolutionary theology. In his work *Encounter with Revolution,* published in 1955, Shaull arrives at the conclusion that in Latin America revolution is already a possibility and a necessity, that the Christian social doctrine of the past cannot adequately interpret the new situation of those countries, and that the Christian message has much to offer to properly guide the revolutionary process.[37] Shaull's work shows the influence of neo-orthodoxy and the theology of secularization.

It is possible to trace in broad strokes the development of Isaline thought by means of a review of the assemblies the movement has held at a continental level. Thus the next section will be a historical sketch of those conferences, pausing at the most important of them to point out some of the predominant elements in the theology of ISAL.

35. Emilio Castro, "Prologue," in *De la Iglesia y la sociedad,* (Montevideo, 1971), p. iii.
36. Ibid., pp. ii-iii.
37. Richard Schaull, *Encounter with Revolution,* p. 115.

CONTINENTAL ASSEMBLIES OF ISAL

FIRST CONTINENTAL ASSEMBLY, HUAMPANI, PERU, JULY 1961: ESTABLISHING THE BASIC AGENDA

This consultation was held with the presence of forty-two people from sixteen Latin American countries. Out of it emerged the Latin American Council of Church and Society in Latin America, which afterwards came to be Church and Society in Latin America (ISAL). The assembly was called by ecumenical organizations from Argentina, Brazil, and Uruguay. Among the advisors in the group were Dr. W. Stanley Rycrofft from the United States of America and Pastor Paul Albrecht, who at that time was the Executive Secretary of the Department of Church and Society in the World Council of Churches. The organizers of the council in Huampani expressed special appreciation to that department of the WCC for the support it gave to them in everything.

The purposes of the council were to gather and exchange information regarding the work that the different churches were carrying out in the social area, to discover how the participants could help one another in the future, to determine from the Christian point of view the significance that social changes have and the common responsibility of Christians toward those changes, and to establish a common strategy of study and future action.[38]

The general theme of the council was the social responsibility of the evangelical church in the face of rapid social change. That theme was divided into three sub-themes: Christian responsibility toward rapid social and cultural changes, the prophetic role of the Christian in the political life of Latin America, and the Christian concern for progress and economic development.

According to spokesmen from ISAL, Huampani represented the first time that evangelicals from the whole continent had come together in order to reflect on "the meaning of Christian responsibility in a situation of rapid social transformation." For the representatives of ISAL, the movement was "a new concept of Christian testimony through service and the fulfillment of the social and political responsibilities which the believer shares with

38. ISAL, *Encuentro y desafío,* p. 12.

every citizen." They also affirm that "Huampani signified at the same time a new awareness and the first important application of a method of analysis which afterward would be repeated with varying results in the series of regional consultations which followed that of Huampani."[39]

In the Isaline evaluation, the most important result of the meeting at Huampani was "the perplexity, the confusion." There it was discovered that the radical transformation of society, that is, the Latin American revolution, "was going through the very hub of the life and organization of the church."[40]

The perplexity turned out to be a creative one. At Huampani certain basic concepts came to the fore which in a way would become guidelines for the development of Isaline thought. Two examples are the concept of *structure,* which comes from the contemporary social and economic lexicon and is useful for social analysis; and the *theological concept of history* as a social event where the action of God is manifested, carrying out the divine will for human redemption and converting man into the subject as well as the object of social transformation. Other ideas that have formed part of the doctrine of ISAL were also heard at Huampani, including the concepts of *secularization* and of *ideology,* the latter considered as "the attempt to interpret historical and social reality from within the realm of secular thought concerning historical change." Ideology, the ISAL spokesmen continue, is

> not only an interpretation, however, but a dynamic framework for orienting social transformation toward precise objectives. . . . The dialogue between the Christian faith and revolutionary ideologies . . . seemed possible and necessary . . . ideology was the proper ambient for the political, for "praxis," that is, the means for taking on the commitment and the action for social transformation in the sense determined by the theological interpretation of history.[41]

Julio de Santa Ana, who became general secretary of ISAL in 1969, summed up the task of Huampani as "an analysis of Latin American social reality in order to confront the results of the same with the life of the churches." But he saw that in the report of the

39. ISAL, *América hoy,* pp. 11, 13-14.
40. Ibid., p. 14.
41. Ibid., pp. 15-18.

consultation the tendency to separate the church from the world, and social reality from church life, persists. "It was from there that there slowly arose an awareness that to observe the process of social changes in Latin America was not enough; it was also necessary to participate in that process." At the same time, Santa Ana emphasized the above-mentioned concepts, which were to shape the theology of ISAL.[42]

In the opinion of José Míguez Bonino, president of the committee responsible for the general consultation at Huampani,[43] ISAL in its early days was "an imported movement, promoted by the ecumenical interest in the problems of development." Míguez Bonino then describes three stages in the evolution of Isaline thought: (1) In the beginning, during the years 1960-1965, ISAL's analysis of the situation oscillated "between a developmentalist focus and another one which was revolutionary," but afterwards it adopted "the sociology of dependence" and a revolutionary strategy "tied to a socialist option." (2) In the years 1966-1968, ISAL transformed its theological prospective "from a theology which was predominantly Barthian to a 'theology of the transforming action of God in history,' strongly influenced by the theology of Paul Lehmann and Richard Shaull, until Rubem Alves gave it a creative expression in critical dialogue with Marcuse on the one hand and with Moltmann on the other." By that time, ISAL had consciously adopted a Marxist analysis and interpretation, although according to Míguez Bonino "it was not a mere stereotype." There were several interpretations. (3) From 1970 onward ISAL had a new interest in the churches, with which it had had little contact. It also emphasized national movements rather than centralized action.[44]

The development in the thought and attitude of the theologians from ISAL would make itself evident in the conferences that followed Huampani, which are important landmarks on the road of Latin American liberationism.

SECOND CONTINENTAL ASSEMBLY, EL TABO, CHILE, JANUARY 1966: GREATER DETERMINATION AMID WORSENING CONDITIONS

Leonardo Franco: pessimism regarding social change. The Latin American panorama of the sixties is described in a paper prepared

42. Santa Ana, *Protestantismo, cultura y sociedad,* pp. 126-27.
43. ISAL, *Encuentro y desafío,* p. 15.
44. José Míguez Bonino, *Doing Theology in a Revolutionary Situation,* pp. 54-55.

by Leonardo Franco on the topic "La Coyuntura Histórica" (The Historical Occasion). Franco says that the Alliance for Progress had failed in its attempt to produce economic and social development, and also that the attitude of the United States towards Latin America had hardened in order to defend the status quo on the continent. Further, he said, "As a counterpart to the interventionist attitude of the United States we find the rise of militarism in various Latin American countries."[45] In April of 1964 a military coup was carried out in Brazil, and a year later North American forces invaded the Dominican Republic.

Franco also laments the crisis of leadership in Latin American leftist movements, because the leftist groups related in one way or another to Marxist ideology had become "the first ones to create a consciousness of the need for social change in Latin America, and have always been at the vanguard of revolutionary transformations."[46]

In his conclusion Franco wants to be realistic, but he sounds pessimistic, in spite of his confidence in the irreversibility of the historical process:

> We have tried to be realistic and show that the possibility of an immediate social change, such as we all long for, is not very great. . . . the birth pangs of the social revolution are greater than what we had imagined several years ago. . . . we cannot do anything other than examine reality as it is; and the fact is that this reality does not allow us to be optimistic.[47]

Richard Shaull: the role of theology. Richard Shaull's report entitled "And a God Who Acts and Transforms History" is of great importance. In its core, Shaull reflects on "the contribution and task of theology." Christian heritage, he says, does not offer us today "a system which embraces all of truth; instead it offers a particular perspective of human life in history, and the possibility that man may fulfill himself and give meaning to his life in this process." In other words it is "a way of understanding *our history* in the light of a specific history, that of the people of Israel and that of Jesus Christ." Thus Christian heritage deals with the human-

45. Leonardo Franco, "La coyuntura histórica," in *América hoy,* p. 28.
46. Ibid., p. 34.
47. Ibid., p. 36.

ization of man and the possibility man has for reaching his "human-ity."[48]

The hermeneutic criterion for relating the biblical testimony to the present human situation is found by Shaull in the theology of Paul Lehmann; says Shaull, "The biblical message describes that which God does in order to provide and maintain the 'human' condition of man." Note that the hermeneutic criterion is not what God *says,* but rather what He *does* in history. Shaull gives the following explanation of the theological task:

> Our task therefore is not to impose certain values, but to recognize and live according to those values that predominate in the world; it is not to give meaning to life, but to discover the meaning that life has in a world which participates in redemption; it is not to establish a new order in the universe, but to participate in a new order of things taking shape through social transformations.[49]

Shaull concludes this section of his paper by proposing a basic method for the theology of liberation, that is, the theological activity in praxis and from praxis for social change:

> I believe therefore that the most important thing for us is to discover how to be present in the midst of man's contemporary struggle, in those frontiers where the struggle is being carried out, and to seek to maintain there a living dialogue between the Christian description of history, and our situation as we understand it and live it concretely. Beginning with this attitude, a new way of thinking theologically can come into being, and also new images, concepts and parables that will be able to describe in a more adequate way what God does in our midst, in strictly secular terms.[50]

Movement toward participation. At El Tabo the Isaline theologians wanted the church to go from dialogue to direct participation in the revolutionary struggle.[51] They had already come to the conviction that "the thing that was necessary was not a 'Christian response' to revolution, but participation in the revolutionary process which stirs our people." Julio de Santa Ana comments that at

48. Richard Shaull, "Y un Dios que actúa en la historia," in *América hoy,* p. 60.
49. Ibid., p. 61.
50. Ibid., p. 64.
51. ISAL, *América hoy,* pp. 117-19.

El Tabo "it is also understood that the Christian is obligated in his action by the revolutionary context."[52] And in that participation, the criterion for determining the significance of the biblical paradigms and for detecting the action of God in history is history itself, the actual events in Latin American reality. The norm for faith and practice is found not in the Scriptures but outside of them. Biblical interpretation is left at the mercy of historical changes and subjectivism.

THIRD CONTINENTAL ASSEMBLY, PIRIÁPOLIS, URUGUAY, DECEMBER 1967: CLEAR POLITICAL COMMITMENT

In the words of René Padilla, starting from the meeting at El Tabo, "the attempt of the movement to project a Christian attitude 'divorced from all political and ideological content' was totally abandoned."[53] Political ideology came to be predominant in the reflection and planning of ISAL. In the Third Assembly the participants were fully convinced that the word of order was "from commission to action," and that there was no way out other than that of a greater participation in the liberating struggle.

A spokesman for the movement recounts that when the Third Assembly was finished "almost all of us who attended were conscious that the road to the liberation of Latin America was necessarily very long." Che Guevara had died, militarism was dominant even in countries that had given signs of democracy, capitalism seemed unstoppable, and the Latin American leftist groups continued to divide. From the point of view of ISAL it was not a very encouraging picture for those who had dreamed of a quick social transformation. However, the difficulty of such an undertaking gave them renewed strength to go on with even greater zeal from reflection to revolutionary action. "For groups like ISAL the only way out was to become auxiliaries of the revolutionary forces and to work principally towards the development of a revolutionary consciousness among popular core groups."[54] After the Third Assembly ISAL tried to tie its participation more directly to the "liberating action" of those core groups.

52. Santa Ana, *Protestantismo, cultura y sociedad*, p. 168.
53. René Padilla, *Fe cristiana y Latinoamérica hoy*, pp. 120-21.
54. Introduction to *América Latina: Movilización popular y fe cristiana*, p. i.

At the same time, due to its strong ideological commitment, ISAL continued to separate itself from the larger sector of Latin American Protestantism, for the "revolutionary church" was an infinitesimal minority. According to the Isaline analysis, the church of those days (Catholic or Protestant) was divided into "reactionary," "reformist," and "revolutionary segments."[55]

Speaking before a small group of evangelical leaders during the celebration of the First Latin American Congress on Evangelism in Bogotá, Colombia, 1969, a prominent evangelical intellectual from South America said that in the theological realm "ISAL was a group of generals without an army and the Latin American evangelical population an army without generals." Without a doubt the members of ISAL were aware of the isolation into which they had fallen. They would change their tactics with regard to the churches in the consultation that occurred four years after Piriápolis.

FOURTH CONTINENTAL ASSEMBLY, ÑAÑA, PERU, JULY 1971: MOBILIZATION FOR SOCIAL CHANGE

The period between 1967 and 1971, that is, between the third and fourth continental conferences of ISAL, was dedicated to putting into practice the decisions made in Uruguay in 1967. One of those decisions was to occupy a place and develop a consistent struggle in the ranks of the "revolutionary church." The Fourth Assembly had as its purpose to consider whether the action of ISAL had been "at the level of the demands set forth by the revolutionary process," and to offer orientation for the future action of the movement.[56]

Growing social radicalism. At the assembly mention was made of tendencies that were making a certain difference between the Latin American situation in 1967 and that of 1971. First, in most Latin American countries the capitalist system was going through "a profound crisis out of which we do not yet know whether it will emerge alive." Second, in many Latin American countries, if not in all of them, "core groups which defend the popular interests have *already* judged in a negative way this irrational solution to

55. Ibid., p. viii.
56. Ibid., pp. viii-ix.

which the capitalist system is currently appealing." Third, "new aspects" were manifesting themselves in the process of liberation of Latin America. For example, the assembly noted that "Marxism is *already* without a doubt being accepted as the uncontested method of analysis for the study of Latin American reality. That is to say . . . the Christian-Marxist confrontation no longer has a reason to exist." Moreover, "a greater infusion of Christians is evident in the forces at the front line which are struggling in each national situation against the dominant system and on behalf of liberation"; the rivalry among Latin American leftist groups was being left behind; there seemed to be a "clear elevation of the popular conscience," which in turn was favorably inclined towards revolutionary struggle; and the basic position of Che Guevara "is being given as an undeniable premise to confront the demands of the struggle for Latin American liberation."[57] Che Guevara had proposed the creation of many Vietnams in Latin America.

Rubem Alves: theology of a new humanity created by political power. I have already mentioned that from 1967 to 1971 ISAL used the methods of Paulo Freire in the training of leaders at the popular level.[58] In the area of theology, the voice of Rubem Alves came to have a certain prominence in the Isaline movement of that time. I have also referred to the Marxist influence of Herbert Marcuse in the thought of Alves, especially in his book entitled *A Theology of Human Hope.*[59] The influence of Freire is also evident in that work.

Alves begins his discussion of the theme of liberation by referring to the search for a language that can express a vision and passion for human liberation. From there he goes on to describe what he calls *political humanism,* which in reality is a new conception of man, or a new anthropological focus. According to Alves, there are three elements in this way of conceiving man: (1) a new awareness of oppression, of "colonial domination" (examples can be seen in the awareness of blacks and students in the United States); (2) new language that expresses the new concep-

57. Ibid., pp. i-vii.
58. Costas, p. 200; quoting the anonymous work *Se vive como se puede: Resultados de una experiencia de aplicación de la pedagogía de Paulo Freire* (Montev-iedo: Tierra Nueva, 1970).
59. Rubem Alves, *A Theology of Human Hope* (see bibliography).

tion of man; and (3) the appearance of a new community, the world proletariat, "an ecumenical phenomenon which joins together people of the third world with blacks, students, and other groups in the developed nations. This awareness does not have, then, national, economic, social or racial limits."[60]

Alves then moves on to contrast political humanism with technology and theology. Following Marcuse in the description of technological language, Alves says that modern society has, in the final analysis, become a system that encompasses, conditions, and determines man.[61] It converts him into a consumer of merchandise, leading him to believe that there is no need for a future and that it is possible to be happy in the present by means of the conquests of technology.

Alves finds points of contact and contrast between *political humanism* and theology. He rejects existentialism because it reduces liberation to the subjective realm. He agrees with Karl Barth in his radical criticism of the present; but he laments the fact that Barthianism does not give enough importance to the future, nor to the work and creativity of man. For Barth, Alves suggests, man is not the creator of his own future.[62]

There is also contrast between political humanism and the "theology of hope" of Jürgen Moltmann. Alves admires Moltmann's emphasis on the future, but does not agree with his idea that the movement toward the future arises in answer to a *promise* that comes from without and makes it possible. That is to say, for Moltmann the renovating movement does not spring forth from the present reality, from the present condition of man through his intervention in history, but comes instead from a promise that is transcendent. Alves to the contrary believes that the future is "a horizon of possibilities, open, to be filled by the creation of freedom mediated to history by action." Man is the creator of a future that is not determined. Political humanism includes the negation of that which is inhuman in the present, concern for the transformation of this present by means of political action, and openness to hope which is based on history itself and not on a promise that is no more than transcendent.[63]

60. Ibid., pp. 1-6.
61. Ibid., pp. 17-27.
62. Ibid., pp. 44-55.
63. Ibid., pp. 55-68.

Alves thinks that the creation of history is only possible by means of power and goes on to explain that the use of power is rooted in politics:

> This is why this new consciousness believes that the new man and the new tomorrow are to be created in and through an activity which is political in character. Politics would be the practice of freedom, the activity of the free man for the creation of a new tomorrow. In this context politics is no longer understood as the activity of the few, the play of power among the elites. It is the vocation of man, because every man is called to participate, in one way or another, in the creation of the future. Politics thus becomes for this consciousness the new gospel, the annunciation of the good news that, if man emerges from passivity and reflexivity, as the subject of history, a new future can be created. It challenges man: "Seek first the kingdom of politics and his power, and all these things shall be yours."[64]

Alves teaches the liberation of man by man himself. It could be said that he abandons the oppressed to their own resources, facing a present that must be denied and a future that is always relative and uncertain. There are no fixed norms to determine whether man in his effort to create the future is going in the right direction. With regard to the content of his book, he affirms:

> Since these reflections arise out of my relative and provisional historical situation, they share the same provisional and relative character. They must, therefore, remain unfinished and open. Someone in a different historical situation could make a different choice. I cannot say that my historical experience is truer than his. There is always the element of personal choice and commitment, the risk of faith involved. . . . From a different perspective the same biblical material could probably be read in a different way. Exegesis is always done from one's relative position in history.[65]

Having departed from the authority of the Scripture, the Isaline theologians are left in complete subjection to historical relativism and subjectivism in their theology and praxis.

Turning local churches into revolutionary bases. The title of the book that compiles the documents of the consultation at Ñaña

64. Ibid., p. 16.
65. Ibid., pp. xiii-xiv.

is very suggestive: *Latin America: Popular Mobilization and Christian Faith*. Its emphasis does not fall on faith but on revolutionary action. The papers focus especially on the theme of the mobilization and participation of Christians in the struggle for social change.

The final document offers a sociological analysis of the Latin American situation and sets forth several bases for the strategy and the program of ISAL. The process of liberation is understood as a "breaking off from the system of economic dependence and exploitation which our countries suffer, a system which is generated by the action of imperialism in alliance with the dominant national classes." In order to overcome that dependence "it is necessary to promote the organization of those segments of the population which are being exploited by the dominant national classes and imperialism."[66] The purpose of liberation is expressed in the following terms:

> Why the process of liberation in Latin America? Simply in order to create a more just society in which hateful class distinctions will disappear and a more rational organization of production will be introduced, taking into account the personal needs of the workers. It will be a society in which power ought to be exercised by the popular classes which today suffer exploitation. To this end it will be necessary to socialize the means of production and democratize the exercise of power. It will be a new society in the sense that the social aspect will be more predominant than the individual.[67]

Christians can and should participate in the effort for liberation, following the example of Father Camilo Torres, who opted for revolution and socialism. There were, according to ISAL, three aspects of the liberating process in 1971:

> a) The discovery, on the part of committed Christians, of Marxist analysis as the most effective means for understanding the Latin American situation and projecting an effective action for radical change within that situation. . . . b) The orientation towards the proletariat, as a result of revolutionary commitment, implies an increasingly greater identification with the working class, making one's

66. ISAL, *América Latina: Movilización popular y fe Cristiana*, pp. 140, 143.
67. Ibid., pp. 143-144.

own the struggle in which that class is involved. . . . c) A task of
"conscientization" is then discovered, one which cannot be put off,
and which can be developed on various fronts of action. First, in the
churches themselves . . . . Second, among the people . . . . Third, by
becoming a part of political parties and organizations belonging to
the popular classes.[68]

It should be noted that the churches were the first objective of
the revolutionary action of ISAL. Before the consultation at Ñaña,
ISAL had been isolated from the churches. Now it wanted to come
back to them, understanding that

> the churches are task fronts, whether as a center of support or as a
> means for promotion and political recruitment, and also as a place of
> ideological struggle in which an effort is made to set free the Chris-
> tian conscience, in order that it may respond to the option and to
> militancy in support of the popular classes.[69]

It is obvious that "a change of the old ecclesiastical structures"
was necessary if the churches were going to cooperate in the
revolutionary struggle. ISAL saw three types of groups in the
churches: opposition groups who due to their ideological position
are in conflict with the hierarchy and who must be "encouraged,
supported and uplifted in their action"; groups who express the
interests of the dominant classes, and who "must be denounced in
a clear and final way"; and majority groups who experience multi-
ple alienations, and who must be instructed in order to be made
aware of their situation.[70] In other words, one of the revolutionary
actions of ISAL would be to destabilize the churches, intensifying
the antagonisms that already existed in them.

The document also gives attention to the theme of intellectual
freedom, with the conclusion that one must avoid the false interpretation that the bourgeois context has given to freedom. There
was agreement in the consultation with regard to two premises
considered to be conclusive:

68. Ibid., pp. 145-47.
69. Ibid., p. 148.
70. Ibid., pp. 149-50.

a) Recognize, on the one hand, that when *freedom* is spoken of, it should be considered in terms of a *socialist society* . . . in terms of the advance of the socialist process. . . . In that sense, there would be here a primacy of the *intellectual function,* above the traditional concepts of the *individual rights* of the intellectual. b) Recognize that it is by these means that the figure of the *being-intellectual* will arise (the critical and creative capacity of man in its broadest aspects), which will finally erase the old image of the "intellectual" created by bourgeois society.[71]

Those premises mean, from my point of view, that it is absolutely necessary to commit intellectual suicide for the sake of the "socialist process." Man is viewed en masse and is thought to be at his best when programmed for strict adherence to the directives of the party.

With respect to theology, ISAL warns:

authentic "theological renewal" should not be understood as anything like the repetition of theological formulas in opulent societies . . . but rather as the effort to understand the symbols and categories of faith in the framework of the process of liberation supporting and not obstructing that process. . . . The Church, then, should . . . give attention to the formulation of a "theology of the people," and not a "theology for the people."[72]

THE DEMISE OF THE ISAL ORGANIZATION

Without a doubt, in the 1971 assembly the Isaline movement turned furiously radical in its ideological commitment to the left. After Ñaña, it participated in the organization and activities of Christians for Socialism in Chile (1972); but at the fall and death of Salvador Allende, the ISAL group there had to disband and reorganize. The Uruguayan government also declared the Isaline movement illegal.[73] The ISAL movement no longer exists in an organizational form. However, Míguez Bonino says that those facts do not invalidate the historical significance of ISAL, "nor its character as a significant manifestation of the new consciousness

71. Ibid., p. 160.
72. Ibid., p. 150.
73. Costas, pp. 210-12.

which is emerging among Latin American Christians."[74] On the other hand, the generous words of Míguez Bonino cannot hide the fact that ISAL has not been able to achieve, as it had hoped to, the objectives proposed for itself in its Fourth Assembly.[75]

EVANGELICAL EVALUATION OF THE THEOLOGY OF ISAL

I will mention here three evangelical authors who directly critique ISAL. Other evaluations dealing with liberation theology or with theologies of liberation in general will be traced in following chapters.

"HUMANIZATION" MEANS MERE HUMANISM: ARANA QUIROZ

According to Pedro Arana Quiroz, Isaline thought is a humanism that is divorced from the sacred Scriptures and seeks the revelation of God only in man and history:

> God reveals himself to us in the movements and in the persons who struggle for the humanization of man. God reveals himself, in that way, in revolution and in the revolutionaries. . . . In the theology of ISAL, God is translated as revolution. The people of God as the revolutionary forces. The purpose of God as humanization. And the Word of God as the revolutionary writings. No one can fail to see that all this is Marxist humanism.[76]

In his book *Providencia y Revolución,* Arana Quiroz opposes the Isaline concept of humanization and advocates a biblical humanism that gives the glory to God.

"A NEW LANGUAGE OF FAITH" MEANS NOT LISTENING TO SCRIPTURE: KIRK

Andrew Kirk focuses on ISAL from the hermeneutical point of view. He begins his criticism by pointing out that within the Isaline writers there cannot be found a "discussion which begins from an

---

74. José Míguez Bonino, *La Fe en busca de eficacia,* p. 62. This note did not appear in the English edition, *Doing Theology on a Revolutionary Situation.*
75. Costas, pp. 212-22, points out some sociological and ecclesiastical reasons for the demise of ISAL.
76. Pedro Arana Quiroz, "La revelación de Dios y la teología en Latinoamérica," pp. 77-78.

exact exegesis of a given text." ISAL, says Kirk, uses the Bible "with the purpose of proving an affirmation, or a generalization which is derived, we suspect, from somewhere else."[77] Dr. Julio de Santa Ana, then president of ISAL, admitted that in ISAL little study had been done on the biblical basis of its task.[78]

Kirk is concerned by the way ISAL interprets the Exodus of Israel as a paradigm of revolution for our time, and he opposes the idea of Rubem Alves that revelation comes through historical events apart from a "vocalized" or verbal revelation. According to Alves, in the event of the Exodus Israel did not possess any idea of God *a priori;* "renovating language arises from historical reality of the liberating events."[79]

Alves's words illustrate the Isaline concept of the revelation of God in the events of history, which implies that He is revealing Himself today in the revolutionary process of Latin America. The biggest problem with that idea is that ISAL ignores the normative character of the sacred Scriptures. Revelation is not in the Bible but in events; it comes from events, and the interpreter has the freedom of deciding where and how God is acting in history. If it is said of a certain political movement that it is of the Lord, then neither the church nor the Christian has any other option than to support it and to embrace it.

Kirk refutes Alves, indicating that the account of the Exodus demonstrates that the people of Israel were, centuries before that event, in alliance with Yahweh, who was revealed to them as the God of Abraham, Isaac, and Jacob independently of the liberating act that was about to happen.[80]

With respect to the search for "a new language of faith," Alves asserts that it is history that creates language and not vice versa. The proposition that "according to the Bible events come before words" is very easy to refute with the Bible itself, according to Kirk. In the Exodus the revelation of that which God purposed to do came before the event itself. "The truth is, that the Bible always gives preeminence to the Word over history, in the sense that history remains silent without revelatory interpretation, and is

77. Andrew Kirk, "La Biblia y su hermenéutica en relación con la teología protestante en América Latina," p. 172.
78. Anana Quiroz, "La Revelación de Dios," citing "Protestantes en América Latina," *Cuadernos en Marcha* 29 (September 1969).
79. Kirk, p. 173.
80. Ibid., p. 174.

always dependent on the initiative of God." Kirk also points out the radically relativistic historical position of ISAL.[81]

Kirk states that ISAL "has rejected revelational theology," and that the problem for the movement now is "how to avoid being left in a simply mute history." The reason for that question is the impossibility of "deducing a theology from a mere historiographic description."[82]

Taking into account the fact that the hermeneutic system of ISAL does not allow the self-criticism of its ideological basis, Kirk sees that it is inevitable for the Isaline theologians to fall deeper and deeper "into a lamentable formalism and ideological conformism."[83] Time has shown that Kirk's 1972 prediction was not mistaken.

THEOLOGY OF REVOLUTION IS NOT THE GOSPEL: PADILLA

C. René Padilla focuses bravely on "the revolutionary gospel" proclaimed by Richard Shaull and his followers. He refers to ISAL without naming it directly, but his criticism of the "theology of revolution" is very cutting:

> All its errors are due to the fact that it begins with the revolutionary situation and interprets the Scriptures on the basis of presuppositions derived from leftist ideologies. Instead of showing the relevance of Revelation to Revolution, it makes Revolution the source of Revelation. The result is a secularized Gospel the dominant notes of which coincide with notes of Marxist tone.[84]

Padilla describes the theology of revolution as "another gospel" that reduces the purpose of God in history to mere humanization and loses sight of the ultimate cause of injustice, which is within man himself. The perspective that this "other gospel" has of man "coincides with that of Marxism, not with that of Christianity, even though it claims to give expression to the latter." Further, "The 'theology of revolution' idealizes man and consequently converts

81. Ibid., pp. 179-80.
82. Ibid., pp. 185-86. Kirk is quoting Julio de Santa Ana, "ISAL, un movimiento en marcha."
83. Ibid., p. 188.
84. C. René Padilla, "Mensaje bíblico y revolución," p. 200.

the Gospel into a utopian ideology which makes use of theological terminology but which has little relation to the eschatological message of the Bible."[85]

Padilla points out that if revolution must be understood as the expression of the redeeming purpose of God in history, then there is no reason for conservatives not to defend the status quo by saying that God's purpose is revealed in it. The revolutionary as well as the conservative can identify the purpose of God with the historical situation. Their theologies can be exactly the same at this point—even though the programs supported by those theologies are poles apart. Padilla states, "Both gods are equally alienating, and mankind needs to be liberated from the one and the other by the living and true God who was revealed in Jesus Christ once for all."[86]

CONCLUDING ASSESSMENT

Although ISAL may not appear to exist any longer as a continental organism, it provoked a certain commotion within Protestant theological circles of Latin America, and its fundamental ideas are still heard in the theology of liberation.

Certainly the Isaline movement has been a challenge for evangelical Christianity in Latin America. ISAL is to be admired for its concern to understand Latin American social reality in depth and for its attempt to formulate within that context a theology that is pertinent to the basic necessities of its people. ISAL came to emphasize for Latin American Protestantism the fact that the human being is also a body, not only a soul, and that we all live and act within a social situation of which we all are a part. Directly or indirectly, ISAL has stimulated us Protestants to read the Scriptures anew in order to find what the Lord would have to say to us regarding our social problems. As Padilla has well said, the greatest challenge of ISAL dwells in its "call to reflection within the context of a concrete commitment and to the use of theology as an instrument of transformation."[87]

We must also recognize that more than a few of ISAL's criticisms

85. Ibid., pp. 200-01.
86. C. René Padilla, "Iglesia y Sociedad en América Latina," p. 141.
87. Ibid., p. 147.

of the church were valid, and they continue to be valid in great sectors of the evangelical population of Latin America. It is our duty to respond to those criticisms with courage to make the necessary changes in the fulfillment of our mission.

At the same time, we have seen that ISAL has serious problems in its theology and its praxis. The Isaline movement represents, for all Latin American evangelicals, a solemn warning concerning the danger of allowing oneself to be obsessed by political problems and pretending to build a theological system not starting from the Scriptures, but from one's context and from social events, under the domination of an ideology. If the biblical norm for making theology is rejected, then there is no stopping on the slippery road that leads to a humanism that struggles to establish the kingdom of God here and now.

The hermeneutic problem of ISAL is acute because its criteria for interpretation are not found in the Word of God but in human reflection and in historical events. The word of revelation, ISAL suggests, does not come to man, but from man, as he struggles to change history. God acts where ideology wants Him to act. Revolution does not only occur within the framework of divine providence; it is the only way that God is using to humanize man. It is suggested that the humanization proposed by Marxism is the same as the one offered by the Christian faith. Therefore, on the political plane only the Marxist option is valid for the Christian, and Marxism becomes the criterion for the interpretation of the Scriptures. Because it does not take seriously the normative character of the written revelation of God, Isaline theology "loses its Christian specificity."[88] The followers of this theology can also lose their freedom of thought and action.

The premises of ISAL, as expressed in Ñaña, Peru, in 1971, regarding intellectual freedom sound alarming. Freedom of thought seems to be one of the last resources left to us in civilizations that try in one way or another, in the East or in the West, to program us for service to an ideology, whichever that might be. It is in internal, individual, personal freedom that true human dignity and liberation can be found.

88. Ibid., p. 141.

4

The New Catholicism And Liberation Theology

Catholic liberation theology springs from soil fertilized by the New Catholicism, a movement whose immediate origin dates from the papal rule of John XXIII, but whose deeper roots extend to the new theology that even then had been developing for several decades. In relation to the theology of liberation, we will consider in this chapter especially what may be called official New Catholicism, which finds expression in the documents of Vatican Council II, in the Latin American Episcopal Conferences of Medellín (1968) and Puebla (1979), and in encyclicals of John XXIII and Paul VI, the reigning pontiffs during the time when the Catholic theology of liberation was conceived.

VATICAN COUNCIL II

The arrival of Angelo Guiseppe Roncalli to the papal throne in 1958 signified the beginning of a new era for the Roman Catholic church. Pope John XXIII, who came to be known as "the good pope," was already an old man of 77 when he was elected the successor of Pius XII; but there was enough youth in his spirit for him to perceive that the Catholic church was falling behind in the process of social change that had been accelerating since the time of the Second World War.

An *aggiornamento,* an updating of sorts, was imperative if the church was going to speak in a relevant way to the modern world. John XXIII accepted that challenge and began to work on the task of renewal. One of his critical decisions was to call an ecumenical council, a meeting of the bishops and other Catholic representatives from the whole world.

There had not been a similar meeting since 1870, when the dogma of the infallibility of the pope was declared. Some Catholics thought that that dogma made another ecumenical council unnecessary, because the pope could now dictate beliefs on any issue of faith and practice. It appeared that the centuries-long conflict between the papacy and the councils had resolved itself in a permanent and unappealable manner in favor of the Roman pontiff.

John XXIII, however, demonstrated that there was still room for a council called and directed from the "Cathedra of Peter." The pope thought it necessary that the shepherds of the Catholic fold should seek together, under the authority of the Vatican and in obedience to the "deposit of faith," the most effective way to respond to the questions of a society in a state of rapid transformation.

A number of the decisions of Vatican II are related, directly or indirectly to Catholic liberation theology. The most significant for this study are the conciliar dispositions concerning the nature and the mission of the church.

THE NATURE OF THE CHURCH—LEANINGS TOWARD UNIVERSALISM

Long before the time of John XXIII some Catholic theologians were already desirous of formulating an ecclesiology that would be more biblical and patristic. The resulting attempt to renovate ecclesiological doctrine was represented in the council by a group of progressive bishops and theologians, who preferred to view the church as the people of God and not as a hierarchical judicial institution that speaks and acts in a spirit of triumphalism. Without denying that organization and hierarchical authority are necessary for the church, they basically saw the church as "the small flock," the pilgrim people that has not yet reached its final and glorious destination. Those ideas were incorporated in the *Dogmatic Constitution on the Church* (*Lumen gentium*) and in other conciliar documents. With regard to the nature of the church, Vatican II affirmed that she is "by her relationship with Christ . . . a kind of sacrament or sign of intimate union with God, and of the unity of all mankind." She is also "the universal sacrament of salvation."[1] This is one of the concepts that serve as a foundation for Gustavo Gutierrez's doctrine of salvation, as we shall see in another chapter. The idea that the church is the universal sacrament of salvation was not new to the participants of Vatican II. For example, Jean Daniélou in his commentary on the ecclesiology of the council quotes a text from Saint Cyprian in which the church is called *"unitatis sacramentum."*[2] Aloys Grillmeier says that since ancient times "the value of sacramental symbolism and efficacious instrumentality in the whole of the divine economy of salvation for all mankind and its history has been ascribed to the church." According to Karl Rahner, the church is "the historically tangible and audible sign of the redemptive grace in Christ." In 1961, Hans Küng had said that the church "as the sacrament of the salvation of the world, is the promise of grace to the world."[3] Of great importance also is the teaching of Vatican II on the church as the Body of Christ. In the use of that symbol the council momentarily approached the New Testament concept of the church. But the conciliar documents also sought to balance that concept with the affirmation of the encyclical *Mystici corporis* of Pius XII (1943), which stated that Christ establishes the Body on earth "as a visible structure," and that there is therefore a need for a hierarchical organization. Karl Adam, one of the precursors of the new ecclesiology, had affirmed that because the church is the Body of Christ it must be a visible organism. And Gustave Weigel has said that there is nothing that is more visible than a body.[4]

But a question arises concerning which church, or visible struc-

1. *Dogmatic Constitution on the Church* (*Lumen gentium*), arts. 1 and 48. Vatican II documents cited in this book are taken from *Documents of Vatican II,* edited by Walter M. Abbott.
2. Jean Daniélou, "El misterio de la Iglesia," in *La Iglesia del Concilio,* (Bilbao: El Mensajero del Corazon de Jesus, 1966), p. 49.
3. Aloys Grillmeier, "The Mystery of the Church," trans. Kevin Smith, in *Commentary on the Documents of Vatican II,* Vol. 1, edited by Herbert Vorgrimler (New York: Herder and Herder, 1967), p. 140; S. Paul Schilling, *Contemporary Continental Theologians* (New York: Abingdon, 1966), pp. 215-16; Hans Küng, *The Council, Reform and Reunion* (New York: Sheed and Ward, 1961), p. 13.
4. Karl Adam, *The Spirit of Catholicism* (Garden City, New York: Doubleday, 1954), p. 31; Gustave Weigel, *Catholic Theology in Dialogue* (New York: Harper & Row, 1965), p. 23.

ture, expresses the unity of the Body of Christ. Traditionally, the answer of Catholicism to that question has been the Roman Catholic church. But Vatican II used a euphemism when it said: "this Church, constituted and organized in the world as a society, subsists in the Catholic Church, which is governed by the successor of Peter and by the bishops in communion with that successor."[5] It has been said that the use of "subsists" in place of "is" represents one of the most significant changes in the ecclesiology of Catholicism, because it allows "theological space" for other ecclesiastical communities.[6] The conciliar text adds that there is the possibility that outside of the structure of the Catholic church "many elements of sanctification and of truth can be found . . . . as gifts properly belonging to the Church of Christ, [they] possess an inner dynamism toward Catholic unity."[7] In other words, all that is good and true outside Catholicism belongs to the church, whose full expression is given only in the Roman Catholic community. The council does not teach that other churches have the same status as the Roman Catholic church. The *Decree on Ecumenism* states:

> For it is through Christ's Catholic Church alone, which is the all-embracing means of salvation, that the fullness of the means of salvation can be obtained. It was to the apostolic college alone, of which Peter is the head, that we believe our Lord entrusted all the blessings of the New Covenant, in order to establish on earth the one Body of Christ into which all those should be fully incorporated who already belong in any way to God's People.[8]

However, Vatican II opens the door for an ecumenism that encompasses much more than the groups that profess to be Christian. In the Constitution *Lumen gentium* the relationships of the one people of God are described by means of concentric circles that begin with the Catholic faithful who are fully incorporated into the church and extend all the way to those who are not Christians, including the Jews, the Muslims, "those who in shad-

5. *Dogmatic Constitution on the Church,* art. 8.
6. Arthur A. Vogel, "The Second Vatican Council on the Nature of the Church and Ecumenism," *Anglican Theological Review* 49 (1967): 245. Vogel cites the Catholic theologian Gregory Baum in his concept of "theological space" for other ecclesiastical communities.
7. *Dogmatic Constitution on the Church,* art. 8.
8. *Decree on Ecumenism,* art. 3.

ows and images seek the unknown God," and those "who without blame on their part, have not yet arrived at the explicit knowledge of God, but who strive to live a good life, thanks to His grace." The *Constitution* continues, "Whatsoever goodness or truth is found among them is looked upon by the Church as a preparation for the gospel. She regards such qualities as given by Him who enlightens all men so that they may finally have life."[9] Grillmeier interprets those words in the sense that such people "profess not to have religion, but in reality they seek and affirm absolute justice and peace, that is, absolute values."[10]

The council seems to avoid the danger of universalism by saying that those who refuse to enter or remain in the Catholic church cannot be saved;[11] but the declarations mentioned above regarding those who practice other religions, or who do not belong to any of them, are open to a universalist interpretation. It is easy to conclude that somehow all belong to the people of God.

Avant-garde Catholic theologians such as Edward Schillebeeckx and Karl Rahner emphasize "presacramental grace," which is manifested in the desire for salvation by those who have not been evangelized. These theologians do not make Reformed theology's distinction between common grace and efficacious grace, and they appear to suggest that there is an efficacious saving grace in non-Christian religions and even outside of all religion.[12] They also speak of the church as "the extension of the incarnation" in the whole world, and of "anonymous Christians" in other religions.[13] I will return to that theme in relation to the teachings of Gustavo Gutierrez in a later chapter.

It is also worthy of mention that, in contrast to the traditional attitude of the Roman Catholic church towards atheism, Vatican II tried to comprehend atheists and to dialogue with them. It rejected atheism but did not anathemize it.[14] At the time of the council a dialogue had been initiated between West German Cath-

9. *Dogmatic Constitution on the Church,* art. 16.
10. Aloys Grillmeier, "The People of God," trans. Kevin Smith, in *Commentary on the Documents of Vatican II,* Vol. 1, p. 182.
11. *Dogmatic Constitution on the Church,* art. 14.
12. Eugene Hillman, *The Church as Mission* (New York: Herder and Herder, 1965), p. 187. Hillman cites E. Schillebeeckx, *Christ, the Sacrament of the Encounter with God* (New York: Sheed & Ward, 1963), p. 179.
13. Karl Rahner, "Christianity and the Non-Christian Religions," in his *Theological Investigations,* Vol. 5 (Baltimore: Helicon Press, 1966), pp. 115-34.
14. *Pastoral Constitution on the Church in the Modern World,* art. 21.

olics and European Marxist intellectuals. By 1967 more than six hundred intellectuals from seventeen countries participated in the Catholic group. Thus Marxist influence in the Catholic theology of Latin America after the council should come as no surprise.

THE MISSION OF THE CHURCH—EMPHASIS ON SOCIAL INVOLVEMENT

The *Dogmatic Constitution on the Church* states that the Christian mission consists of "communicating to men the fruits of salvation" and making an effort to meet the needs of the poor and the suffering in whom the church recognizes "the likeness of her poor and suffering Founder."[15] The objective of the Christian mission is spiritual and cultural, or social. The *Decree on the Church's Missionary Activity (Ad gentes)* exhorts:

> Let the faithful labor and collaborate with all others in the proper regulation of the affairs of economic and social life . . . Let the faithful take part in the strivings of those peoples who are waging war on famine, ignorance, and disease and thereby struggling to better their way of life and to secure peace in the world . . . The laity must strive by their civic and apostolic activity to set up a public order based on love and justice.[16]

That is not a new emphasis in Catholicism. The council was simply following the model established by the ecclesiastical *magisterium* and by Catholic theologians concerning the Christian responsibility to permeate the temporal order with the spirit of the gospel. Leo XIII, in his encyclical *Rerum Novarum,* had already focused on social issues of great importance and had exhorted the Catholic faithful to promote the welfare of society. What Vatican II set forth had been "drawn from the treasures of Church teaching."[17] In the *Pastoral Constitution on the Church in the Modern World (Gaudium et spes),* where more details concerning Christian social responsibility are given, there is to some extent a synthesis of the declarations that the popes—from Leo XIII to Paul VI—had made about social issues. Of course, the dominant influence was

15. *Dogmatic Constitution on the Church,* art. 8.
16. *Decree on the Church's Missionary Activity,* arts. 12, 19.
17. *Pastoral Constitution on the Church in the Modern World,* art. 91.

that of John XXIII, due to his famous encyclicals *Mater et Magistra* and *Pacem in Terris.*

Speaking concretely about the mission of the church, *Gaudium et spes* clarifies that "Christ, to be sure, gave His Church no proper mission in the political, economic, or social order. The purpose which He set before her is a religious one." But precisely "out of this religious mission itself came a function, a light, and an energy which can serve to structure and consolidate the human community according to the divine law."[18]

The church can help man to discover the meaning of his own existence, of his dignity, and of his death. The church rejects all slaveries, whose roots are found in sin; it warns that all human talent must be at the service of God and used for the good of humanity; it proclaims human rights at the same time that it opposes a false autonomy of man with respect to divine norms; it promotes unity among individuals and nations; it recognizes what good there is in current social change; it defends the dignity of work and the rights of workers, and denounces injustices in the social order: "While an enormous mass of people still lack the absolute necessities of life, some, even in less advanced countries, live sumptuously or squander wealth. Luxury and misery rub shoulders . . . Hence, numerous reforms are needed at the socio-economic level, along with universal changes in ideas and attitudes."[19]

According to *Gaudium et spes,* "God intended the earth and all that it contains for the use of every human being and people." Consequently, "by its very nature, private property has a social quality deriving from the law of communal purpose of earthly goods."[20]

In view of its great social responsibility, nothing is irrelevant to the church in the economic, political, family, social, or international orders, and in all those spheres the church must fulfill its mission. The text of *Gaudium et spes* reflects the presuppositions of so-called developmentalism, but provides an opening for a more radical transformation in the social order.

In his response to *Gaudium et spes,* the Protestant ecumenical leader Robert McAfee Brown points out, among other things, that

18. Ibid., art. 42.
19. Ibid., arts. 41-42, 63.
20. Ibid., arts. 69, 71.

it assumes a positive attitude toward the world, a willingness to learn from the world; that there are some signs that "the Council Fathers have listened to the gospel of Marx as well as the gospel of Mark;" and that instead of condemning communism, the document promotes dialogue between persons of different convictions.[21]

Without a doubt, Vatican II marked the beginning of a new era for the Roman Catholic church. Without reaching fundamental dogmatic changes, the council set in motion currents of renewal, in spite of the fact that the participants were divided between conservatives and progressives. The former were looking principally to the past, whereas the latter were looking with great concern at the signs of the times and were asking for profound changes for their church. One of the results of that conflict of interests was the ambivalence of the final documents of the council. That ambivalence explains up to a point the diversity of opinions concerning some conciliar teachings. Vatican II was "an open council," and to the interpretation of its teachings it remains open.

With respect to social transformation, the fresh breeze that John XXIII allowed to enter into the council has become for Latin America a theological wind so strong that the Catholic church itself has been unable to contain it. Liberation theologians have taken refuge in Vatican II in order to launch their revolutionary ideas into the theological arena. They have also sought support in the social encyclicals of the two pontiffs who governed the Catholic church during the time of the council.

THE SOCIAL DOCTRINE OF JOHN XXIII AND PAUL VI

To hear modern popes speaking about social issues is not at all unusual for the Catholic fold, especially since the days of Leo XIII's *Rerum novarum* in 1891. But what is surprising is the shift of the two Vatican II popes towards the left in the social and political realm, in contrast to their predecessors' attitude toward socialism.

JOHN XXIII: A VISION OF A SOCIAL ORDER ESTABLISHED BY GOD FOR THE COMMON GOOD

In his encyclical *Mater et magistra* (1961) "the good Pope" repeats and carries further some of the social teachings of previous

---

21. Robert McAfee Brown, "A Response," in Walter M. Abbott, ed., *The Documents of Vatican II*, pp. 309-16.

pontiffs. For example, he emphasizes the dignity of the human being, indicating that the church is concerned for the temporal good of people. Economics, he says, is primarily a product of private enterprise, but it is necessary that the intervention of the state be more extensive today than before. With regard to the working class, the pontiff considers that one way of meeting the demands of justice is for workers to "gradually acquire some share in the enterprise" in which they work, although in everything the common good should be taken into account. That should also be the criterion in the case of economic expansion at the international level.[22]

John XXIII asks that economic development and social progress go hand in hand in such a way that "class differences arising from disparity of wealth not be increased, but lessened so far as possible." He defends private property on the basis of natural law, and reiterates the teaching of Leo XIII regarding the social function of private property.[23]

It seems to John XXIII that "perhaps the most pressing question of our day concerns the relationship between economically advanced commonwealths and those that are in process of development." The answer to that acute problem, according to the pope, is found not only in economic assistance to the needy countries on the part of the nations that have a superabundance of consumer goods. Scientific, technical, and financial cooperation is also necessary. But a new colonialism should be avoided, and there should be an effort to distribute the resulting wealth among all of the citizens of the country.[24] That is a theme that liberation theologians take up under the rubric of dependence and underdevelopment.

The pope denounces those ideologies that "neither encompass man, whole and entire, nor . . . affect his inner being." He advocates the establishment of a social order founded upon God.[25]

On April 11, 1963, fifty-three days before his death, John XXIII directed his encyclical *Pacem in terris* (Peace on earth) not only to the bishops and the Catholic faithful, but "to all men of good

22. John XXIII, "Mater et magistra," in *The Gospel of Peace and Justice* (Maryknoll, N.Y.: Orbis, 1976), arts. 51-55, 77, 78-81.
23. Ibid., arts. 73, 109, 119.
24. Ibid., arts. 157, 168, 171.
25. Ibid., arts. 212-17.

will." It appeared during the interval between the first and second sessions of Vatican II. It is said that never had a papal document made such an impact on the world, especially on international entities such as the Geneva Conference on Disarmament, the League of Human Rights, the European Council, and the United Nations.[26]

Pacem in terris exalts the name of God, human dignity, natural law, and the common good. It explains the rights and duties of man and the basis of human coexistence. The relationship between the state powers and the citizen should be founded on the order established by God and on the common good. Relationships between states should have as their norms truth, justice, common solidarity, and liberty. With respect to disarmament, John XXIII affirms:

> Justice, right reason and humanity, therefore, urgently demand that the arms race should cease; that the stockpiles which exist in various countries should be reduced equally and simultaneously by the parties concerned; that nuclear weapons should be banned; and that a general agreement should eventually be reached about progressive disarmament and an effective method of control.[27]

Once again the pope defends the socially and economically weak nations and asks the wealthy countries to deal justly, fairly, and respectfully with those that are more needy. The pontiff also suggests that the only way of attaining the universal common good is to establish, by general agreement of the nations, a world authority.[28]

Of special interest for the ecumenical movement is the liberty John XXIII gives to the Catholic faithful to dialogue and cooperate with separated brethren and also with non-Christians "in the pursuit of objectives which are of their nature good, or conducive to good." With regard to relationships with non-Catholics, two distinctions should be made:

26. "Introduction to *Pacem in terris*," in *Ocho grandes mensajes* (Madrid: Biblioteca de Autores Cristianos, 1973), p. 203.
27. John XXIII, "Pacem in terris," in *The Gospel of Peace and Justice*, art. 112.
28. Ibid., arts. 120-25, 132-41.

one must never confuse error and the person who errs, not even
when there is question of error, or inadequate knowledge of truth,
in the moral or religious field. . . . It must be borne in mind, furthermore, that neither can false philosophical teachings regarding the
nature, origin and destiny of the universe and of man be identified
with historical movements that have economic, social, cultural or
political ends, not even when these movements have originated from
those teachings and have drawn and still draw inspiration there-
from.[29]

Evidently those principles clear the way for cooperation even
with those who hold to materialism or atheism. Before Vatican II,
John XXIII had created the Secretariat for Christian Unity, but
during the Council the Secretariat for Non-Christian Religions and
the Secretariat for Dialogue with Non-Christians were established.
In that way the doors of Roman Catholic ecumenism were opened
for all mankind. The results of that universal opening were not
long in coming, as can be seen in Latin American liberation theology. The introduction to *Pacem in terris* in the edition of Madrid's
Biblioteca de Autores Cristianos states that John XXIII offers "a
prudent and very well-lighted passage up to the still-closed door
of communism."[30] At the same time, following in the footsteps of
Pius XII, John XXIII does not opt for revolution, but for evolution:

In human institutions . . . it is not possible to renovate for the better
except by working from within them, gradually. This was also proclaimed by our predecessor of happy memory, Pius XII, in these
terms: "Salvation and justice are not to be found in revolution, but in
evolution through concord. Violence has always achieved only destruction, not construction."[31]

However, it could be said that *Pacem in terris* was carrying within
itself the revolutionary seed for those peoples who had not found
a solution for their economic and social problems in the thesis of
development.

PAUL VI: OPENING THE DOOR FOR MARXIST REVOLUTION

On June 21, 1963, Cardinal Giovanni Montini was elected to
succeed John XXIII in the pontifical chair and took the name of

29. Ibid., arts. 157-59.
30. "Introduction to *Pacem in terris,*" in *Ocho grandes mensajes,* p. 204.
31. John XXIII, "Pacem in terris," in *The Gospel of Peace and Justice,* art. 162.

Paul VI. His first official encyclical, which was signed August 6, 1964, has as its theme the church and opens the door to dialogue.

Such dialogue, he said, should be effected within the Catholic church and outside of her with all men. There are three concentric circles outside the church with which there should be dialogue. The closest circle to Catholicism is that of "the world that calls itself Christian," or the so called ecumenical dialogue. Then there is the circle of those who believe in God, including the Hebrews, the Muslims, and the followers of "the great Afro-Asian religions." The farthest circle represents "all that is human." Paul VI recognized that in that immense circle are found great numbers who do not profess any religion, and who "furthermore call themselves, in many diverse ways, atheists."[32]

Paul VI asserts that "the theory on which the negation of God is based is fundamentally erroneous," and denounces "those ideological systems that deny God and oppress the Church; systems which frequently are identified with economic, social and political regimes, among them especially atheistic communism." However, his discourse immediately takes a conciliatory turn when he says that this condemnation "does not come from us," and he adds: "Our reproach is, really, a lament of victims more than a sentence of judges."[33] The pontiff wants to keep the doors of dialogue open.

On March 26, 1967, almost a year and a half after the conclusion of Vatican II, Paul VI published his famous social encyclical *Populorum progressio*. As the title indicates, the pope focuses on the need for promoting the development of all peoples. It is a call for the integral development of man and the mutual development of humanity.

The first part of the encyclical deals with people's economic needs and aspirations and the problems of economic development. Paul VI recognizes the errors of colonialism, but he does not generalize, and he notes that the colonizers also carried out a positive work in favor of the countries that were under their dominion. But there is a growing imbalance in modern economy; "rich peoples enjoy rapid growth whereas the poor develop slowly," and social conflicts have taken world dimensions. There are "glaring inequalities" in the enjoyment of possessions and the exercise of power. To all of this can be added the clash between

---

32. Paul VI, "Ecclesiam suam," in *Ocho grandes mensajes,* arts. 91-92, 100, 102.
33. Ibid., art. 93.

traditional civilizations and the new elements of industrial civilization, as well as the generation gap.[34]

According to Paul VI, "development cannot be limited to mere economic growth. In order to be authentic it must be complete: integral, that is, it has to promote the good of every man and of the whole man." It is necessary to have total development, a "transcendental humanism." The description of development offered by this encyclical has become famous: "for each and all the transition from less human conditions to those which are more human." "Less human" refers to material and moral deficiencies, the oppressive structures resulting from social injustice. "More human" means liberation from misery, the possession of necessities, the growth of knowledge, the acquisition of culture, increased esteem for the dignity of others, cooperation for the common good, the desire for peace, the acknowledgement of supreme values that have God as their source and finality, and especially faith in Him for the unity of all human beings in the love of Christ.[35]

In order to achieve such development, it is necessary, according to the pontiff, to take some urgent and direct measures in the economic realm. For example, it should be admitted that "private property does not constitute for anyone an absolute and unconditional right." That right should not be exercised "to the detriment of the common good." Sometimes the common good even demands expropriation: "If certain landed estates impede the general prosperity because they are extensive, unused or poorly used, or because they bring hardship to peoples or are detrimental to the interests of the country, the common good sometimes demands their expropriation."[36]

Furthermore, *Populorum progressio* vigorously denounces the system that considers "profit as the key motive for economic progress, competition as the supreme law of economics, and private ownership of the means of production as an absolute right that has no limits and carries no corresponding social obligations." Unregulated economic liberalism leads to dictatorship and produces "the international imperialism of money.[37] Therefore the

34. Paul VI, "Populorum progressio," in *The Gospel of Peace and Justice,* arts. 7-10.
35. Ibid., arts. 14, 20-21.
36. Ibid., arts. 23-24.
37. Ibid., art. 26.

economy should always be at the service of man. Another of the better-known paragraphs of this encyclical speaks of revolution:

> There are certainly situations whose injustice cries to heaven. When whole populations destitute of necessities live in a state of dependence barring them from all initiative and responsibility, and all opportunity to advance culturally and share in social and political life, recourse to violence, as a means to right these wrongs to human dignity, is a grave temptation.
>
> We know, however, that a revolutionary uprising—save where there is manifest, long-standing tyranny which would do great damage to fundamental personal rights and dangerous harm to the common good of the country—produces new injustices, throws more elements out of balance and brings on new disasters. A real evil should not be fought against at the cost of greater misery.[38]

Violent revolution is not rejected absolutely. In certain circumstances it may be necessary.

For Paul VI development involves being concerned as much for social progress as for economic progress. All programs of reform must be at the service of the person, and man must constitute himself as "the author of his own advancement" in keeping with the faculties which the Creator has given him.[39]

In the second part of *Populorum progressio,* the pope identifies himself with the underdeveloped countries of the whole world with a demand for equity in commercial relations between rich and poor countries. "The poor nations remain ever poor while the rich ones become still richer because the developed nations continue applying the rule of free trade in international commercial relations, without taking into account that they are at an advantage due to the inequality in economic conditions from country to country. Consequently Paul VI declares that free trade cannot be fair unless it is subject to the demands of social justice. In order to achieve justice and peace in international relations, Paul VI proposes, as did John XXIII, the establishment of "a world authority capable of acting effectively in the juridical and political sectors."[40]

Finally, there is a call to Catholics, to other Christians and

38. Ibid., arts. 30-31.
39. Ibid., art. 34.
40. Ibid., arts. 57-58, 78.

believers, and to all men of good will to work for a more human life for all peoples and to seek world peace and solidarity.[41]

After reading *Populorum progressio* one is not surprised that it has been acclaimed in many parts of the world as a document with great beneficial implications for humanity, especially for underdeveloped countries. On the other hand, neither is it surprising that one publication of the powerful financial institutions of New York would call this papal message "Marxism warmed over." According to the author who quotes those words, the plea of the hungry countries to those who live in affluence is "ineffective if it is peaceful; suicidal if it is revolutionary. Paul VI dares to attempt to make it energetic and concrete."[42]

The "developmentalist" language of the encyclical is obvious, but it has elements, such as those mentioned above, in which liberation theologians could find encouragement and guidelines. It can be said that the social doctrine of both popes of Vatican II encouraged, directly or indirectly, the development of theological liberationalism in Latin America.

The Second Latin American Episcopal Conference: "The Justification of a Praxis of Liberation"

The Latin American Episcopal Council (CELAM) was born on the occasion of the first General Conference of Latin American Bishops which was called by Pius XII and held at Rio de Janeiro, Brazil, from July 25 to August 4, 1955. The topics discussed at that time indicate the area of major interest for the Latin American bishops of preconciliar times: the clergy, the religious orders, the seminaries, Masonry, the development of Protestantism in Latin America, the separation of church and state, superstition, spiritism, communism, and the problem of immigrants. The emphasis falls on the defense of the Catholic faith and clerical problems.

CELAM was created to study issues of interest to the church in Latin America, to coordinate pastoral activities, and to plan future conferences of Latin American bishops called by the Holy See.[43]

41. Ibid., arts. 81-86.
42. "Introduction to *Populorum progressio*, in *Ocho grandes mensajes*, pp. 319-20.
43. "La evangelizacion en el presente y en el futuro de America Latina," document of the Episcopal Conferences, in preparation for the Third Latin American Episcopal Conference held in Puebla, Mexico, 1979 (Mexico: CELAM, 1978), p. 21.

According to Monsignor Aloisio Lorscheider, president of CELAM, this entity has achieved the following results among others:

> It has stimulated the development of indigenous pastoral theological thought. . . . It has called attention to the need for a more just society on a Christian continent in order for evangelization to be truly effective. It has cooperated in the balanced renewal of the Church in Latin America within the spirit of Vatican II. . . . It has helped to clarify increasingly the physiognomy of the Church in Latin America, a *poor* church with a definite *liberating* function.[44]

When the second Latin American Episcopal Conference was held in 1968 in Medellín, Colombia, the Catholic church throughout the world was already experiencing the effect of the currents of renewal that Vatican II had set into motion. Medellín was definitely a sequel to that council. José Míguez Bonino has called the conference in Medellín "the Vatican II of Latin America." Monsignor Alfonso Lopez Trujillo, Secretary of CELAM, has said that "Medellín would have been impossible without the Council." The Second Latin American Episcopal Conference made every effort to apply the renewal initiated by the council to Latin America as the theme of Medellín clearly shows: "The Church in the Contemporary Transformation of Latin America in the Light of the Council."[45]

What was Medellín? Monsignor Lopez Trujillo answers that it was the spirit of renewal of the church; an early fruit of conciliar renewal; an echo of the pontifical *magisterium,* especially based on *Populorum progressio*; a pastoral response stemming from the discerning of "the signs of the times"; and an effort towards integral evangelism, which includes the proclamation of the gospel and the commitment to work for justice and authentic human liberation. Medellín was an ecclesiastical accomplishment; "it is not a political manifesto, but a prophetic presence of the Church. And it should be interpreted as such."[46]

Of particular interest, says Trujillo, are the great choices made

44. Aloisio Lorscheider, "Que es el CELAM? [What is CELAM?]," pp. 8-10.
45. José Míguez Bonino, "El nuevo catolicismo," in *Fe cristiana y Latinoamerica hoy,* p. 91; Alfonso Lopez Trujillo, "Medellín: una mirada global," p. 12; *La Iglesia en la actual transformacion de America Latina a la luz del concilio* (see bibliography).
46. Lopez Trujillo, pp. 12-16.

at Medellín: to opt for man, for our peoples integrally conceived, for the poor, for integral liberation, that is, liberation as integral development as prescribed by *Populorum progressio.*[47]

Monsignor Lopez Trujillo wrote his observations several years after Medellín and paused to consider the concept of liberation according to his understanding of the conference and its documents:

> Liberation is conceived as an integral part of the theology of redemption. . . . It is historical and transhistorical liberation. . . . It requires a commitment for our peoples and for the Church. . . . The corresponding commitment is made according to the essential mission of the Church. . . . Liberation is found in the process of *injustice* and *sin* (as the situation), *conversion* and *reconciliation* (as the goal). . . .
>
> Many of the circumstances of underdevelopment and misery are the consequence of injustice. . . . Liberation aims at profound personal and social conversion, which leads to the change of structures. . . . Medellín supposes simultaneous action upon the person and the structures, in which the *personal* pole, so characteristic of the Christian faith, occupies the principal place. . . . The profound conversion is an encounter with God and with the brethren and a commitment to struggle for justice and to bold structural reforms. . . .
>
> The liberating pastoral option demands a spirit of true *reconciliation.* . . . Social conflicts are neither denied nor unrecognized. . . . It does not identify itself with an attitude of traditional *pacifism.* . . . It has to be present in the struggle for justice. . . . It opposes a form of *class struggle* which is proper to Marxist analysis. . . . The occurrences of class consciousness are not denied. . . . There are forms of class struggle in which the Christian may, and in some occasions should, participate . . . without enmity or mutual hatred . . . based in the love for justice.[48]

Even that moderate evaluation of the meaning of Medellín can open the way for Latin American theological liberationism. Enrique Dussel, Catholic historian and theologian, says that "CELAM will develop the theology of liberation as its own theology." And regarding the conference at Medellín he comments:

47. Ibid., pp. 16-17.
48. Ibid., pp. 17-22.

At any rate Medellín opens the door for a clear class commitment, and it allows the taking of positions in defense of the interests of workers, peasants and those who have no voice in society. In whatever act of repression a Christian may be involved in the following years, he will always justify his actions from the documents of Medellín. Therefore, for a Rockefeller, for the intelligence agencies, even for the military and the police, Medellín became the justification of a praxis of liberation.[49]

In the opinion of the Catholic writer Roberto Oliveros Maqueo, the fundamental contribution of Medellín was to reflect on the faith from the context of misery and injustice under which large groups of Latin Americans are suffering.[50]

It is worth keeping in mind that Gustavo Gutiérrez, without a doubt the best known of the theologians of liberation, was one of the theological consultants for CELAM, and at Medellín he was a member of one of the most important task forces, the Peace Commission.[51] Hugo Assmann mentions that the document of Medellín on "Liberating Education" fundamentally took its inspiration from the ideas of Paulo Freire,[52] With respect to justice, Dussel claims that Medellín's document on "Human Promotion," by opting for a theology of liberation that "has primarily a biblical and political foundation," surpasses the theology of development and the theology of revolution "promoted in Protestant circles by Richard Shaull."[53]

It can be said that Medellín officially opened the door to the theology of liberation; but there also have been complaints because the message of the second conference of CELAM has not been carried out always and everywhere to its final consequences.

REVOLUTIONARY FERMENT IN THE NEW LATIN AMERICAN CATHOLICISM

At the time of Vatican Council II seventeen bishops from Asia, Africa, and Latin America gathered in Rome to sign a document

49. Enrique D. Dussel, "Un analisis contextual de la Iglesia Catolica en America Latina," pp. 38-39.
50. Roberto Oliveros Maqueo, *Liberacion y teologia*, p. 120.
51. Dussel, "Un analisis contextual," p. 38.
52. Hugo Assmann, bibliographical appendix to *Pedagogia del oprimido* by Paulo Freire (Montevideo: Tierra Neuva, 1970), p. 247.
53. Enrique D. Dussel, *A History of the Church in Latin America*, p. 145.

that according to Dussel "expresses one of the basic teachings of the Council." The first to sign it was the Bishop of Olinda and Recife (Brazil), Dom Helder Camara. The document appeared for the first time in *Témoignage Chrétien* (Paris, 31 July 1966) the year after the council had finished its labors. "The document . . . stated that the Church does not condemn revolution in principle, that revolution is acceptable when it serves the cause of justice, and that frequently it is the rich and not the poor who begin class struggle and violence."[54] That interpretation of Vatican II encouraged Catholics desirous of involving themselves in one way or another in the struggle for the change of social structures in Latin America.

ERNESTO CARDENAL: POET, PRIEST, REVOLUTIONARY

Catholic revolutionary ferment has manifested itself in different ways. It even has its own poetic expression in the protest verse of the Nicaraguan poet and monk Ernesto Cardenal, who began his literary battle several years before Vatican II was held. Cardenal was born in Granada, Nicaragua, in 1925. He studied philosophy and letters at the Universidad Autonoma de Mexico, after which he did graduate work at Columbia University. He took part in the rebellion of April 1954 against President Anastasio Somoza (the elder). At that time he wrote four revolutionary poems under the suggestive title *Hora O* (*Zero Hour*), in homage to Cesar Augusto Sandino. In 1957, after the death of Somoza (September 1956), Cardenal entered the monastery of Our Lady of Gethsemane in Kentucky, where he was a novice under Thomas Merton, the well-known Trappist writer distinguished for his broad ecumenical interests. Finding the climate of Kentucky disagreeable, Cardenal transferred to the Benedictine monastery of Santa Maria de la Resurreccion in Cuernavaca, Mexico, and then went to Colombia to finish his studies in theology. He returned to Nicaragua in 1965 and was ordained a priest in the Cathedral of Managua.

On the island of Solentiname in the Great Lake of Nicaragua, Cardenal formed a community of contemplation and service. He helped the islanders by means of a school and a medical clinic. In *The Gospel in Solentiname*, Cardenal compiled ideas expressed by his brethren in response to the reading of the gospels.

54. Ibid., pp. 140–41.

In an interview televised on Channel 11 in Guatemala on September 25, 1978, Cardenal admitted that he was a member of the Sandinista National Liberation Front and affirmed that he did not see a dichotomy between the gospel and politics, because the gospel is political. He clarified that he had not participated in the armed struggle, because his age did not allow it, but his struggle was being carried out "with poetry and preaching." By that time the international news media were already calling Cardenal "the ideologist of the Sandinista Movement in Nicaragua." At the present time Cardenal is a member of the revolutionary cabinet in his country. He has been the head of the Ministry of Culture since the triumph of the revolution that overthrew President Somoza (the son). In September of 1979 he declared to the press, "This is a Christian revolution. The people of Nicaragua are, in the great majority, Christian, and that is why the people carried out the revolution. . . . The church never condemned recourse to weapons for a just cause. Pope Paul VI said that armed struggle and violence were legitimately moral in the case of evident and prolonged dictatorship—and ours was truly prolonged."[55]

According to the journalist José Ramon Enriquez, "it cannot be said that Cardenal is in the first place a poet or in the first place a Christian or a revolutionary. . . . He is a poet, Catholic priest and revolutionary at the same time and for identical reasons."[56] In an interview with José Steinsleger, responding to the question "What is Christianity for Ernesto Cardenal?" the poet-priest affirms,

> For me Christianity is the Christianity of the Gospels, a Christianity that has been disfigured through the centuries, but which in essence is authentically revolutionary. In Latin America there are now a number of priests, religious, and theologians who have understood that Christianity and Marxism are not incompatible but, on the contrary, have a common goal; the Kingdom of God on earth, as the Gospel calls it; the perfect communist society, according to Marxism.[57]

55. *Prensa Libre* (Guatemala), 14 September 1979.
56. José Ramon Enriquez, "Ernesto Cardenal: Nuestro delito es anunciar el paraiso," *La Hora Dominical* (Guatemala), 23 May 1976.
57. José Steinsleger, "La meta comun del cristianismo y el marxismo," *La Hora Dominical,* (Guatemala), 7 March 1976.

Concerning the experience of Solentiname, Cardenal explains: "That contemplative or semi-contemplative life which we lived there has also led us to revolution, to revolutionary solidarity. Our road has led from contemplation to revolution, and from the Gospel to Marxism." Cardenal does not think of God except as the one who intervenes in defense of the oppressed and in judgment against the oppressors. Nor is there for him any other true church than the one that identifies itself with the cause of the dispossessed of this world.[58]

CAMILO TORRES: REVOLUTIONARY ACTION OUT OF "LOVE FOR MY NEIGHBOR"

From the pulpit or the classroom it is possible to go to the street demonstrations or to the public square where the so-called "live forces of the country" unite to protest against the established order, and even to the trenches where the stammering of the machine guns is much louder than the voice of reason and of feelings. This was in a way the pilgrimage of the Colombian Father Camilo Torres Restrepo, who has become the symbol of those Latin American Catholics who are willing to carry their revolutionary commitment to its final consequences.

Camilo Torres was born to a home of the upper urban class in Bogotá on February 3, 1929. After finishing his seminary studies he went to Louvain to study sociology. Upon returning to his country he was named chaplain of the National University, where he won the affection of the students. He also became involved in various works of aid and development. His mother recalls that from childhood Camilo manifested his solidarity with those who were rejected by society. When he was hardly more than a child, he would take the medical samples of his father, who was a doctor, and give them to the needy. Even the money given to him to go to the movies he would distribute to the children of the poor neighborhoods. "That immense love for the poor led him to believe that only if the majority class took power would there be an "effective change in the situation."[59]

There are those who suggest that Camilo opted for a retreat to

58. Ibid.
59. German Guzman Campos, *El Padre Camilo Torres*, pp. 1-3.

the mountains "not because he believed in guerrilla warfare, nor in its effectiveness, nor in its methods," but only because it was there "that he felt secure." It is also said that he did not die with a rifle in his hand—indeed, he never even held one. It is admitted, to be sure, that he was a guerrilla and present in combat with the army (which cannot be denied), but at the same time it is affirmed that he "never shot at anybody, nor did he ever kill anybody."[60]

What is certain is that Camilo felt the need to follow the road of guerrilla warfare, the path of violent action in revolutionary praxis. He felt that in poor countries Christians not only can but should involve themselves in the transformation of structures for the benefit of the majorities. Finally he came to the profound conviction that armed violence is the only way left for "all sincere revolutionaries." His proclamation to Colombians on January 7, 1966, ends with the words "Liberation or death!"[61] And death he found on February 15, 1967, "facing heaven, facing Colombia, and facing this Indian and mestizo America. Face to face with the conscience of free men," according to the words of one of his biographers.[62]

Camilo found theological justification for revolutionary commitment in the nature of love for one's neighbor. After requesting a reduction to lay status, he made a public declaration in which the following words appear:

> I opted for Christianity considering that in it was found the purest form of serving my neighbor. I was elected by Christ to be a priest eternally, motivated by the desire to give myself full time to the love of my neighbors. As a sociologist, I desired that that love should be effective, by means of technology and science; in analyzing Colombian society I have become aware of the need for a revolution to be able to feed the hungry, to give drink to the thirsty, to clothe the naked and to bring about the welfare of the majority of our people. I consider that the revolutionary struggle is a Christian and priestly struggle. Only through it, in the concrete circumstances of our country, can we put into practice the love that men ought to have for their neighbors.[63]

60. "¿Camilo Torres: Sacerdote o Guerrillero?" *Protesta,* no. 20.
61. Camilo Torres, *Cristianismo y revolucion,* pp. 341, 571.
62. Guzman Campos, p. 263.
63. *Cristianismo y revolucion,* p. 376.

In his message to the Christian public on August 26, 1966, he declared:

> The most important thing in Catholicism is love for one's neighbor. "He that loveth another hath fulfilled the law" (St. Paul, Rom. 13:8). In order for this love to be genuine, it must seek to be effective. . . . It is necessary, then, to take the power from the privileged minorities in order to give it to the poverty-stricken majorities. . . . Revolution is not only permitted but obligatory for those Christians who see in it the only effective and far-reaching means of making love for all a reality. . . . I believe that I have dedicated myself to the Revolution in love for my neighbor.[64]

Such language had to sound subversive to the powerful, and there has been no lack of those who identify Camilo with communism. However, in his "Message to Communists" on September 2, 1965, he declared that neither as a Columbian, nor as a sociologist, nor as a Christian, nor as a priest, was he, or would he be, a communist. At the same time he denied that he was anticommunist and stated his willingness to fight at the side of the communists, without being one of them, "for common objectives: against the oligarchy and the control of the United States, and for the coming to power of the class of the masses." His hope was "to build socialism without destroying what is essential in Christianity." He dreamed of fomenting a revolution that would be socialistic but also nationalistic, "without falling completely within the Soviet block," but maintaining a neutral stance towards the competition between the great world powers.[65] Although the church did not approve of his radically revolutionary action, Camilo did not abandon his Catholic faith.

HELDER CAMARA: NONVIOLENT ACTION LEADING TO "PERSONALIST SOCIALISM"

In contrast to Camilo Torres's desperate and violent response to the problems of Latin America, there arose within Latin American Catholicism the firm but at the same time peaceful voice of Helder Camara, who has been called "the red bishop of Brazil" and "Lenin

64. Ibid., pp. 525-26.
65. Ibid., pp. 429, 527-28.

in a priest's cloak," due to his arduous struggle on behalf of the poor. His passion is to speak in the name of those who cannot do so for themselves, to be the voice of those who have no voice.[66]

Helder Camara was born in Fortaleza, Brazil, on February 7, 1909. He received his priestly ordination in 1931, and his first work was among university students in his native city. At that time he allowed himself to be captivated by Fascism. In 1936 he was named the technical assistant for the Secretariat of Education of Brazil's capital. He became a member of the Superior Council of Education, remaining in that post until 1964, when he moved from Rio de Janeiro to Recife.

In 1955 the first conference of CELAM was held in Rio. Cardinal Barros Camara, archbishop of that city, entrusted to Dom Helder the organization of the international eucharistic congress of Rio, held in conjunction with CELAM I. Dom Helder demonstrated his excellent gifts as an organizer. It is said that on that occasion Cardinal Gerlier of Lyon told Helder: "Do you think it decent to display such religious pomposity in a city surrounded by slums? Why don't you use your gifts to solve this problem?" Those questions seem to have contributed towards a tremendous change in the life of Helder Camara. One of the first signs of that change was the campaign that Helder carried out to aid the slum dwellers, "since the inhuman conditions in which they live are a collective sin, for which all should feel guilty."[67]

Politically, Camara arrived at the following conclusion:

> For the underdeveloped countries I find no solution either in capitalism or in neocapitalism. Nor do I find one in existing socialism, either from Cuba, or from Russia, or from China. . . . If you wish, you may say socialism, but a socialism that respects in reality—not only in theory—the human person, and that doesn't fall into dictatorship. Not a government dictatorship or a party dictatorship.[68]

In other words, Dom Helder proposes that the solution should be sought in a form of socialization, or a "personalist socialism." In March of 1968, in a conference of the Catholic Institute of Recife, he indicated that Christians do not need to fear a world

66. Feliciano Blazquez, *Helder Camara: El Grito del Pobre*, pp. 9-12.
67. Ibid., p. 35.
68. Ibid., pp. 38-39.

movement toward socialism because "Christians 'can offer a mystique of universal fraternity and incomparable hope far more comprehensive than the narrow mystique of historic materialism. . . . The Marxists, conversely, feel the need of revising their concept of religion.' "[69] At the same time Camara, following the example left by the great pacifists Mahatma Gandhi and Martin Luther King, rejects the idea that violence is the remedy for our social evils: "He does not believe in the strength of weapons; he hates war; he feels himself a pilgrim of peace; he trusts in the efficacy of non-violence and does not hope for any solution from government, which tends to be a docile and well-directed instrument at the service of the great powers."[70]

Dom Helder maintains that violence begets violence without solving the problem of the oppressed masses. He speaks of three kinds of violence. The first is that which is suffered by the weak under the thumb of the mighty. Injustice "is the first of all violences, the first violence." As a reaction to the violence of injustice there arises the second violence, the revolution of the oppressed "or of a youth determined to fight for a more just and more human world." Then comes repression on the part of the authorities to rescue the public order or to restore it. That is the third violence. "The conclusion is evident," says Camara; "there is a real threat that the world may enter into an escalated violence, that it may fall into a spiral of violence."[71]

But if Camara does not believe in the strength of weapons, what then is the solution for the problem that confronts the oppressed peoples? In a lecture given at Rome on December 1, 1965, Dom Helder said, "I have the fraternal confidence to suggest that within each country of Latin America, the hierarchy, without forgetting in any way its directly pastoral work, lend its moral support, if the case demands it, to a movement of nonviolent action capable of stimulating the weakness of 'feudal lords' who still find themselves in the middle ages."[72] That action, which according to Camara will be of "justice and peace," will exercise a moral liberating pressure that will help in a peaceful but effective way to change the socioeconomic, political, and cultural structures of the underdeveloped

69. Dussel, *A History of the Church*, pp. 163-64.
70. Blazquez, p. 120.
71. Helder Camara, *Espiral de violencia*, pp. 18-19, 30.
72. Blazquez, p. 121.

countries. At the same time it will induce the developed countries to radically change their policies of foreign trade with underdeveloped countries.[73]

The call by the "bishop of the poor" to action for justice and peace is ecumenical. He addresses all men, without regard to racial, social, linguistic, geographical, or religious barriers so that they may unite in the task of demanding in a peaceful way "justice as a prior condition for peace."[74]

Camara makes a special appeal to youth to join the "Abrahamic minorities," the movement of men and women of good will who hope against all hope and believe in the triumph of peace through justice. Hoping to win them, Dom Helder does not condemn the younger generation; on the contrary, he makes an effort to understand them and even praises them. He uses moral persuasion with them. He invites them to dialogue constructively and to discuss openly and sincerely his proposal to exert moral liberating pressure to produce a more just and human world.[75]

Helder Camara is not blind to the great obstacles that lie in the path of nonviolence, but he believes that "time is on the side of Gandhi" and the pacifist movement that he initiated. "Before long," states Dom Helder, "Gandhi will be recognized as a prophet." One reason for maintaining such an optimistic hope is that people will become convinced of the absurdity of war. Moreover, there are minorities who, in opposition to the forces of hatred and violence, know full well that in the final analysis war is useless for the attainment of peace among human beings. They realize that the "only real answer to violence is to have the courage to confront the injustices which constitute the first violence."[76]

Of course, there are those who question Bishop Camara's teaching and attitude. They say that he argues for nonviolent violence, since nonviolent resistance also disturbs the established order. Others wonder if Dom Helder's well-intentioned words can find a responsive chord in hearts that do not possess peace with God and cannot, therefore, have peace with man. What is undeniable is that fourteen years after the publication in French of Camara's now famous book *Spiral of Violence*, the fertile soil of Latin America

73. Camara, p. 59.
74. Ibid., p. 55.
75. Ibid., pp. 65-81.
76. Ibid., pp. 47-48.

continues to be dampened with the blood shed by those who are guilty of the violence that "the Bishop of the poor" condemns.

POPE PAUL VI: AN ELEMENT OF BALANCE

Politically, Camara did not find himself alone among his colleagues in the priesthood. His preference for a special socialism tailored to Latin America was and is shared by other Roman Catholic clergy. I have already mentioned the meeting of Christians for Socialism and the case of Father Camilo Torres. Bishop Mendez Arceo of Cuernavaca, Mexico, and Archbishop Jorge Enrique of La Paz, Bolivia, have also opted for a socialist system that would be compatible with Christianity.[77] The attitude of those prelates reflects in a certain way the spirit of Vatican II and of popes John XXIII and Paul VI, who carried the Catholic church from anathema to dialogue in its dealings with socialism. Helder Camara, Camilo Torres, Mendez Arceo, and many other Catholics in different parts of the world are evidence of the phenomenon that the French writer and journalist Jacques Duquesne calls "Christ's left."[78]

Pope Paul VI tried to be an element of balance among the warring ideological factions within the Catholic church. For example, when he visited Colombia on the occasion of the Second Latin American Episcopal Conference in 1968, he said to the peasants of that country:

> "Man shall not live by bread alone" . . . your conditions as poor people are more propitious for reaching the kingdom of Heaven. . . . Finally allow us to exhort you not to put your confidence in violence or in revolution: such an attitude is contrary to the Christian spirit and may also delay rather than promote the social advancement to which you legitimately aspire.[79]

Seven years later, in his encyclical on "The Evangelization of the Contemporary World" (*Evangelii nuntiandi*), Paul VI wrote:

77. Blazquez, pp. 40-41.
78. Jacques Duquesne, *La Izquierda de Cristo.*
79. Paul VI, "Mensaje a los campesinos colombianos," [Bogata, 23 August 1968] in *La Iglesia en la actual transformacion a la luz del concilio,* 1:252-53.

The Church associates, but never identifies, human liberation and salvation in Jesus Christ, because it knows by revelation, by historical experience and by reflection of faith, that not all notions of liberation are necessarily coherent and compatible with an evangelical vision of man, of things and of events; that it is not sufficient to instate liberation, create welfare and development for the kingdom of God to come about.

Furthermore, the Church is fully convinced that all temporal liberation, all political liberation . . . —no matter how much it may pretend to be the theology of today—carries within itself the seed of its own negation and falls short of the ideal which it itself proposes. . . .

The Church cannot accept violence, above all that of armed force—which is uncontrollable when unleashed—nor the death of whomever it might be, as the road to liberation, because it knows that violence inexorably begets new forms of oppression and slavery, sometimes worse than those from which it seeks to bring freedom.[80]

However, there already had been an awakening of the revolutionary consciousness within the Catholic church, and it seemed impossible that it could in any way reverse its own history.

THIRD CONFERENCE OF CELAM: A CONSERVATIVE SHIFT

By the time that the Third Conference of Latin American Bishops was held (Puebla, Mexico, 1979), Catholic theology of liberation was already in its heyday. It was natural, therefore, to wonder if the bishops would continue or impede the process of renewal, or even of revolution, that had been sponsored by Vatican II, by the Conference of Medellín, and by the social doctrine of Popes John XXIII and Paul VI. Another topic of much speculation was the attitude that the new pope, John Paul II, would assume concerning the theology of liberation and its consequences in the ecclesiastical, political, and social realms. As the date of the event at Puebla drew near, the air of expectation increased, questions and commentaries multiplied, and hopes and fears grew. Whatever would happen in Puebla would have great repercussions in the universal church, and especially in the so-called Third World.

80. Paul VI, *La Evangelizacion del mundo contemporaneo* (*Evangelii nuntiandi*), arts. 35-37.

The discourses of John Paul II in Puebla, as well as the final document of the conference, lend themselves to more than one interpretation, as often happens with official declarations of contemporary Catholicism. For more than a few observers the pope gave the impression of rejecting completely the theology of liberation and condemning all political activism by priests.[81] But it was also reported that upon his return to Rome John Paul II declared that liberation theology is necessary not only for Latin America, but for the whole world.[82] Enrique Dussel believes that the news media "and above all the political Right inside and outside the church," distorted the Pope's thought in their reporting of the speeches delivered by the pontiff in the Mexican republic.[83]

Be that as it may, it is clear that John Paul II adopted an attitude that was quite conservative and gave a new thrust to popular religiosity, including the excesses in the veneration of Mary. The image that the pope projected to the world was that of an extreme devotee of Mary. It is also possible to say that the pontiff and the conference itself were moderating elements in the ideological field and, if they did not give a great thrust to liberationism, neither did they condemn it. The theologians of liberation were not invited to participate officially and directly in the conference, but they made their presence felt at Puebla by means of their ideas. The final document approves neither capitalism nor Marxism, and offers a broad opening for other historical alternatives in favor of the poor.

Dussel comments that those who opposed the popular revolutionary movements within the church were defeated in the conference; but with regard to the ministry of denunciation entrusted to the church they attained their goals, because in Puebla very little was said and with very little force about that particular issue; "a text was produced, largely of compromise." Dussel concludes that Medellín was a point of departure and inspiration for the Third Conference and that Puebla is in the tradition of Medellín: "The doors have been left open so that Christians can continue to opt for the interests of the people, of the poor and oppressed."[84]

On the other hand, the Catholic priest Francisco Interdonato,

81. *Time,* February 12, 1979.
82. *La Prensa* (Managua, Nicaragua), 4 May 1979.
83. Enrique D. Dussel, "Un analisis contextual," p. 72.
84. Ibid., pp. 66-67.

who opposes the theology of liberation, says that "Puebla has not wanted to point out directly the positive mistakes of the theology (or theologies) of liberation, but the negative imperfections, that is, what it lacks, with the goal of perfecting or completing the concept of *liberation,* not with the critical analysis of a theologian, but as an Episcopal *magisterium.*" Interdonato does not believe that the objective of Puebla expressed in the final document has been in any way to impede "the liberating effort in the socio-economic-political sphere, nor to spiritualize it, making it innocuous. No! It conserves it in its own being, but links it essentially to the direct mission of Christianity." According to Interdonato, Puebla neither condemns nor canonizes the theology of liberation; what it does is to complete it, integrating it into the living tradition of the church, into its *magisterium,* as an "integral liberation."[85]

In the following chapters I will say more about the response of Roman Catholic conservatives to the theology of liberation. This chapter has intended only to portray in broad strokes the New Catholicism, which, as most people see it, had Vatican II as its starting point, and which during the decades of the sixties and seventies aided the development of the theology of liberation in Latin America.

85. Francisco Interdonato, *Teología Latinoaméricana: ¿Teología de la Liberación?,* pp. 154-57.

5

The Immediate Origin of Liberation Theology

The currents of thought mentioned in the previous chapters flow into liberation theology in various ways. It is necessary now to describe the development of Roman Catholic liberation theology in the Latin American context.

There is more than one way to trace the origin of Catholic liberation theology. For example, J. Andrew Kirk approaches the topic by referring briefly to several of the matters that have been treated in the previous pages such as contemporary European theology, the documents of Vatican II and Medellín, and the social doctrine of John XXIII and Paul VI.[1] The Catholic writer Alfred Garland, in his analysis of postconciliar Catholicism in Peru, begins by associating it with the protest movement which he considers to be "the crisis" of the Catholic church. That phenomenon has its archetype in the famous "May movement" of 1968 in Paris, when thousands of students confronted the police in open rebellion against the established order. Garland says that after Vatican II the protest groups within the church sought to imitate "the French May," interpreting at their whim the teachings of the council under the banner of radicalism.[2] And the editors of the documents pre-

---

1. J. Andrew Kirk, *Liberation Theology: An Evangelical View from the Third World*, pp. 23-28.
2. Alfredo Garland, *Como lobos rapaces*, p. 27.

sented at the encounter in El Escorial, Spain (July 1972), in which several Latin American theologians participated, affirm that there is a unanimous feeling that liberation theology began to make itself explicit especially after Medellín (1968).[3]

But perhaps the most helpful analysis of the development of Catholic liberation theology has come from Latin American historian Enrique D. Dussel.

THREE STAGES OF LATIN AMERICAN THEOLOGY

Dussel describes three periods in the development of Latin American theology in recent times. In the first period Latin American professors from seminaries and faculties of theology went to study in Europe. In the second period courses of study were organized for the purpose of understanding in depth the Latin American reality. The emphasis at that point was not so much theological as sociological. "The third stage, that is, the 'birth' of theology not 'in' Latin America nor 'with' sociographical Latin American themes, but a 'Latin American' theology, will come only when . . . the political relations . . . are seen."[4]

Dussel explains that before Latin American theology could come into being it was necessary for the way to be opened by "prophets," such as those who opposed militarism in Brazil in 1964, or those who defended the socialist movement, or those who went beyond the total condemnation of violence to try to understand it and do it justice. Liberation theology came later, when the dialectic of dominator-oppressed became understood. In that way the church progressed from conservatism to liberalism, then to developmentalism, finally opening itself "to a posture of liberation." According to Dussel one of the greatest differences between European political theology and Latin American liberation theology is that the second movement views the dialectic of oppressor-oppressed on the *international* level. "Latin America is in the position of the Third World: dominated and oppressed. The dialectical suppression of this opposition is the beginning of liberation."[5]

For Dussel, the theme of liberation is properly biblical and is

3. *Fe cristiana y cambio social en America Latina,* p. 394.
4. Enrique D. Dussel, *A History of the Church in Latin America: Colonialism to Liberation* (1492-1979), pp. 244-45.
5. Ibid., p. 245.

found throughout all Christian tradition. It was a topic of discussion, for example, in the Tübingen School long before the Second Vatican Council. Nevertheless Dussel points out that in Latin America alone has the idea of liberation taken on strong political overtones:

> The term began to be used in 1964 but without an awareness of its political implications. Paulo Freire and his Brazilian MEB (Basic Educational Movement) utilized the method of liberation as a basic component: the conscientization as a correlative of liberation, that is, pedagogically it was a "liberating education" or an "education as the practice of freedom." When the "Message of the Bishops for the Third World" (1966) and Medellín (1968) employed the idea and term "liberation" in its political sense, that is, as liberation from the structures of neocolonial domination, the question was definitively set forth. A short time later the term began to appear in the Chilean episcopal documents and thereafter has been generally used.[6]

The three stages that Dussel sets forth and his explanation of the political origin of liberation theology are very useful for understanding the immediate origin of Latin American theological liberationism.

IDEAS FROM EUROPE

With regard to the first stage mentioned by Dussel, that of studies undertaken in Europe by Latin American professors of theology, it should be noted that one of those theologians was the Peruvian priest Gustavo Gutiérrez Merino, an enthusiastic Catholic militant in his home country. Years later he would become known throughout the world as the author of *A Theology of Liberation*. Garland states that Father Gerardo Alarco, principal professor of the Catholic University in Peru, discovered that Gutiérrez was extremely intelligent and encouraged him to continue his studies in Chile, Louvain, and Lyons. Alarco had been influenced by the Catholic "New Theology" during his studies in Europe and came to be known in Lima as a "renovating rebel."[7]

At that time there was great concern in Europe for the state of

6. Ibid., p. 246.
7. Garland, pp. 55-56.

poverty in Latin America and for the threat of communism. Scholarships were provided for Latin American students with the hope that they would help to counter that threat, eliminating poverty and establishing "a just and Christian order."[8] Louvain had been a stronghold of the Christian Democratic Movement under the inspiration of Jacques Maritain, but his political ideas were no longer received with enthusiasm in university classrooms.

The University of Louvain, a center of intense sociological studies, took in several students from Latin America. Among those students were Gutiérrez and the Colombian priest Camilo Torres Restrepo. Evidently the two became friends in Louvain. Later their paths crossed in consultations or study programs in South America. Gutiérrez did not believe that the decision of Camilo to join the guerrilla movement was a wise one.[9]

Gutiérrez dedicated himself to teaching in the Catholic University of Lima and to working with Catholic Action, especially with the organization of Catholic university students. In 1960 the Catholic student movement had opted for Christian Democracy and its ideology of the New Christendom. By 1963 it had changed its emphasis from the religious to the political sphere under the influence of Gutiérrez. The rupture between the National Union of Catholic Students (UNEC) and Christian Democracy began, according to Garland, during 1964 and 1965. Garland points out that at that time the doctrinal position of the UNEC became more extreme, emphasizing the Marxist analysis of reality under the guidance of Gutiérrez, who by then had begun to outline his theology of liberation.[10]

That was the period of Vatican II. The winds of renewal had begun to be felt in the Catholicism of Latin America. There was great expectation regarding the results of the council. The more optimistic observers expected profound changes in the attitude of the church toward the serious economic, social, and political problems of the world. Meanwhile, the more progressive Latin American Catholic theologians continued to reflect on the social reality of which they were a part.

8. Ibid., p. 57.
9. Ibid., pp. 58-59.
10. Ibid., pp. 66-67.

In the second period of the development of Latin American theology, study courses were organized in different parts of the continent. Dussel mentions some of the organizations that sponsored encounters to study the Latin American reality, for example, the Pastoral Institute of Latin America (IPLA), which in 1964 organized meetings in Puerto Rico, Uruguay, and Ecuador.[11] The Chilean priest Segundo Galilea together with Monsignor Leonidas Proaño of Riobamba, Ecuador, founded the IPLA, "which from the city of Quito began to dictate the pastoral norms for the Young Church, converting it into a sort of parallel church.[12] Besides Proaño and Galilea, the teachers in those get-togethers for priests included José Comblin, Lucio Gera, Juan Luis Segundo, Ivan Illich, Gustavo Gutiérrez, and others.

From the sociological emphasis of these meetings a step would be taken to the third stage in the development of Latin American theology—to what we now know as Catholic liberation theology. The revolutionary theological ferment encouraged by Vatican II and by the social doctrine of the conciliar popes continued to grow among the priests of several Latin American countries.

The case is well known, for example, of the fifty Colombian priests who gathered in July 1968 in the Golconda farm near the town of Viota, Cundinamarca, Colombia, to study the encyclical *Populorum progressio* of Paul VI. Toward the end of the same year they met again in Buenaventura and produced a document that drew its inspiration mainly from the constitution *Gaudium et spes* of Vatican II and from the conclusions of Medellín. Their document analyzes the situation in Colombia and blames national and foreign centers of power for the underdevelopment and dependency that afflict the people of Colombia. It affirms, furthermore, the need for including the temporal aspect in the salvation process and the responsibility of the priests to commit themselves to the process of social change. It includes a strong denunciation of capitalism and the national bourgeoisie. As they probably expected, the priests of the Golconda group suffered persecution.[13] Some people called the Golconda movement "the revolution of the cassocks."

11. Dussel, *History of the Church,* p. 245.
12. Garland, p. 74.
13. Dussel, *History of the Church,* pp. 200-01.

In Peru the movement known as the National Office of Social Investigation (ONIS) came into being in 1968 as an expression on the part of the priests of their interest in the solution of social problems. "Some two hundred and fifty priests (two out of every seven in Peru) adhered to it"[14] and exerted a degree of pressure on the episcopate in favor of church renewal and immediate social changes in the country. Gutiérrez was one of the more prominent members of ONIS.

In Argentina a small group of priests and bishops organized in 1965 the movement "Priests for the Third World" as an expression of solidarity with their people. The movement grew and came to opt for a socialism that was nationalistic, populist, Latin American, humanistic, and critical.

Monsignor Ivan Illich, director of the Center of Documentation (CIDOC) in Cuernavaca, Mexico, advanced several ideas that led to a decree from Rome against CIDOC in January 1969. Illich had the backing of the bishop of Cuernavaca, Monsignor Sergio Méndez Arceo. After a pastoral letter from that bishop, the Vatican removed the restrictions set forth in its decree. Méndez Arceo became famous not only for his liturgical reforms in the cathedral of Cuernavaca, but especially for his socialist position. After a visit to Cuba, Garland reports, the bishop said in one of his Sunday homilies that it is necessary to reconcile the kingdom of God and the thinking of Marx. The presidential council of the Mexican Episcopal Conference went on record as disassociating itself from the bishop's words. In Mexico other movements also sprang up, such as the "Solidarity Church" and "Priests for the People."[15]

In Puerto Rico the priest S. Freixedo let out a cry of pain born, according to him, of his love for the church: "It is a cry of anguish upon seeing that my Mother Church sleeps when the world needs her most."[16]

DISAGREEMENT WITH DEVELOPMENTALISM

The examples of priests concerned with the social problems of Latin America could be multiplied. A new consciousness had

14. José Míguez Bonino, *Doing Theology in a Revolutionary Situation,* p. 52.
15. Garland, pp. 86-87, 103; Dussel, *History of the Church,* pp. 204-5.
16. S. Freixedo, *Mi Iglesia duerme,* p. 19.

begun to take hold of them as they became aware of the social doctrine of the conciliar church and of the ideas of their colleagues who were developing the theology of liberation. Prominent among those theologians was Gutiérrez, whom Roberto Oliveros Maqueo considers "the most representative of the theology of liberation" and "as the one who steps beyond the paths of the theology of development to those of liberation, with his openness to Marxist fact and language."[17] Those words reveal two essential ingredients of liberation theology: its strong opposition to the thesis of development and its openness to Marxism.

According to the theory of *development,* technological progress is most needed. The model of development comes from countries of the North Atlantic. In other words, the developed countries provide the pattern for the economic, social, and political progress of the underdeveloped ones. The latter should, therefore, accumulate capital, introduce planning, increase technology, and stimulate the investment of foreign capital to reach the level of development of the North Atlantic nations. The Alliance for Progress tried to accelerate such development.

I have already mentioned that the Catholic church of Vatican II adopted the concept of *integral development,* which subordinates technical aspects to moral ones. Oliveros Maqueo thinks that the European Catholic theologian Joseph Comblin, who was professor of theology in Chile, Brazil, and Ecuador and one of the pioneers of the new Latin American theology, represents "an echo of the European theology of development,"[18] which fails to take into account the situation of dependency as the determining cause of Latin American underdevelopment. Comblin proposes integral development in contrast to that which is merely technological.[19]

It should not be forgotten that the ideas of underdevelopment and dependency are foundational in the sociological analysis that gives impulse to the theology of liberation. One criticism liberation theology makes against developmentalism is that the North Atlantic nations depended on the colonies for their development. Because that situation does not exist today the process cannot be

17. Roberto Oliveros Maqueo, *Liberación y teología,* pp. 102, 104.
18. José Comblin, *Cristianismo y desarrollo* (see bibliography).
19. Oliveros Maqueo, p. 142.

repeated.[20] The theory of development does not grasp "the impossibility of following the path of the United States seeing as how the greatness of that nation is sustained by the riches sucked off from dependent nations."[21] As Dussel has said, the theology of liberation arises when it perceives "the dialectic of oppressor-oppressed at the *international* level."[22]

THE CONTRIBUTION OF GUSTAVO GUTIÉRREZ

Gustavo Gutiérrez does not oppose the thesis of development with a theology of revolution, which in the opinion of some Catholic writers is promoted by Richard Shaull.[23] Shaull's theology does not come out of the context of underdevelopment and dependency, but out of the opulent situation of the North Atlantic nations. Its goal is the reformation of the Western system. Gutiérrez opposes developmentalism with a *theology of liberation,* which, in the light of faith, reflects on the revolutionary situation of Latin America, "backed by a social analysis that helps it to be less naive."[24] Several publications and theological gatherings in which Gutiérrez participated mark the development of his thought.

EARLY IDEAS: LOVE OF ONE'S NEIGHBOR AND IDENTITY WITH THE POOR

In a meeting of Latin American theologians at Petropolis, Brazil, in 1964 the contributions that stand out are those of the Catholic theologians Juan Luis Segundo from Uruguay, Lucio Gera from Argentina, and Gutiérrez from Peru. Segundo focused on the theme of evangelization, taking as his point of departure social change in Latin America. Gera considered the responsibility of the Latin American theologian, proposed extensive changes in the

20. Míguez Bonino: "The theory of development . . . makes at least three fundamental mistakes. . . . The first is to believe that history is unlinear and that society can move to previous stages of other existing societies. . . . Secondly, the model did not take into account the political factors. . . . Thirdly, the theory took for granted that the developed countries were the 'normal' model for the underdeveloped" (*Doing Theology,* p. 26).
21. Oliveros Maqueo, p. 141.
22. Dussel, *History of the Church,* p. 247.
23. Oliveros Maqueo, p. 191; Dussel, *History of the Church,* p. 145.
24. Oliveros Maqueo, p. 192.

theological seminaries, and exhorted theologians to identify themselves with the life of the people so that they could effectively communicate the Christian message.

In his presentation, Gutiérrez asked how to establish saving dialogue with the Latin American man. He criticized the pastoral options in Latin America and proposed a new pastoral focus that would respond to the needs of the people. Gutiérrez was already concerned with themes such as social vindication, revolutionary struggle, and violence. In this presentation may be found in embryonic form some of the ideas that he would develop later in his theology of liberation.[25]

Gutiérrez's first publication was a work entitled *Christian Charity and Love* (Lima, 1966).[26] In it he tried to overcome the dichotomy between love for God and love of one's neighbor. Human love involves love for God because man is God's temple. That would come to be one of the themes of Gutiérrez's well-known book, *A Theology of Liberation.*

In Montreal in 1967 Gutiérrez taught a course titled "The Church and Poverty." Poverty is another of the themes that would occupy a prominent place in *A Theology of Liberation,* published four years later. In Montreal the Peruvian theologian declared that poverty opposes evangelical justice and should not be attributed to the will of God. Christians need to fight for the suppression of that scandal, which is the fruit of social sin. The church is called to identify itself with the poor, assuming poverty, ceasing to be a rich church in the midst of destitution.[27]

LIBERATIONISM: A CLEAR CALL TO SOCIAL REVOLUTION

The Pastoral Mission of the Church in Latin America was published in 1968 shortly after the conference of Medellín, although Gutiérrez had developed the topic for a meeting in February 1967.[28] Gutiérrez showed that he had deepened his criticism of

25. Ibid., pp. 60-63. According to Oliveros Maqueo, the documents of the meeting in Petropolis in mimeographed form are in the archives of the Centro de Estudios Bartolome de las Casas, Lima, Peru.
26. Oliveros Maqueo, p. 108.
27. The notes for Gutiérrez's course on "The Church and Poverty" are also found in the archives of the Centro de Estudios Bartolome de las Casas in Lima, Peru.
28. See Oliveros Maqueo, pp. 106, 110-11.

the different types of pastoral ministry of the church. He focused
on the pastoral ministry, which he called "prophetic." He had also
continued to develop the concept of the integration of creation
and salvation in a single historical process in which man is not
simply a spectator but rather a protagonist and a transformer of
history. The influence of Marx was clearly evident in that concept.

A meeting in Chimbote, Peru, took place shortly before the
conference of bishops in Medellín. Gutiérrez titled his lecture
"Toward a Theology of Liberation."[29] In it can be seen more clearly
than before the themes of his liberation theology. He forcefully
rejected the theology of development and proposed a search for a
new historical project that would have as its point of departure
the situation of the poor in Latin America. Faith, said Gutiérrez,
has a political dimension. History is one; man is a protagonist in it
and can change it. Oliveros Maqueo says that the conference at
Chimbote "marks the appearance of liberation in the theological
ambience, in the technical sense of faith as a commitment to the
poor in the search for a new historical project."[30]

In his Chimbote address, Gutiérrez also referred to theological
method, to the new way of doing theology. Undoubtedly that is
one of the dominant points of the lecture. There he suggested that
theology is an intellectual pursuit that is progressive, and in a
sense, variable. It is a reflection, a second act coming after action.
Commitment precedes theology; commitment is action. Charity is
central, and to have charity is to commit oneself to action. Theology comes later.

A conference in Cartigny, Switzerland, in 1969 was organized
for the purpose of studying in depth the theology of development.
Gutiérrez presented "Notes for a Theology of Liberation." Those
notes were a sort of prelude in outline form of the book *A Theology of Liberation*. Gutiérrez indicated that "one of the functions
of theology is to be a critical reflection of the pastoral action of
the Church."[31] He opposed the theory of development, contrasting
it with liberation; he pointed to dependency as a key element in

29. Gustavo Gutiérrez, *Hacia una teologia de la liberacion.* See Oliveros Maqueo,
    p. 112.
30. Oliveros Maqueo, p. 113.
31. Gustavo Gutiérrez, "Notes for a Theology of Liberation," *Theological Studies,*
    31 (1970): 243-61. This article summarizes Gutiérrez's lecture in Cartigny,
    Switzerland.

the interpretation of Latin American reality; and he emphasized the need to radically change that situation.

Regarding the very important theme of the relationship between salvation and liberation, Gutiérrez tried to build a bridge between the two through the concept of the unity of history: there are not two histories, one sacred and the other profane, but only one. Furthermore, Gutiérrez saw that there is unity between creation and salvation: creation is the first saving act. Eschatological promises also give unity to history; the eradication of poverty and exploitation is a sign of the coming of the kingdom. The Christian hope is creative as it enters into contact with the social realities of today's world. But what is the relationship between eschatology and politics? Gutiérrez did not yet have a definitive answer to that question. He saw that it is difficult to establish ahead of time the exact norms that should rule the conduct of the church. He affirmed that it will be necessary to act according to the demands of the moment with the light that is already available and with the desire to be faithful to the gospel. One thing at least was clear: for Gutiérrez the mission of the church is defined in the fact of social revolution. There is no other alternative.

> Only by repudiating poverty and making itself poor in protest against it can the Church preach "spiritual poverty," i.e., an openness of man and the history he lives in to the future promised by God. Only in that way can it fulfil honestly, and with a good chance of being heard, the critico-social function that political theology assigns. For the Church of today, this is the test of the authenticity of its mission.[32]

Gutiérrez sent an exposition to a symposium in Bogotá in 1970 entitled "An Outline for the Theology of Liberation." In that work he affirmed that his point of departure is a dependent Latin America. He proposed a theology that would arise out of the Latin American Christian community and asked that community to reflect critically on its faith, without separating itself from social reality. He insisted again on the unity of history. He opposed the establishment of a division between the world of salvation and the world of history, between sacred and profane history. From God's point of view, said Gutiérrez, there is only one history. He creates

32. Ibid., p. 261.

human beings in order for them to be His sons. Creation presupposes salvation; the two come together in the concept of liberation.[33]

JUAN LUIS SEGUNDO AND RUBEM ALVES

It was also in 1970 that Juan Luis Segundo published under the title *From Society to Theology* a collection of articles that focus on themes of the developing theology of liberation. Segundo accepted the thesis that dependency on the international level is the cause of both underdevelopment in Latin America and great prosperity in the North Atlantic countries, particularly the United States of America. Latin American countries are, according to Segundo, the proletariat, the exploited ones, not partners in international trade. Consequently, Segundo's analysis included the concept of class struggle. Regarding the mission of the church, Segundo concluded that salvation needs to be related to the events of history. The Christian ethic is social; faith has a political dimension. Consequently, the Christian should identify himself with efforts to bring about social change.

On the basis of the gospel, which condemns covetousness, Segundo said that it is a Christian duty to reject capitalism, which makes financial gain its supreme objective. Because the gospel does not offer any social and political model, the Christian does not have to defend any particular pattern and can adopt a critical attitude toward any political system in order to defend the dignity of man.

Segundo expressed the hope that in Latin America dependence in the theological realm would also be overcome, that Latin Americans would no longer limit themselves to a repetition of European theology. It would be necessary to translate the Christian message for the reality of our continent. Latin America should not listen to Europe but to the Word of God.[34]

In the same year, 1970, Rubem Alves published in Uruguay his book *Religion: Opio o instrumento de liberation?* The English edition had appeared in the United States in 1969, with an intro-

---

33. *I Simposio sobre teologia de la liberacion,* (see bibliography).
34. Juan Luis Segundo, *De la sociedad a la teologia.* See Oliveros Maqueo, pp. 143-55.

duction by Harvey Cox, under the title *A Theology of Human Hope* (see Chapter 3 of this book). The Catholic writer Oliveros Maqueo dedicates several pages to the thinking of Alves, recognizing that this Protestant theologian from South America has made significant contributions to liberation theology.[35]

A POINT OF ARRIVAL

By 1970 the Catholic theology of liberation was already systematized, especially in the thinking of Gutiérrez, who at the end of the previous decade had formulated the essential concepts of his theological system. In reference to the meeting in El Escorial, Spain (July 1972), in which Gutiérrez participated, Alfonso Alvarez Bolado says of him:

> He is not simply a characteristic author of liberation theology. In a sense he is the one who molds, the one who formulates the fundamental intuitions of his theology in simple, expressive and sober language, a theology which he does not invent but gathers out of his pastoral immersion in Christian movements, a reflection which detects the aspirations of a continent made up of a majority of Christians, which becomes conscious of the fact that the liberation of God is not a "fading heroic act" out of the past, but rather a summons in the present, a historical step of the Lord (Passover), a call to a new form of humanity which cannot be that unless it takes up its responsibility of transforming its natural and historical world.[36]

In contrast to other theologies that have tried to respond to the social problems of contemporary man—for example, existential theology, political theology, secular theology, or the theology of revolution—Gutiérrez and his companions are certain that the point of departure for Latin American theology must be the situation of poverty in Latin America. They assume that Marxist analysis is the most adequate means to understand that situation. Underdevelopment is the product of economic dependence on an international level, and capitalism is responsible for the sad state of

35. Oliveros Maqueo, pp. 155-75, commenting on Rubem Alves, *A Theology of Human Hope.*
36. Alfonso Alvarez Bolado, "Introduccion," in *Fe cristiana y cambio social en America Latina,* p. 23.

affairs in Latin America. It is indispensable to open the way for a
Latin American socialism for Latin Americans, with a view toward
the formation of a new man and a new classless society.

Liberation theologians are also convinced that there is only one
history in which God acts, and God expects man to cooperate
with Him in order to transform it. Salvation is not separate from
the process of social transformation. Faith has a political dimension. Scripture supports the church's involvement in the process
of social change. That participation involves an act of commitment
to the poor in their liberating struggle. Faced with that commitment, the church is put on trial to see whether it is truly authentic.

Those convictions, and others like them, demand a new way of
doing theology. In view of the scandal of poverty and its national
and international causes, liberation theologians believe it is imperative to reflect, in the light of faith, on praxis, in praxis, and from
praxis in order to write, along the way of revolutionary commitment and as a "second act," the chapters that will point toward
authentic Latin American theology.

The Brazilian Catholic theologian Hugo Assmann first published
his work *Opresion-Liberacion: Desafío a los cristianos* in 1971. It
was the same year in which Gustavo Gutiérrez published, for the
first time as well, his now-famous *A Theology of Liberation*. Because from the standpoint of liberation theology both books are "a
theology of the road," it should be said that they are simply *a point
of arrival* and *a point of departure* on the pilgrimage begun by
Catholic liberation theologians. In liberation theology further
chapters will always be written, to the extent that theologians and
the community of faith become involved in the liberating praxis
of the Latin American people. Gutiérrez says:

> But in the last instance we will have an authentic theology of libera-
> tion only when the oppressed themselves can freely raise their voice
> and express themselves directly and creatively in society and in the
> heart of the People of God, when they themselves "account for the
> hope," which they bear, when they are the protagonists of their own
> liberation. For now we must limit ourselves to efforts which ought
> to deepen and support that process, which has barely begun.[37]

37. Gustavo Gutiérrez, *A Theology of Liberation: History, Politics and Salvation*,
p. 307.

It is significant that Gutiérrez wrote those words at the end of his major book on liberation theology. Evidently his theology, initiated and developed under the theological and sociological influences that have been mentioned in previous chapters, has not arrived at its final destination and will not be able to do so as long as the liberation of the poor in Latin America remains an unfinished process. Each step forward in that process will be at the same time a new point of departure toward total liberation. Consequently the liberation theology we now know, thirteen years after Gutiérrez published *A Theology of Liberation,* is not definitive. Nevertheless it represents an important landmark along the road of Latin American Catholic theology.

Part Three

The Method of Liberation Theology

6

A New Way of Doing Theology

I have suggested that liberation theologians move from sociology to politics and from politics to theology. How are those transitions effected? How do the elements provided by the sociological analysis of Latin American reality tie in with the sources of the faith ("the objective faith of the church")? Or to put the question in a simpler way, how is the relationship between sociological analysis and theology established? Why do liberation theologians call their work theology and not sociology? In order to answer those and similar questions, it is indispensable to remember that in liberation theology we are confronted with a new theological method having its own point of departure, its own special relationship to the theology of the church, its own hermeneutic norm, and, of course, its own philosophical framework.

THE POINT OF DEPARTURE

Liberation theologians differ regarding positions on certain themes, but they concur on several fundamental points, thereby making a general evaluation of their theological system possible. There is consensus, for example, that the point of departure is the Latin American situation and the historical activity that seeks to change that situation radically. Such is the teaching of Gustavo Gutiérrez, Hugo Assmann, and other liberation theologians.

THE "TEXT" IS THE LATIN AMERICAN SITUATION

Hugo Assmann says:

> Perhaps the greatest merit of the theology of liberation is its insist-
> ence on the starting-point of its reflections: the situation of "domi-
> nated (Latin) America." . . . One thing virtually all the documents so
> far published agree on is that the starting-point of the theology of
> liberation is the present historical situation of domination and depen-
> dence in which the countries of the Third World find themselves.[1]

According to Segundo Galilea, a Chilean Catholic theologian, one
distinctive of liberation theology lies in the fact that it emerges
out of a context of underdevelopment, in contrast to theologies
that have been written in highly developed societies. "The Latin
American theology of liberation is formed in a Christian context
of poverty, dependence, and underdevelopment."[2]

Assmann clarifies that there is no pretension of limiting the
notion of liberation to the Latin American context. That context
is only a "first reference"; two-thirds of the world's population find
themselves basically in the same problem:

> If the state of domination and dependence in which two-thirds of
> humanity live, with an annual toll of thirty million dead from starva-
> tion and malnutrition, does not become the starting-point for *any*
> Christian theology today, even in the affluent and powerful countries,
> then theology cannot begin to relate meaningfully to the real situa-
> tion. Its question will lack reality and not relate to real men and
> women.[3]

Once the thesis is accepted that underdevelopment is not a simple
economic setback or primitivism but a form of dependence, and
that developmentalism is a failure, all Christians, whether in underdeveloped countries or in highly developed countries, should assume a new posture in their theological reflections. That is why
even the theologians of rich countries are exhorted to take the
situation of Third World poverty as a point of departure for their
theological task. All should develop theology for the benefit of the

1. Hugo Assmann, *Theology for a Nomad Church*, pp. 38, 53.
2. Segundo Galilea, *Teología de la liberación: ensayo de síntesis*, p. 17.
3. Assmann, *Theology*, p. 54.

poor countries, because the underdevelopment of those countries is the fruit of economic dependence at the international level.

For theologians of rich countries, the dependence and underdevelopment of the Third World is not the only problem. They also have to contextualize their theology by answering the problems of their own social environment—for example, the contemporary atheism, whether theoretical or practical, of North Atlantic society. Segundo Galilea perceives that the participant in the dialogue of European theology is "the unbeliever" in the first place.[4] Furthermore, there are ethical situations peculiar to a "post-Christian" society that do not have any direct relationship to the state of poverty of the Third World (unless they are attributed to the opulence resulting from the dependence that underdeveloped countries suffer.) But it is not correct to give a purely economic explanation to specific ethical problems, whether personal or social. There are also sins common to rich and poor people, oppressors and oppressed, highly developed countries and underdeveloped countries. Of course, such considerations do not excuse theologians of the North Atlantic from focusing with courage on the responsibility that their own countries may have for the underdevelopment of the Third World. Jürgen Moltmann acknowledges that responsibility:

> As the Third World moves over the horizon of our awareness, we recognize more and more clearly that what are so often called underdeveloped nations have become the political and economic victims of European expansion. And we see too *how* this has happened. It also becomes more and more clear to us that our nations are living at the cost of the peoples of the Third World. And we see too *how* this is so. In the slums of the mass cities of the Third World, surely something like the tragedy of the western Gulag Archepelago is being played out. When we begin to look these facts in the face, all that is left to us is either personal and public conversion, and the search for ways to a juster world-wide community, or to close our eyes again as quickly as possible, and to look the other way. The liberation of the oppressed world depends on our conversion; and world peace depends on the liberation of the Third World.[5]

4. Galilea, p. 17.
5. Jürgen Moltmann, *The Power of the Powerless*, pp. 165-66.

Assmann explains that to take the concrete historical situation as a point of departure for reflection concerning the Christian faith "does not mean that the concept of liberation has to be restricted to the economic plane, but it is on this plane that the priorities become dramatically obvious."[6] What is being sought, according to Assmann and Gutiérrez, is "the continuous creation of a new way of being human, a permanent cultural revolution."[7]

In any case, the point of departure is not the biblical text, but the social context. That is why Assmann says, the "'text' is our situation."[8]

THEOLOGY AS CRITICAL REFLECTION IN COMMUNITY

Liberation theologians take Latin American reality as a point of departure for their reflection, but not without analyzing it according to the social sciences under the direct influence of Marxist thought.

In the first chapter of *A Theology of Liberation,* Gutiérrez critically contrasts his way of doing theology with classical ways of doing theology. He begins by saying that in every believer there is a rough outline of a theology, an effort to understand what the faith is. Theological reflection is not an exclusive privilege of a few Christian thinkers but is the task "of all those who have accepted the gift of the Word of God." It is on the foundation of the believer's reflection in community, "and only because of it," that the structure of theology can be erected "in the precise and technical sense of the term."[9]

The Christian community in its activity of reflection is, according to Gutiérrez, a point of departure and much more: "it is the soil into which theological reflection stubbornly and permanently sinks its roots and from which it derives its strength."[10] Theology thus becomes deindividualized. It becomes an issue of the community. It stops being the prerogative of an ecclesiastical elite.

6. Assmann, *Theology,* p. 54-55.
7. Ibid., p. 55, quoting from Gustavo Gutiérrez, *Liberación, opción de la iglesia en la decada del 70,* p. 17.
8. Ibid., p. 104.
9. Gustavo Gutiérrez, *A Theology of Liberation: History, Politics and Salvation,* p. 3.
10. Ibid.

Already at the opening words of Gutiérrez's theology the conservative evangelical begins to have serious questions as he becomes aware that the point of departure and the foundation for the theological task is not Holy Scripture but the theological reflection of the Christian community.

What Gutiérrez expects from Christians is not traditional theological reflection, but a theology that comes out of a life of faith that seeks "to be authentic and complete." Later he explains that Christianity is authentic and complete when it opts for the poor and commits itself to the struggle to liberate them. Moreover, for Gutiérrez theology should be a *critical* reflection on itself, on its own bases, and on the economic, social, and cultural conditionings of the life and thought of the Christian community. It should be a critique both of society and of the church.[11] The critique of the economic, social, and political order is a function of theology. Only in such a way can theology have a basis and a point of departure that will give it validity in light of the reality of Latin America and the Third World.

The analytical content of liberation, according to Assmann, includes "denouncing of domination; perception of the mechanics of dependence; opposition to "development" and the capitalist economic system; and a break with the 'unjust established order.'" European theology, even that of a political nature, has not taken into account that particular social analysis. Its objective has not been to respond specifically to Latin American social problems; rather it is a theology developed in the opulence of the North Atlantic. Assmann also suggests that theologians of highly developed societies have not assumed the responsibility of their own countries for the phenomenon of underdevelopment in the Third World.[12] It is the Latin American theologians of liberation who have integrated into their thought the relationship between dependence and underdevelopment. Segundo Galilea says that, in contrast to the schools of theology developed in Europe or North America, the participant in the dialogue of liberation theology "is not primarily the unbeliever . . . but the 'un-man,' the one whom exclusion and destitution keep in a subhuman situation."[13]

11. Ibid., pp. 3, 11.
12. Assmann, *Theology*, pp. 56, 58. But see also the quotation of Moltmann above (n. 5).
13. Galilea, p. 17.

Furthermore, it is pointed out, the traditional theology of the North Atlantic finds itself generally under the influence of a philosophy that gives precedence to reflection, to the cognitive element, and not to action. Such theology, more concerned with orthodoxy than with orthopraxis, more interested in theory than in action, does not respond adequately—according to liberation theologians—to the distressing problems of the Latin American people. The urgent need is to change the world, not to explain it. It is more important to do than simply to know.

Inevitably a new way of doing theology becomes necessary in light of the demands of the situation in the Third World and in light of the limitations of traditional theology. Behind the new way of doing theology there is a new way of philosophizing, the immediate origin of which is evident. Karl Marx said, "Philosophers have limited themselves to interpreting the world in different ways; but transforming it is what it is all about."[14]

CRITICAL REFLECTION UPON PRAXIS AND FROM THE PERSPECTIVE OF LIBERATING PRAXIS

If in the previous section the key word was critique, we now turn to the much-used word *praxis*. *Praxis* is of Greek origin, deriving from *prasso*, to work, to execute. It is of very ancient use. The title of the book of Acts, say Richard J. Dillon and Joseph A. Fitzmyer, was related in antiquity to "a Hellenistic literary form that recounted the deeds of outstanding men (such as Alexander the Great, Hannibal, or Apollonius of Tyana)."[15] With regard to the use of *praxis* in the theology of liberation, its socio-political meaning and its strong Marxist tone are quite obvious. Xosé Miguélez comments: "Although the term praxis is a Greek legacy (in Spanish it has been normally translated 'práctica'), its technical use, not translated, is very much tied in modern philosophy to the origin and development of Marxist thought." However, Miguélez does not believe that the assimilation of the word in the theology of liberation "supposes an undiscerning and unconscious appropria-

14. Karl Marx, "Tesis sobre Feuerbach (1845)," in his *Sobre la Religion*, p. 161.
15. Richard J. Dillon and Joseph A. Fitzmyer, "Acts of the Apostles," in *The Jerome Biblical Commentary*, edited by Raymond E. Brown, Joseph A. Fitzmyer, and Roland A. Murphy, 2 vols. in 1 (Englewood Cliffs, N.J.: Prentice-Hall, 1968), 2:166.

tion of the global Marxist vision regarding history, man and God." But he concludes his extensive study on *praxis* in Gutiérrez and Assmann by finding in them "a Marxist use of the term, but it is conscious and critical."[16]

Traditional method or a "Copernican Revolution"?

Gutiérrez refers to the "classical tasks of theology": theology as "wisdom" of a biblical and spiritual nature but also isolated from the world, platonic and neoplatonic; and theology as "rational knowledge," that is, theology as an intellectual discipline, the fruit of the encounter between faith and reason. Both classical tasks of theology have, in Gutiérrez's opinion, a permanent value in spite of the deformations they have suffered through the centuries. The theological task proposed by Gutiérrez—that is, "critical appraisal of historical praxis" in the light of the Word—does not replace the other functions of theology; on the contrary, it needs them but redefines them, motivating them so that they may have "ecclesiastical praxis as their point of departure and their context."[17]

Gutiérrez explains that liberation theology "offers us not so much a new theme for reflection, as a *new way* to do theology." To be sure, there are antecedents of this type of reflection in the first centuries of the church. Gutiérrez cites as an example *The City of God* by Saint Augustine. That work, Gutiérrez says, "is based on a true analysis of the signs of the times and the demands with which they challenge the Christian community."[18]

Segundo Galilea is of the same opinion, affirming that liberation theology is not "an absolute new way" of doing theology because it inserts itself in the best tradition; it belongs to "one of the most traditional ways of doing Catholic theology." It has Latin American antecedents in the works of Francisco de Vitoria, Bartolome de las Casas, and other defenders of the American Indians of the sixteenth century.[19]

Even so, the clarifications of Gutiérrez and Galilea do not seem to plumb the depths of the new way of doing theology. In fact, it has been said that this method is a "Copernican revolution" in the

16. Xosé Miguélez, *La Teología de la liberación y su método,* pp. 39, 49.
17. Gutiérrez, *Theology of Liberation,* pp. 3-6, 14.
18. Ibid., pp. 6, 15.
19. Galilea, pp. 16-17.

realm of theology.[20] The theologians of liberation follow a philosophy that gives primacy to praxis. That philosophy is described as "historical" because it takes place in the realm of earthly realities, in human events.

Faith linked to transforming the world. Gutiérrez lists several factors that have contributed to the understanding of the Christian faith as a commitment to liberating praxis: (1) the fruitful rediscovery of *charity* as the center of the Christian life; (2) the significant evolution of Christian *spirituality* towards a fruitful synthesis between contemplation and action; (3) "greater sensitivity to the *anthropological aspects* of revelation," by which man is seen as the protagonist in the transformation of history; (4) the new *philosophical emphasis* on human action as the point of departure for all reflection; and (5) the rediscovery of the *eschatological dimension* in theology, which has brought to the fore the central role of historical praxis. In constructing history as a political task, "man orients and opens himself to the gift which gives history its transcendent meaning: the full and definitive encounter with the Lord and with other men."[21]

The influence of Marxism. Gutiérrez acknowledges that his concept of praxis is influenced by "*Marxist thought,* focusing on praxis and geared to the transformation of the world." Later he says that in Marx there is an "epistemological break" with previous thought, so that for Marx knowledge is found "indissolubly linked to the transformation of the world through work." Gutiérrez seems to agree with Sartre that "Marxism, as the formal framework of all contemporary philosophical thought, cannot be superseded." He says that "it is to a large extent due to Marxism's influence that theological thought, searching for its own sources, has begun to reflect on the meaning of the transformation of this world and the action of man in history."[22]

Segundo Galilea sees three tendencies in liberation theology. The first begins with the biblical idea of liberation. The other two tendencies have a more interdisciplinary method. Within that

20. The Yugoslav theologian Miroslav Volf develops this theme in "Doing and Interpreting."
21. Gutiérrez, *Theology of Liberation*, pp. 6-11.
22. Ibid., pp. 9-10, 29-30.

method, one tendency "gives more importance to the cultural soul of the Latin American people, to their historical process (since the conquest) of oppression-liberation; to popular religiosity as an important factor of liberation." In the other tendency "there are points which coincide with some elements of Marxist analysis, legitimately according to them, since they are those elements which are accepted by contemporary sociology and economics as valid contributions." There is a fourth tendency that, by virtue of its subjection to Marxism, comes closer to an "ideology of liberation" than to a theology. Galilea says that what "some critics present as the theology of liberation which is predominant in Latin America, is precisely this current which has no theological credits."[23] On the other hand, to call those theologians of the third tendency Marxists is, according to Galilea, a sign of ignorance. But in his analysis he does not seem to take sufficient note of the Marxist philosophical influence in this third tendency within the theology of liberation.

Theology as a product of pastoral activity. The obvious result of that philosophical influence is that for Gutiérrez the *point of departure* for theological reflection is not only Latin American society analyzed by the social sciences, nor only the theological reflection that seeks to answer theoretically the questions of the Latin American man, but praxis itself, the effort to transform social structures. In this way, liberation theology is more a reflection *from* revolutionary praxis than a reflection *on* that praxis. Assmann did well when he entitled the Salamanca edition of his book *Theology from the Praxis of Liberation.*
Gutiérrez states very clearly:

> To reflect on the basis of the historical praxis of liberation is to reflect in the light of the future which is believed in and hoped for. It is to reflect with a view to action which transforms the present. But it does not mean doing this from an armchair; rather it means sinking roots where the pulse of history is beating at this moment and illuminating history with the Word of the Lord of history, who irreversibly committed himself to the present moment of mankind to carry it to its fulfillment.[24]

23. Galilea, pp. 27-28.
24. Gutiérrez, *Theology of Liberation,* p. 15.

According to Gutiérrez, then, the point of departure for theological reflection is "the presence and activity of the Church in the world." Theology is the product of pastoral activity. That which comes first is the commitment of love in service. "Theology *follows*; it is the second step." Praxis precedes reflection. Appealing to the Hegelian concept of philosophy, Gutiérrez thinks that it can also be said of theology that "it rises only at sundown,"[25] at the end of a day that has been dedicated to action. Theology has to emerge from historical liberating praxis. That is definitely the point of departure for the theological task. The theologian has to be immersed in the transforming struggle and proclaim his message from that point. Liberation theologians are very far from taking the sacred Scriptures as the point of departure for their theological task.

THEOLOGY OR SOCIOLOGY?

Liberation theology does not consist only of a critical, sociological analysis of the Latin American situation. It includes much more than a description of economic, social, and political reality. Even on the philosophical level the emphasis falls on action, on praxis, not on knowledge for its own sake. It is a philosophy of the transforming action of society. It strives to change the situation of poverty and underdevelopment. Furthermore, liberation theologians do not stop at that which is merely philosophical and sociological. If they had done so, their work would be described as a philosophy or sociology, not *theology,* of liberation. But they make an attempt at theology, taking as a point of departure the Latin American situation, as analyzed by the social sciences, and responding to that situation with a new way of doing theology.

The word "theology" means, etymologically, "discourse about God." In academic circles it is recognized that a variety of theologies exists within Christianity. Conservative evangelical theologians also distinguish between biblical theology and unbiblical or anti-biblical theologies. But it is interesting that all of them— whether true or false—are called theologies. Even "liberal theology," which has been the number one enemy of conservative evangelicalism, receives that name. Thus there can be said to be a

25. Ibid., pp. 8, 11.

consensus among us with regard to the use of the word. In light of those considerations there is no reason to say that liberation theology is only sociology and not theology, just as there is no reason to affirm that liberal thought should not be called theology but philosophy. But it remains to be determined whether the Catholic theology of liberation accords with the teachings of Scripture or not.

Assmann responds to the objection of the "sociologization of theology" by saying that it is an impossible dream to forge a theology that does not take the analysis of reality by means of the human sciences as a point of departure. He adds:

> "theological purism" cannot stand up to contact with the Bible; exegesis cannot dispense with the secular sciences in its attempt to reach the true meaning of the biblical texts. When it tries to do so, it not only fails to get to grips with the real challenge of the Bible, but—much worse—fails to make the biblical text speak in a meaningful way to the problem-laden men of today.[26]

However, Assmann also asks whether critical reflection on historical praxis is theology. He admits that in this field there are many things that "yet remain to be finally made clear" but concludes:

> Critical reflection on human history becomes theological to the degree that it looks for the presence of the Christian faith in historical experience; it is this that distinguishes theology from other ways of reflecting critically on this experience. If reference to faith in history is laid aside, then there is no theology. In this sense, "in the light of faith," "in the light of revelation," and so on . . . denote the essence of theological reflection.[27]

Gutiérrez affirms that reflection in light of faith should be accompanied constantly by the pastoral action of the church. That is due to two fundamental reasons. First, theology relativizes historical accomplishments. For example, it does not give absolute character to a revolution, however popular the revolution might be. By relativizing a historical accomplishment, theology "helps safeguard society and the Church from regarding as permanent what is only

26. Assmann, *Theology,* p. 63.
27. Ibid., p. 62.

temporary." There is always more ground to conquer; no achievement in the present is complete, permanent, and absolute. Therefore, theology finds itself in contrast to an ideology "which
rationalizes and justifies a given social and ecclesial order." Second,
calling to mind the sources of revelation helps guide pastoral
action, putting it in a broader context, and helping to keep it from
falling into activism and immediatism. Theology thus fulfills a
liberating function, avoiding all fetishism and narcissism.[28]

Gutiérrez's scheme may seem attractive for a fruitful relationship
between theology and the social sciences and for a revolutionary
praxis in which the church can maintain its critical reservation
based on revelation. But, to quote a popular saying, "it is easier
said than done." In the theological encounter held at El Escorial,
Spain (July 1972), at which several liberation theologians of Latin
America were present, José Míguez Bonino talked about the radicalism of ISAL, which ended up requiring the submission of faith
to ideology and the submission of ecclesial praxis to politics.
Míguez Bonino recognizes the great danger that by bringing the
Christian faith to the level of the strategic and tactical, it may lose
its theological content and fall into the sectarianism of an ideology.[29] That problem is real and unavoidable.

THE VIEW OF SCRIPTURE

But what do expressions like "the Word of God," "the gospel,"
"in light of faith," and "the sources of revelation" mean to the
Catholic theologians of liberation? An answer must begin with a
reminder that the Catholic concept of revelation is much broader
than that of Protestantism. In Catholic teaching, normative revelation for the church includes tradition as well as the holy Scriptures,
which according to Catholicism have more than sixty-six books.
That idea of revelation is already a serious problem for the dialogue
between the Catholic theologians of liberation and conservative
evangelicals.

Moreover, it must be asked what concept of the Scriptures
themselves the Catholic theologians of liberation have: what do

28. Gutiérrez, *Theology of Liberation,* p. 12.
29. José Míguez Bonino, "Vision del cambio social y sus tareas desde las iglesias
    cristianas no-catolicas," in *Fe cristiana y cambio social en America Latina,* pp.
    201-2.

they think of biblical inspiration and authority? It is well known, for example, that Vatican II's concept of biblical inspiration is not as high as that of conservative evangelicals. Vanguard Catholic theologians seem to be more willing to submit themselves to the dictates of rationalistic criticism than to the authority of the Bible. After all, the Scriptures are losing more and more their absolute character in the view of many contemporary theologians. Dennis P. McCann, a Catholic theologian, comments that for liberation theologians the way in which the church reads the Bible is subject to the vicissitudes of history. Biblical meaning is always relative, dependent on the social context.[30]

The way in which liberation theologians use the Bible will be discussed in greater detail later. For now, we should acknowledge that they have tried to relate their philosophical and sociological reflection to the content of their faith. We have already seen that Gutiérrez believes that the theology of the church and the text of the Scriptures themselves contain elements that have contributed to the formation of the idea of a historical liberating praxis. There are several biblical factors that liberation theologians use to justify their critical reflection on historical praxis. Such use of the Scriptures is part of the new way of doing theology.

Examples of biblical elements that have been incorporated in liberation theology include creation, the Exodus, prophetic denunciations, the political implications of the ministry of Jesus, and the eschatological promises. Those elements of biblical revelation serve, when interpreted in a "liberationist" way, as a unifying bridge between theology and the critical reflection that claims to be based on human sciences, but which invests heavily in a Marxist analysis of society with its philosophy of praxis for social change.

An exegetical criticism of the use of the Scriptures by liberation theologians will be considered later. For now it is enough to have shown that they attempt to synthesize ideology and theology by means of a new method for the theological task. As a result of that method, theology becomes subordinated to sociology and to liberating praxis.

THE HERMENEUTIC CRITERION

We now come to what from the hermeneutic point of view can be called the marrow of liberation theology. We have established,

---

30. Dennis McCann, *Christian Realism and Liberation Theology,* p. 159.

based on declarations by representatives of this theology, that the point of departure for their reflection is the Latin American context and, above all, praxis for social change. We have also seen that the reflection of liberation theologians on the church and society, and on historical liberating praxis, is *critical,* because it is based on the social sciences and especially on the sociological analysis that derives from Marx. But the reflection is carried out also in the light of faith, that is, in light of the Scriptures and of the teachings of the Roman Catholic church. Such are the basic elements that enter into the new way of doing theology: the social situation, the critical or "scientific" analysis of that situation, the praxis for social change, and the contribution of Roman Catholic theology.

Several critical questions now emerge. For example, what is the criterion that determines if theology is correct, or if praxis is going on the road that it ought to follow, or if a social struggle is serving the interests of justice on behalf of the oppressed? Who has the last word? Where is the norm for the correct interpretation of the biblical text? In the attempt to answer those questions, I shall describe what some liberation theologians say about the hermeneutic criterion and offer evangelical responses to them.

GUTIÉRREZ: THEOLOGY AS "A SECOND ACT"

Truth that changes. Gustavo Gutiérrez has told us that theology has a liberating function in its close relationship to historical praxis. But when he speaks of "theology" he does not have in mind *orthodoxy,* "which is often nothing more than fidelity to an obsolete tradition or a debatable interpretation." Gutiérrez is not thinking of a theology "which has as its points of reference only 'truths' which have been established once and for all." That kind of theology "can be only static and, in the long run, sterile." Gutiérrez advocates a theology "which both grows and, in a certain sense, changes,"—a truth "which is also the way."[31] Some lines that have become very popular express Gutiérrez's vision: "Traveler, there is no road; the road is made by walking."

Gutiérrez seems to quote approvingly the words of J. B. Metz: "The so-called fundamental hermeneutic problem of theology is

31. Gutiérrez, *Theology of Liberation,* pp. 10, 12-13.

not the problem of how systematic theology stands in relation to historical theology, how dogma stands in relation to history, but what is the relation between theory and practice, between understanding the faith and social practice."[32] Gutiérrez is also in agreement with the hermeneutic principle of Edward Schillebeeckx: "The hermeneutics of the Kingdom of God consist especially in making the world a better place. Only in this way will I be able to discover what the Kingdom of God means." The conclusion of Gutiérrez is inevitable: "In the last analysis, the true interpretation of the meaning revealed by theology is achieved only in historical praxis." That praxis is after all the hermeneutic criterion, even for understanding the significance of theology—which involves the Scriptures as well. Such are the "political hermeneutics of the Gospel."[33] Critical reflection on praxis is theological when it discovers in this liberating praxis the presence of the Christian faith. Gutiérrez does not go into much detail on his hermeneutic method, but it can be said that he is not as radical as other liberation theologians in their attitude toward Scriptures.

Movement toward the Word of God? In an article entitled "A New Gustavo Gutiérrez?" C. René Padilla comments briefly on an exposition Gutiérrez presented in a theological workshop held in Lima, Peru, in 1981. Padilla says that in that exposition are elements that seem to suggest that "the Peruvian theologian has made peace with the traditional definition of theology," without denying "the priority that Gutiérrez wants to give to Christian experience in relation to theological reflection, nor his rejection of the rationalist categories of traditional theology."[34]

Taking into account the fact that according to Gutiérrez theological reflection should be a theology of the way, progressive, variable, unfinished, always open to new achievements, it is logical to expect that he himself will make adjustments or changes in his work. It would be better if he made them in the direction of the authority of the Scriptures, and not merely in the search for a contemplative attitude that would reinforce liberating praxis, always leaving theology as "a second act." But we should continue to become informed about what liberation theologians say or

---

32. Ibid., p. 244, note 62, quoting J. B. Metz, *Theology of the World,* p. 112.
33. Gutiérrez, *Theology of Liberation,* p. 13.
34. C. René Padilla, "¿Un nuevo Gustavo Gutiérrez?" p. 21.

write. Gutiérrez said in 1970 that "there are certain chapters of theology that can only be written afterwards."[35] Let us be attentive to the publication of those chapters.

Segundo Galilea believes that in the reflection of the most representative liberation theologians, liberating praxis is not an autonomous theological criterion independent of the Word of God. He says that "theology of liberation is made by interpreting, deepening, criticizing, purifying all praxis of liberation (which can be ambiguous, which can become degraded) by confronting it with the objective values of the faith which the Church transmits to us."[36]

Unfortunately what we have discovered in Gutiérrez is that in the final analysis liberating historical praxis determines the meaning of theology. The same thing occurs with other theologians of liberation, some of whom are more radical.

HUGO ASSMANN: THEOLOGY AS "THE SECOND WORD"

Unreliability of the Bible. Assmann cannot depend upon the biblical text enough to use it as a hermeneutic criterion. Revelation does not exist for him as a reality or criterion in itself except as historically mediated. The Bible, says Assmann, "is not a direct source of criteria." Its text "has come down to us formed, deformed, reformed and deformed yet again by the actual history of Christianity." Thus Assmann, as noted earlier, believes it is impossible to reach "theological purism" because secular sciences are indispensable to the exegesis of the biblical text, to understanding its real challenge, and to answering the problems of contemporary man.[37]

For Assmann the "purely theological criteria" are not sufficient for critical reflection on praxis, if by those criteria one means those that come only "from the supposedly exclusive resources of theology." The reference to faith and to its historical testimonies is not sufficient either, in the opinion of Assmann, "to distinguish

---

35. Gustavo Gutiérrez, "Notes for a Theology of Liberation," p. 258. See also Gutiérrez, *Theology of Liberation,* p. 272, and *We Drink from Our Own Wells,* pp. 136-37. Gutiérrez adds spirituality to praxis as a source for theology.
36. Segundo Galilea, p. 22.
37. Hugo Assmann, *Theology,* pp. 60-61, 63.

good theology from bad." Nor can biblical exegesis be the hermeneutic criterion: "the usual views of exegetes who 'work on the
sacred text' are of little use to us, because we want to 'work on
the reality of today.'" In addition to the distinctive note of theology
("in light of the faith"), one must take into account "criteria of
reference to the historical value of experience, such as the process
of liberation in history, and these can only be formed through the
secular sciences." "In the Bible," says Assmann, "no message is
valid unless it 'is made true' in practice." Assmann does not believe
in a truth that exists "of itself," independent of human action. He
rejects dogmatism, authoritarianism, and reactionism, and prefers
to talk about faith as practice. Rejecting the old debate of orthodoxy versus orthopraxis, Assmann says that "faith must be understood as basically its practice, its working out in history rather
than the simple sense of 'practicing the faith.' This is stressed more
and more strongly by contemporary theology."[38]

Uses of the natural sciences in theological reflection. The supremacy of historical praxis over theology, and even over the Bible,
stands out in the thought of Assmann. But he also says that it is
necessary to take into account the contribution of the human
sciences in the critical reflection on praxis. The expression "in the
light of faith" can be the distinctive or typical note of theological
reflection, but not its exclusive characteristic:

> The theology of liberation takes a decisive step in the direction of
> the secular sciences by admitting that the fact of human experience,
> on which the secular sciences have the first word to say, is its basic
> point of reference, its contextual starting-point. One might say that,
> by defining itself as critical reflection based on the inner meaning of
> the process of liberation, the theology of liberation can be seen not
> only as the "second act" after the "first act" of action, but as the
> "second word" after the "first word" of the secular sciences—which
> is not to be understood as presuming to be the "last word."[39]

Theology, then, should be humble and should avoid "the old vices
of . . . [having] the last word . . . [and] the presumed omniscience

38. Ibid., pp. 64, 76, 80, 105.
39. Ibid., p. 62-63.

so characteristic of the traditional categories of theology."[40] Devout Christians may well say that theology is "the last word," but that affirmation would be methodologically dangerous, according to Assmann, because theology has had the habit of not listening enough to the human sciences.

Assmann wants to give those sciences their due place in theological reflection. But are they the final criteria? The answer cannot be affirmative, due to the limited, though progressive, character of any science. Assmann recognizes that scientific instruments cannot measure the "most basic liberating content" of human activity. "There is a limit to all criteria of quantification and qualification, because what they are analyzing is the infinite variety of human activity itself." It is also obvious that theology "shares in this limitation," and can only propose hypotheses about the final human dimension of action.[41]

Assmann not only recognizes the limitations of the human sciences; he also views with mistrust scientific instruments of analysis, because they "easily hide ideological prejudices." Consequently, the human sciences are not adequate as a criterion for theological reflection either. The only thing left for Assmann is historical praxis as the norm of truth. It becomes imperative to dignity the *political option* in any effort to interpret a historical situation. But that political option has to be liberated from its ideological domination. One should make an effort to liberate the criteria and "bring together interpretations of present-day reality and a discovery of relevant criteria in the history of Judaeo-Christianity." Praxis is still supreme, but also relative, unknown in its final human dimension. Assmann says that in view of the impossibility of knowing that dimension analytically, it is necessary to pursue "the quest for the mysterious efficacy of love in the complexity of all aspects of human activity . . . this quest for love in action, is the basic root of the quest for the liberating political efficacy of human action."[42]

The insufficiency of Assmann's theology. Love, however, can also be very subjective and relative apart from the objective revelation of the Word of God. Assmann points out that there are two

40. Ibid., p. 84.
41. Ibid., p. 85.
42. Ibid., pp. 85, 105.

fundamental theological gaps in liberation theology: the Christological gap and the hermeneutical gap. Evidently he has not been able to fill either of them in *Theology for a Nomad Church*. In Assmann's work, what Juan Gutiérrez calls "the evaporation of theology" seems to take place.[43]

JON SOBRINO: THEOLOGY OF FOLLOWING JESUS

Praxis over orthodoxy. Jon Sobrino, a Spanish Jesuit residing in El Salvador, has written a Christology that, together with the work of Leonardo Boff, *Jesus Christ Liberator,* has come to fill in a certain way the Christological void that concerned Hugo Assmann. In contrast to Assmann, Sobrino approaches the biblical text with an exegetical interest in order to contribute to the development of theology from the perspective of liberating praxis in Latin America. He attempts to give a New Testament basis to his Christology, defending the thesis that following Jesus is a condition for knowing Him; that is, only from the point of view of Christian praxis is it possible to draw near to Christ. Praxis prevails over orthodoxy. Jesus Himself, says Sobrino, condemned abstract orthodoxy, placing it in opposition to praxis. Concrete orthodoxy is an expression of praxis.

> The assertion that Christ is the way to the Father can have meaning only for someone who follows the same road. . . . Even from the standpoint of orthodoxy itself, therefore, it is obvious that orthodoxy is impossible without some praxis. Orthodoxy can be rendered concrete and Christian only through a specific praxis. . . . Viewed from the standpoint of praxis, the ultimate supremacy of praxis over orthodoxy is evident. It is evident in the case of the historical Jesus, who stresses the importance of doing the Father's will over crying "Lord! Lord!" This assertion is not based just on the natural view that action holds supremacy over knowledge. It is based on the very essence of Christian revelation. What happens in divine revelation? We do not get some abstract knowledge about God or some doctrine; we get a manifestation of God in action. What we get in revelation is the historical and historicized love of God. Viewed theologically, the life of the Christian does not consist in knowing about that love but in

43. Juan Gutiérrez, *The New Libertarian Gospel.* The Spanish edition is titled *Teología de la Liberación: Evaporación de la Teología.*

receiving it and sharing it. Knowledge of it is subordinate to that process, though it is not to be disdained.[44]

Sobrino makes an effort to demonstrate the supremacy of Christian praxis on the basis of the Scriptures. He indicates that it is not only on the natural plane (as in the case of Marxism) that praxis is supreme over knowledge. It is also the case in the New Testament. The hermeneutic problem related to the resurrection of Jesus is resolved by Sobrino when he says:

> Understanding the resurrection of Jesus today, then, presupposes several things. One must have a radical hope in the future. One must possess a historical consciousness that sees history both as promise and as mission. And one must engage in a specific praxis that is nothing else but discipleship—the following Jesus. . . . The last condition seems to be the most necessary because it is praxis inspired by love that concretizes Christian hope as a hoping against hope, and because love is the only thing that opens history up.[45]

Evangelical response: We need the authority of the Bible. The evangelical Christian makes an effort to understand the resurrection of Jesus from the revealed text. On the other hand, no evangelical Christian would deny the need for manifesting faith by means of good works. There certainly needs to be in the Christian life a practice of faith and love that is in harmony with the knowledge of the Word of God. But that is very different from suggesting that there is a hierarchical order according to which praxis is supreme. According to evangelical doctrine, Christian conduct has its norm in the objective revelation of the holy Scriptures. In that sense, the Christian has to know certain principles before acting. Faith and obedience, for example, are an answer to the revelation that God has given of Himself and His works in the Bible. There is already an object of faith and obedience. Otherwise we would not know what to believe or what to obey.

Faith, obedience, love, and knowledge are intimately related to each other in the New Testament. In a sense none of those elements is complete in itself. They need each other. The order in which their relationship is described in the New Testament can

44. Jon Sobrino, *Christology at the Crossroads,* pp. 390-91.
45. Ibid., pp. 380-81.

vary. For example, in John 14:15 love precedes obedience: "If you love Me, you will keep My commandments." In Ephesians 3:17-18 love is a precondition for knowledge. James teaches in his epistle that authentic faith is that which produces works (2:14-26). In John 7:17, the Lord Jesus Christ says: "If any man is willing to do His will, he shall know of the teaching, whether it is of God, or whether I speak from myself." According to that text, obedience (the willingness to do God's will) precedes knowledge. William Hendriksen comments:

> The only logical conclusion, in view of these various and (at first glance) seemingly (though never *really*) conflicting representations, is this: when we speak of *knowledge, love* and *obedience,* we are not thinking of three altogether separate experiences, but of one single, comprehensive experience in which the three are united in such a manner that each contributes its share, and all cooperate unto man's salvation and God's glory. This experience is *personal* in character. Hence, we can no longer speak of the primacy of the intellect or of the primacy of the emotions or of the primacy of the will, but of the primacy of the sovereign grace of God influencing and transforming the entire personality for the glory of God.[46]

We can also add that neither is it possible, on the basis of the New Testament, to speak of the primacy of Christian praxis with respect to knowledge; nor much less to affirm that theology must be the product of Christian praxis, a "second act" that follows action.

In John 7:17 the issue is knowing not so much the teaching itself as its origin. Unless the hearers of Jesus were prepared to submit themselves to the divine will, they would not come to know whether the teaching was coming from Himself or from the Father. Jesus had already spoken to them. It was not a matter of producing revelation, but of believing it. To us revelation has already been given in the Scriptures. The existence of that revelation does not depend on our response to it. At the same time we realize that we cannot grow as we should in our knowledge of the written revelation if we are not prepared to obey it. But in any case our responsibility is to submit praxis to the Word, instead of giving supremacy to praxis.

46. William Hendriksen, *The Gospel of John* (Grand Rapids, Mich.: Baker, 1979), p. 11.

Sobrino's emphasis on praxis can be positive, as long as it reminds us that correct theology should be accompanied by correct conduct. The balance must be maintained between knowing and doing, between theory and practice. Furthermore, we have to admit that our hermeneutic can be influenced by our way of living and thinking. We do not come "chemically pure" to the biblical text to interpret it. We may approach it with a previous understanding. It is not easy to recognize our own personal, theological, ecclesiastical, and political prejudices; it is even more difficult to abandon them in the face of the majesty of the revelation of God. But that fact, which is so human and overwhelming, is not a valid excuse for abandoning the conviction that God has spoken and is speaking to us by means of the sacred Scriptures, and that written revelation is the supreme authority in every issue of faith and practice. The principle of *sola Scriptura* has not lost its relevance for us. We recognize the seriousness of hermeneutic problems, but we do not believe that the solution to them is found in exalting Christian praxis above what God has revealed to us.

JOSÉ PORFIRIO MIRANDA: THE DIALECTICAL METHOD

The lack of exegesis in Hugo Assmann is compensated in a sense by the Mexican Catholic theologian José Porfirio Miranda, who published *Marx y la Biblia: Crítica a la filosofia de la opresion* in 1970 (Mexican edition), and then in Salamanca, 1972. The English translation, *Marx and the Bible: A Critique of the Philosophy of Oppression,* was published in 1979. Because the title can be misunderstood, Miranda warns that his purpose is not to seek parallelisms between Marx and the Bible, but simply to understand the Bible without ignoring its coincidences with Marx that may emerge along the way of his investigation. He asserts that his method is "the most rigorous and scientific exegesis."[47]

The Spanish Catholic theologian J. I. González Faus focuses on the work of Miranda as if it were entitled "Capitalism and the Bible."[48] At the foundation of Miranda's work is the thesis that the Bible denounces western capitalist society in a devastating way. The fundamental coincidence between Marx and the Bible is this:

47. José P. Miranda, *Marx and the Bible,* p. xvii.
48. J. I. González Faus, "La Teologia Latinoamericana de la liberacion," p. 360.

"What Marx criticizes in western science is the same thing that today prevents it from being challenged by the fact, which is recognized by this science itself, that to a great degree Marx coincides with the Bible."[49]

Critique of Western philosophy. According to Miranda, the root of capitalism was already "in Western and Greek philosophy, which was later diversified into various specialized sciences." It is the philosophy of power, of knowledge as domination, that conceives reality (to quote Marx) "only in the form of *object* or of *contemplation*" without questioning the subject that acquires the knowledge. Man himself comes to be the object of observation and manipulation. Miranda says: "Indeed, Greek philosophy was born to neutralize reality and prevent it from disturbing us, to reduce it to a cosmos in which everything is all right."[50] Miranda makes an effort to free himself from the Greek mentality that has dominated philosophy, science, and theology in the western world. He prefers the dialectical method of Marx, who goes beyond the facts discovered by science, points out the conflictive situation in society, and reveals that man finds himself dehumanized by unjust economic structures. According to Miranda, Marx concluded that reality is moral, and in that he is in harmony with the Bible, which sees that reality is contaminated by sin. Consequently, the method of Marx is today the best method for understanding the biblical text in a way that is pertinent to our contemporaries. J. Andrew Kirk refers to the epistemological decision of Miranda in the following terms:

> In other words, because of the uniform use made today of Greek rationalistic epistemology, within the total scientific endeavour of Western civilization, the only way we can capture afresh the message of an essentially non-Greek book, is by reconsidering the positive contribution of dialectical epistemology. Miranda denies that this contribution implies a necessary search for parallels between Marx and the Bible. It simply aims at producing a new understanding of the Bible, from its own perspective (i.e., from within its own view of reality as conflictive) rather than from a so-called neutral but, in fact, ideologically determined standpoint.[51]

49. Miranda, *Marx and the Bible*, p. xvii.
50. Ibid., pp. xviii-xx.
51. J. Andrew Kirk, *Liberation Theology*, p. 82.

God is known only in the act of justice. The results of Miranda's project are not simply stated, but a few important conclusions deserve comment. One conclusion to which he comes in the study of the Old Testament is that God is not known in abstract, as is the case in a theology that is powerfully influenced by Greek epistemology with its speculations about the nature of being. Rather we know Him in His acts of justice on behalf of the oppressed. Only in the act of justice is God accessible.[52]

God intervenes in history for the cause of justice as the savior of the oppressed and punisher of the oppressors. Abraham was chosen to practice justice and defend the rights of the oppressed against the oppressors. Genesis 18:18-19 deliberately interprets in social terms the promise of 12:3: "in you all the families of the earth shall be blessed." The justice of which Genesis 18 and 19 speak is of a social character; it is that justice done on behalf of the oppressed, the poor, the widow, and the orphan.[53]

Judgment—that is, God's intervention—consists of liberating the oppressed. The final judgment will be the definitive implantation of justice and the turning over of the earth to the just. But even before that conclusion the great objective of the Law was to protect the rights of one's neighbor. The commandments of the Lord are justice (*mishpāṭ*). The specific reason for Yahweh's rejection of Israel was injustice, the exploitation of the poor and destitute.[54]

In the New Testament, says Miranda, sin is *adikia* (injustice)— social injustice in terms that encompass the whole of humanity. The key text is Rom. 1:16-3:20. In the gospel is revealed "the justice of God which saves precisely from all this *adikia*" which abides in all people.[55] The meaning of "sin" is found in Rom. 3:9,

52. Miranda, *Marx and the Bible,* p. 48.
53. Ibid., pp. 92-96, 122.
54. Ibid., pp. 122-27, 155-56, 168.
55. Ibid., p. 169; see the entire section, pp. 160-92. According to Miranda, the structure of the letter to the Romans has as its basis the description of *adikia* (injustice) in 1:18—3:20. This injustice is of a social nature. The concept is, acording to Miranda, from the Old Testament. The unjust are the oppressors. What this is dealing with is "the justice of God as a new reality with social dimensions in human history" (p. 173) of "collective guilt." "But these authors do not develop this point, nor do they realize that if Paul's concern is with societies, civilizations, and cultures, and not with individuals as exegesis and theology have generally supposed, the meaning of the Letter to the Romans changes completely" (p. 176). "Romans 3:9, 19-20 and the entire letter deal with the problem of society . . . , of human civilization" (p. 178).

and is "specified as interhuman injustice for the whole rest of the letter."[56]

The eschaton *and earthly justice.* Social justice is carried out by means of faith, which can also be a reality of social dimensions. "It is faith, enkindled by the proclamation called Gospel, which makes the *eschaton* arrive, not in fantasy but in reality." Miranda explains that "the *eschaton* is physically and existentially the *ultimum* of history, something really new and definitive."[57] It is equivalent to the kingdom in its fullness. Pauline faith and that of the whole New Testament consists of believing that the definitive kingdom of justice and life has arrived. Even resurrection is the fruit of justice: "We should not be surprised that for him [Paul] the transformation of material creation and even the resurrection of bodies depends on justice."[58] Miranda wants to be freed from Greek philosophy, which looks down upon matter. González Faus believes that Miranda has defended himself from the accusation that his theology reflects a "Marxist-Pelagianism" when he teaches that justice is the fruit of love that God sheds abroad in our hearts.[59] But Miranda's emphasis still falls on the idea that the *eschaton* comes not so much through divine intervention as through human faith and action.

For Miranda, faith is not so much believing *in* Jesus, as believing *that* He is Messiah. And His messiahship is believed in because of the historical fact that the kingdom has come. Biblical faith understands itself as hope, a hope that knows no limits: "(1) Faith is believing that there is hope for our world; (2) faith is believing that there is hope for our world because God intervenes in human history; (3) faith is believing that there is hope for our world because God intervenes in our history precisely in the historical event called Jesus Christ."[60] In Miranda's thought, faith as a horizontal cause is what produces justice on earth:

56. Ibid., p. 281. Miranda also says, "according to Paul sin is incarnated in social structures . . . in this civilization and in the ideology which supports it . . . in history and in the civilization whose axis is the law" (pp. 182, 188, 191).
57. Ibid., pp. 244, 246.
58. Ibid., pp. 276-77; cf. pp. 240-42.
59. González Faus, p. 379.
60. Miranda, *Marx and the Bible*, p. 227.

Evangelizing is really efficacious by virtue of the faith which it arouses. The *proclamation* that the kingdom *is arriving* has to *make* the kingdom *arrive*. . . . When one is convinced that the moment of justice has arrived for the whole earth, this conviction (which is New Testament faith-hope) causes the *eschaton* effectively and really to come. They were perfectly right in accusing Jesus of subversion (cf. Luke 23:2).[61]

The compatability of Marx and the Bible. Miranda has accepted Marxist premises without trying to conceal "the abysmal difference between Marx and the biblical authors, a difference stemming from the fact that the latter believe in God and his intervention and Marx does not." Miranda also believes that Marx should be reproached because of his lack of attention to the problem of death—the greatest contradiction in human reality—but in this case reproached not for lack of faith in God, but for "insufficient dialectics."[62]

At the same time, Miranda sees points of convergence between Marx and the Bible. For example, they both see that evil encompasses the whole world; injustice has become structured into civilization. There is coincidence, furthermore, in the affirmation that sin has come to be systematized institutionally "in a flawless civilizing structure," making humanity "aware of the infernal machinery which it has assembled and to be definitively delivered from it." Another coincidence between Marx and the Bible is the possibility of definitive liberation: "The most revolutionary historical thesis, in which, in contrast with all Western ideologies, the Bible and Marx coincide, is this: Sin and evil, which were later structured into an enslaving civilizing system, are not inherent to mankind and history; they began one day through a human work and can, therefore, be eliminated." Besides, "both Marx and the biblical writers believe that man can cease being selfish and merciless and self-serving and can find his greatest fulness in loving his neighbor."[63]

The fact that Miranda is an apologist of Marx is demonstrated also in his book *Marx Against the Marxists.* But the "abysmal difference" that he himself sees between Marx and the Bible

61. Ibid., p. 245.
62. Ibid., pp. 278-79.
63. Ibid., pp. 254-55, 258.

persists. Whereas the Bible teaches that the *eschaton* comes by the direct intervention of God in history when Messiah returns to the world, Marx depends upon human praxis for the establishment of the golden age in history.

Miranda's use of the Bible examined. The biblical erudition of Miranda and his tremendous exegetical efforts are impressive as he tries to demonstrate the validity of his global thesis, which is the opposition of the Scriptures to the oppressive capitalist system. But without defending that system or doing it an indirect service, I feel obligated to say that I do not see that the hermeneutic criterion for Miranda's theological reflection is, in the last instance, the written revelation of God. Exegetes can undertake a detailed examination of the conclusions to which Miranda arrives in his biblical study. What is evident is his tendency to impose an ideology on the Scriptures. That can be seen, for example, in his approach to themes such as the Being and the judgment of God in the Old Testament, or sin, faith, and justice in the New.

It must be asked if, in the Old Testament, God is indeed accessible "only in the act of justice," even when that affirmation is restricted to theological epistemology. For Miranda the justice of God and His judgment have to do with the punishment of oppressors and the liberation of the oppressed. Was God knowable only in His action of justice, or are there also other relationships in the Old Testament in which God gave communication about Himself?

Without a doubt the Lord presents Himself as the defender of the oppressed, the widows, the orphans, the strangers, and all the needy. But with regard to the moral responsibility of the human being before the Creator, is it correct to say that God takes sides with a particular social class in the administration of His justice? It should also be asked whether a conscientious examination of the Old Testament will support the thesis proposed by Miranda, based on Genesis 18:17-22, regarding the meaning of the blessing promised to all nations in the Abrahamic covenant. Miranda underlines the words "justice and judgment" (18:19, KJV) as the key to interpreting that blessing, giving preeminence to its global aspect. It cannot be denied that the blessings in the Old Testament generally encompassed the totality of human existence, without making a clear distinction between that which is spiritual and that which is material. But at the same time it is interesting to observe that when Paul refers to the universal promise of the covenant of God with Abraham (Gal. 3:6-18), he does not give it the same emphasis as Miranda.

Furthermore, if, as Miranda thinks, justice and judgment have to do principally with the problem of the oppressors, the case of Sodom becomes an anomaly. Sodom was destroyed because, with very few exceptions, its inhabitants were "wicked." They were all unjust, although there must have been both oppressors and oppressed in that social structure. There were no doubt slaves there; the judgment of God fell on all social classes. To be wicked, then, does not only consist of oppressing one's neighbor socially and economically. There are other kinds of wickedness that Yahweh punishes. For example, what about idolatry, which the prophets condemned in the name of Yahweh? Weren't multitudes practicing it in Israel and Judah? Wasn't the captivity also a punishment for the idolatry of both the weak and the powerful, of the oppressors and the oppressed?

Miranda's interpretation of the New Testament also causes serious questions to be raised, as when he magnifies the social aspect of *adikia* (injustice) and insists that Paul is primarily denouncing social and structural sin throughout the letter to the Romans. Once more we have to perceive and acknowledge the importance of the social implications of the biblical message. Without a doubt the epistle to the Romans is a severe condemnation of the individual and collective sins of Greco-Roman society. However, the apostle also individualizes his message, saying that "there is none righteous, not even one" (Rom. 3:10), and multiplying references to the personal responsibility that believers in Christ have in their relationship with God and with their neighbor. Miranda admits that "isolated individuals can very well be just and fulfill, with an authentic transformation of the heart, the true will of God (Rom. 2:13-15, 26-29)." But then he says: "Paul's gospel has nothing to do with the interpretation which for centuries has been given to it in terms of individual salvation. It deals with the justice which the world and peoples and society, implicitly but anxiously, have been awaiting."[64] In the light of that affirmation, the meaning of soteriological passages such as Romans 1:15-18; 3:9-31; 5:1-11; and 10:8-13 would be primarily collective, national, and universal.

64. Miranda, *Marx and the Bible,* pp. 178-79.

Bible interpretation and ideology. To our questions about his hermeneutic method, Miranda could answer that our basic problem is an epistemological one. We come to the biblical text under the influence of the Greek way of thinking, and we do not take into account the mentality of the biblical writers; we do not think dialectically. Miranda believes that the dialectical epistemology of Marx is the best tool for drawing out the biblical meaning. It is natural, therefore, that there should be Marxist influence in his interpretation of the Scriptures. In his hermeneutic, Miranda substitutes the epistemology of Marx for the way of thinking of the Greeks.

To say that we evangelicals have also been, consciously or unconsciously, under the influence of an ideology in our approach to the biblical text does not give us a valid excuse to exchange one ideology for another. We cannot approach Scripture "chemically pure." But as evangelicals we also testify to our full confidence in the capacity of the Holy Scriptures to speak to us. We have, furthermore, the ministry of the Holy Spirit, who can guide us "into all the truth" (John 16:13). As C. René Padilla has well said:

> A better option is a theology that reads the Bible with the firm determination of allowing it to speak for itself, without forcing it into an ideological mold and without imposing limitations on the Word of God. The alternative is not: a "pure" biblical theology, or a theology which intentionally puts the biblical text at the service of an ideology. There is a third option: a theology which continuously seeks the coherence between the Scriptures and present obedience by means of a "synthetic act" in which the past and present—the Word and the Spirit—are fused together.[65]

JUAN LUIS SEGUNDO: THE HERMENEUTIC CIRCLE

Among the Catholic theologians of liberation who try to integrate the biblical text with their reflection, Juan Luis Segundo of Uruguay also has a prominent place. In his work *The Liberation of Theology,* Segundo says that the hour for epistemology has come, that is, the "time to get down to analyzing not so much the content of Latin American theology but rather its methodological approach and its connection with liberation."[66]

---

65. C. René Padilla, "La Teologia de la liberacion," p. 21.
66. Juan Luis Segundo, *The Liberation of Theology,* p. 5.

Traditional and liberationist theology. Segundo begins by explaining the difference between a traditional academic theologian and a theologian of liberation, and indicates that academic theology is primarily an interpretation not of man and society but of a book, the Bible.[67] It is a theology that takes into account sciences that help it to understand the past, but it declares itself autonomous with regard to the sciences of the present. The liberation theologian, says Segundo, begins exactly in the opposite way; he "feels compelled at every step to combine the disciplines that open up the past with the disciplines that help to explain the present." In so doing he attempts to interpret the Word of God as it is directed to us here and now. According to Segundo, without that connection between theology and the sciences in order to understand the past as well as the present, the theology of liberation cannot exist. The method that tries to link the past with the present, while dealing with the Word of God, demands what Segundo calls a *hermeneutic circle,* which he defines as:

> the continuing change in our interpretation of the Bible which is dictated by the continuing changes in our present-day reality, both individual and societal. "Hermeneutic" means "having to do with interpretation." And the circular nature of this interpretation stems from the fact that each new reality obliges us to interpret the word of God afresh, to change reality accordingly, and then go back and reinterpret the Word of God again, and so on.[68]

Accomplishing the hermeneutic circle in theology. Two conditions are necessary. First, out of the present there must arise questions that will force us to change our usual manner of interpreting human existence and our cultural and social reality. There must be at least a general suspicion with regard to our ideas and value judgments concerning life, death, knowledge, society, politics, and the world as a whole. Only a change in, or at the very least a pervasive suspicion about, our perception and evaluation of

67. Segundo prepared the basic material of *The Liberation of Theology* for a course in the Divinity School of Harvard University in 1974. This circumstance explains in great measure certain aspects of his approach to the theme, such as the description of Christianity as the religion of one *book,* and academic theology as an effort to interpret the Bible. Segundo has his audience and the country where he is teaching very much in mind (p. 7).
68. Segundo, *Liberation of Theology,* p. 8.

those things "will enable us to reach the theological level and force theology to come back down to reality and ask itself new and decisive questions."[69]

The second condition is that theology must change its usual interpretation of the holy Scriptures to answer the new questions that arise from present reality. Only in that way will the hermeneutic circle be possible. Segundo affirms that without the circle theology is always a conservative way of thinking and acting. "For progressive theology, on the other hand, liberation deals not so much with content as with the method used to theologize in the face of our real-life situation."[70]

There are four decisive points in the hermeneutic circle:

> *Firstly* there is our way of experiencing reality, which leads us to ideological suspicion. *Secondly* there is the application of our ideological suspicion to the whole ideological superstructure in general and to theology in particular. *Thirdly* there comes a new way of experiencing theological reality that leads us to exegetical suspicion, that is, to the suspicion that the prevailing interpretation of the Bible has not taken important pieces of data into account. *Fourthly* we have our new hermeneutic, that is, our new way of interpreting the fountainhead of our faith (i.e., Scripture) with the new elements at our disposal.[71]

Segundo presents four examples of what could be a hermeneutic circle in such authors as Harvey Cox, Karl Marx, Max Weber, and James Cone. According to Segundo, Harvey Cox in his work *The Secular City* (New York: Macmillan, 1965) interrupts the circle from the first point, because he does not really identify himself with the problems of the urban and pragmatic man to whom he desires to communicate the message of Christianity. Segundo insists that the hermeneutic circle always supposes a "partiality" consciously accepted with human criteria.[72]

Segundo takes Marx's critique of religion as his second example. He says that the influence of Marx in Latin American theology cannot be denied: "Whether everything Marx said is accepted or

69. Ibid., pp. 8-9.
70. Ibid., p. 9.
71. Ibid.
72. Ibid., p. 13.

not, and in whatever way one may conceive his "essential" thinking, there can be no doubt that present-day social thought will be
"Marxist" to some extent: that is, profoundly indebted to Marx. In
that sense Latin American theology is certainly Marxist."[73]

With regard to the hermeneutic circle, Marx reaches the second
point when he brings religion under ideological suspicion, but he
does not take the next step. He disqualifies religion as something
purely spiritual; he does not become interested in determining
whether there has been a distortion of the Christian message, or if
it is possible to reinterpret it in favor of the proletarian struggle.
Marx is interested in changing the world, not in changing theology.[74]

The third example is that of Max Weber and his book *The
Protestant Ethic and the Spirit of Capitalism*. Weber is not defending the thesis that capitalism is a product of the Protestant Reformation of the sixteenth century. He recognizes that some
modalities of the capitalist economy already existed before the
Reformation. His investigation is limited to establishing "whether
and to what extent religious influences have contributed to the
characteristics and quantitative expansion of the 'spirit' throughout the world, and what aspects of capitalist civilization are due to
them."[75]

Weber concurs with Marx on the fact that there are relationships
between economic and cultural forms. However, he admits that
economic attitudes can be a result, to some measure, of religious
beliefs. He corrects in that way the excessive emphasis of Marxism
on the economic realm. Weber does not complete the hermeneutic circle either. He does not go beyond the effort to establish the
relationship between the religious ideas of Calvinism and certain
economic attitudes. He is not interested in transforming theology,
nor does he want the Bible to be reinterpreted in answer to the
ideological suspicion. He takes the step from the second to the
third point of the circle, and stops there.[76]

According to Segundo, only James Cone completes the herme-

73. Ibid., p. 35, note 10.
74. Ibid., p. 17.
75. Max Weber, *The Protestant Ethic and the Spirit of Capitalism* (New York:
    Scribner's 1948), p. 91.
76. Segundo, *Liberation of Theology*, pp. 22-23.

neutic circle in his book *A Black Theology of Liberation*.[77] Cone fulfills the requirement of hermeneutic partiality by identifying himself plainly with his own people, the black community in North America. At the first point of the hermeneutic circle Cone demonstrates that he has changed his way of perceiving and evaluating the reality in which he lives. At the second point he accuses traditional theology of being "a theology of the white oppressor" and "the theology of Antichrist." Cone has had a new experience of theology, and at the third point of the circle he declares that in order to be Christian, traditional theology should stop being white theology and should transform itself into black theology, "denying whiteness as a proper form of human existence and affirming blackness as God's intention for humanity."[78] At that point in his reflection, Cone has to take the fourth step in the hermeneutic circle: the new interpretation of the Bible to answer the ideological and exegetical suspicion.

The meaning of the circle. The circle is complete; but because this is a circular hermeneutic, the new biblical interpretation changes reality, and the new reality in turn produces another change in the interpretation of Scriptures, and so on successively. The circle continues its movement. Segundo says that to complete the circle is not in itself "a sufficient proof of the truth of the theology in question;" it is only a proof that a certain theology is alive, that it is connected to historical reality.[79] What then is the hermeneutic norm in this unending succession of changes? For Cone the norm is Jesus, who as the black Christ gives the necessary spirit to black liberation. "The norm of Black Theology, which identifies revelation as a manifestation of the Black Christ, says that he is those very black men against whom white society shoots and kills."[80] Attempting to answer one of the questions that Cone raises, Segundo affirms:

77. Note that both *A Black Theology of Liberation* (1970) and *Black Theology and Black Power* (1969) were published before the *Theology of Liberation* of Gustavo Gutiérrez (1971).
78. Cone, *Black Theology of Liberation*, pp. 22, 25, 32-33.
79. Segundo, *Liberation of Theology*, p. 25.
80. Cone, *Black Theology of Liberation*, p. 80.

Unless I am mistaken, he is asserting that orthodoxy possesses no ultimate criterion in itself because being orthodox does not mean possessing the final truth. We only arrive at the latter by orthopraxis. It is the latter that is the ultimate criterion of the former, both in theology and in biblical interpretation. The truth is truth only when it serves as the basis for truly human attitudes. "Doers of the truth" is the formula used by divine revelation to stress the priority of orthopraxis over orthodoxy when it comes to truth and salvation.[81]

Segundo recognizes that there are many hermeneutic dangers in this way of biblical interpretation; but he seems to accept it, pointing out that "one cannot rule out a particular theological method which is consistent, just because it entails dangers." Thus the hermeneutic circle is justified, along with its interpretation of the Scriptures, due to "the continuing changes in our present-day reality, both individual and societal."[82] Orthopraxis precedes orthodoxy as a final criterion, in theology and in the interpretation of the written Word of God.

SUMMARY AND ASSESSMENT

Fundamentally, what distinguishes the theology of liberation most from other theologies is its *method.*

A NEW CONTEXT

Liberation theology is "a new way of doing theology." It is new in its *context:* the historical, economic, cultural, social, and political reality of Latin America. Without failing to give credit to the writings of Bartolomé de Las Casas and other defenders of the American Indians, it can be said that since colonial times theology in Latin America has been just an echo of that which has been written in other latitudes. The point of origin of that theology has been Europe and North America. Liberation theologians make an effort to change the situation of theological dependence and

---

81. Segundo, *Liberation of Theology,* p. 32.
82. Ibid., pp. 8, 32. Segundo defends the thesis that the criterion of truth of the faith depends on historical efficacy, on its liberating capability (*The Sacraments Today,* p. 55). In another work he says: "We deny that even one dogma can be studied under any final criterion other than that of its impact upon praxis." ("Capitalism-Socialism," p. 232).

underdevelopment, and take Latin American reality as the context for their reflection. They say that their reflection is "critical" because it analyzes the situation of Latin American countries on the basis of the human sciences, including, of course, Marxist sociological interpretation. Furthermore, it takes a critical attitude toward theology itself and toward the church.

COMMITMENT TO ACTION AS A PRECONDITION TO THEOLOGY

The point of departure for liberation theology is "historical liberating praxis," that is, the effort to change the situation of dependence and underdevelopment, of poverty and helplessness, in which millions of Latin Americans live. It is a reflection *upon* praxis, *in* praxis, *from* liberating praxis. The commitment to the liberating struggle is the *first act*; theology comes after as the *second act.*

Gustavo Gutiérrez indicates that Marxism, with its emphasis on the priority of action over reflection, is one of the factors that has led to the emphasis on revolutionary praxis in Latin American theology. Marx not only wants to explain the world but to change it. Revolutionary praxis has to be the source of reflection for philosophy, and, according to the theologians of liberation, also for theology. That is how the domination of *orthopraxis* over *orthodoxy* comes about in the theological task. Consequently, it is emphasized that the theologian has to opt for the poor and identify himself with them in their liberating struggle in order to be able to speak from the vantage point of that revolutionary commitment the message that the people need. That explains why Gutiérrez and other theologians of liberation consider their theology to be an unfinished task. It is a theology whose chapters have to be written in the midst of the process of social change. It is a theology of the way, progressive and variable. Therefore one cannot speak of a definitive theology of liberation, and it would be naive to want to write a definitive work on this theological system.

Neither do liberation theologians believe that it is possible to understand the truth immediately and totally on the purely intellectual or spiritual plane. It is necessary to pursue it, discovering it step by step, in commitment to the neglected social classes. Truth cannot be found in the abstract, in a purely theoretical field, or in doctrinal propositions. It is imperative to "do truth" on the

way of orthopraxis. Revolutionary praxis is the first act and liberation theology the second act.[83]

NEW UNDERSTANDING OF THE WORD OF GOD

Up to the second act there is no theology, strictly speaking. The
human sciences can by themselves analyze Latin American reality,
and there are many revolutionaries who are not Christians, who
fight to their death in order the change the social structures. Out
of that revolutionary praxis, which would be called *orthopraxis*—
the correct praxis—by its protagonists, can emerge a whole reflection of a philosophical or scientific nature. What right then do
Gutiérrez and his colleagues have to call their reflection theology?
Why do they speak of "theology of liberation" and not of "sociology of liberation?" Assmann answers those questions by saying that
"critical reflection on liberating historical praxis" is theology because it is carried out "in light of the faith," or "in light of the
Word of God."

There are, therefore, three basic elements in liberation theology:
(1) The Latin American social context, analyzed by the human
sciences; (2) liberating praxis, as a point of departure and as a
preferred place for the theological task; and (3) the Word of God,
or "the sources of revelation."

Liberation theologians believe that in the midst of historical
praxis it is possible to understand the Word of God in a new way.
Such theological reflection gives a broader and deeper dimension
to the liberating struggle; it points out the relative character of all
human achievement, it prevents the church from becoming set on
that which is provisional, and it always moves forward, beyond the
present manifestations of the kingdom of God to the total fulfillment of the eschatological promises. Therefore, they say, critical

83. "Therefore this faith does not consist in intellectual adherence to a certain
body of revealed content as the definitive solution to theoretical or practical
problems. Nor does it consist in having confidence in one's own salvation,
thanks to the merits of Christ. Instead it entails the freedom to accept an
educational process that comes to maturity and abandons its teacher to launch
into the provisional and relative depths of history (Gal. 4:1 ff.; Rom. 8:19-23;
1 Cor. 3:11-15)" (Segundo, *Liberation of Theology*, p. 122). In the same work
he says that "doers of the truth" is the formula used by divine revelation to
stress the priority of orthopraxis over orthodoxy when it comes to truth and
salvation" (p. 32).

reflection on praxis is *theology,* not only sociology. Obviously, the evangelical Christian has sufficient reason to fear that sooner or later theology may evaporate in liberationist thought.

THE FINAL CRITERION

The most important question about the method of liberation theology is this: What, according to that theology, is the final hermeneutic criterion? The general impression that one gets on reading liberation theologians is that for them the hermeneutic norm is not the written Word of God—that is, the Bible in and of itself. The final criterion rather is praxis, or the ideology that moves that praxis. Action is supreme over reflection. We must *do* in order to *know,* and hope that orthodoxy will arise from orthopraxis.

For Hugo Assmann, neither the Bible, nor theology, nor the human sciences are sure sources of criteria. But we can become involved in liberating praxis with the hope of discovering in it the norm that we need for our faith, our conduct, and our theological task. Because praxis by itself cannot offer a final criterion either, Assmann seems to find his last recourse in love as a norm for praxis; but love that is not sustained by the objective teachings of the Scriptures can drag one into subjectivism or situational ethics. In reality, the hermeneutic criterion for Assmann is his political option, or his ideology.

Liberation theologians who give a prominent place to the Scriptures in their reflection are also unable to offer a final criterion other than ideology, or revolutionary praxis. Miranda accepts the dialectical epistomology of Marx in order to free himself from the Greek way of thinking. Miranda believes that the thought of the biblical writers is also dialectical, and that therefore the best epistemology for understanding their thought is the Marxist one. One result is that Miranda emphasizes class struggle and collective or social sin. Divine justice reveals the sin of the oppressors, and the judgment of Yahweh consists in the liberation of the oppressed and the punishment of the guilty. In his letter to the Romans, the apostle Paul is thinking primarily of social justice and the salvation of society, of the whole of humanity, not of the sin and salvation of individuals.

The Catholic priest Francisco Interdonato says that liberation theologians reject traditional theology because it uses "Greek" categories, but "they do not do so in the name of biblical categories but of sociological ones and, incidentally, a specific one."[84] That the biblical exegesis of liberation theologians leaves much to be desired is obvious to anyone who studies the Scriptures diligently.

THE INFLUENCE OF IDEOLOGIES: EVANGELICAL RESPONSES

It is not valid to approve the method of liberation theology by using the excuse that conservative evangelicals also come to the Scriptures under the influence of an ideology. The solution to the hermeneutic problem is not found in exchanging one ideology for another, nor in giving in to the idea that it is impossible for the Bible to speak to us here and now under the illumination of the Holy Spirit, nor in beginning a supposed orthopraxis with the hope that we will discover the truth in it by doing it.

We must continue to believe in the fact that the Bible *is* the Word of the living and true God, and that in the hands of the Holy Spirit it is capable of communicating its message to us for our life and for the Latin American people. This in no way means that we will adopt an attitude of pious ignorance that has little appreciation for the contribution of the biblical sciences to the intelligent study of the written Word of God. Neither does it mean that we should be indifferent to the cries of the Latin American people, limiting ourselves to continually repeating, without thinking, a theology that, because it has been written in other latitudes, does not deal in a direct way with the problems of Latin American countries. The social context must be seriously taken into account for a legitimate contextualization of the biblical text. But the interaction in the theological task between the biblical text and the social context is only valid as long as Scripture is allowed to speak for itself, without imposing on it the meaning that according to the exegete is the most convenient for contemporary society. When it comes to contextualization, liberation theology presents a challenge to us that we should gladly accept.

If, however, under the influence of one ideology or culture we

84. Franciso Interdonato, *Teologia Latinoamericana, p. 29. ¿Teologia de la Liberacion?*

A New Way of Doing Theology

have been naive, we have no reason to continue being so under the influence of another ideology or culture. It has been said that liberation theologians are ready to criticize everything—traditional theology, the church, and society—except their own method. If liberation theology is found to be heavy in the scales, and is found faulty, then the whole system falls. Evangelicals are convinced that the scale must be the Word of God—that is the Bible—which is totally inspired, and not a social or political prejudice.

CRITICS OF LIBERATION THEOLOGY

The "new way of doing theology" has been seriously questioned from different points of view. For example, in the Roman Catholic realm, Fr. Bonaventura Kloppenburg asks penetrating questions of liberation theology. He wonders "if the persistent accent given to the existential aspect (meaning of the revelation 'for us') does not tend to underestimate the ontological dimension (meaning of the revelation 'in itself') of faith . . . [and] if the proclaimed orthopraxis does not insensitively lead to heteropraxis."[85] Interdonato sees that the major problem of liberation theology "consists in the taking of historical praxis as a criterion for evaluating Christianity, its fruits, and even its own 'efficacy.' " He continues:

> however, this pretended dogma of infallibility of historical praxis cannot withstand the minor confrontation not only with Christianity, but even with axiology or epistemology. . . . It is not possible to take praxis as a criterion, since it itself must be submitted to a criterion; it must be judged. Taking action is not truth by itself; it is if it accords with the truth.[86]

Similarly, before the plenary assembly of the International Theological Commission (Catholic) held in Rome in October 1976, the theologian Karl Lehmann said:

> The concrete situation of humanity, with its hopes and miseries, and especially that of the people of God, can constitute a "locus theologicus" in a broad sense, but it cannot be said that this is *theologically*

85. Bonaventura Kloppenburg, "Cuestiones pendientes en la accion cristiana para la liberación," pp. 357-58.
86. Interdonato, pp. 88, 90.

normative in itself. This situation does not have in itself an absolute value. For the Christian, the light of the word of God as it is in the church and through the ministry of the ecclesiastical magisterium constitutes the primary criterion with which every artificial situation which pretends to be a fountain of theological knowledge must be contrasted.[87]

On the evangelical side are voices such as Andrew Kirk's declaring that the most significant aspect of liberation theology is its use of Marxism as an ideological instrument for liberating theology and, consequently, the church, to the end that it may come to be a means of social change. According to Kirk, liberation theology has made a penetrating critique of contemporary theology without offering an alternative that might be at all viable. Kirk concludes that the only way in which the fourth segment of the hermeneutical circle proposed by Segundo can function freely, and the only way that theology may come to be an instrument of liberation, is for revelation to be accepted as a court of final appeal. There are two reasons why that is so: (1) Marxism can also create a false consciousness and an illusory hope, and is limited in its ability to liberate theology from within. (2) The only way out is found in a serious exegesis of the biblical text, to proclaim to humanity the total message of liberation.[88]

Another evangelical opinion is that of the Latin American theologian C. René Padilla, who evaluates liberation theology without avoiding its challenge and without naively using arguments frequently used in the North Atlantic against that theology:

> The conclusion is that if theology must be a critical reflection on praxis in the light of faith, the hermeneutical circulation between past and present, in scripture and historical situation, is inevitable. The answer for a rationalistic theology preoccupied by orthodoxy, as well as for a pragmatic theology preoccupied by orthopraxis, is a contextual theology preoccupied simultaneously by loyalty to the word of God and pertinence to the historical situation.[89]

87. Karl Lehmann, "Problemas metodológicos y hermenéuticos," pp. 17-18 (author's emphasis).
88. J. Andrew Kirk, *Theology Encounters Revolution,* pp. 128-30. A free and condensed translation has been made of Kirk's thought, endeavoring to express his ideas faithfully.
89. Padilla, "La teología de la liberación," p. 18.

Without a basic knowledge of the theological method I have tried to describe in broad strokes in this chapter, it is impossible to understand the content of liberation theology. Juan Luis Segundo has had more reason than perhaps even he suspects to say that "now . . . it may be time to get down to analyzing not so much the content of Latin American theology but rather its methodological approach and its connection with liberation."[90]

90. Segundo, *Liberation of Theology,* p. 5.

Part Four

Some Fundamental Themes
of Liberation Theology

7

Salvation and Liberation

There is good reason to say that Gustavo Gutiérrez is a systematizer. He demonstrates that in *A Theology of Liberation.* The subtitle, *Perspectives,* is actually the title of the fourth part of the book. After having set forth the Latin American social problem and having evaluated the efforts that have been made to solve it, Gutiérrez focuses again on that problem, taking into account the theological reflections it elicits. His purpose is "to indicate the basic directions of the work to be done in this field." Gutiérrez wants a reflection that will not be separated from praxis. That is why he speaks of theology and "work." What is his point of departure? It cannot be any other than the one he has already set forth in the first chapter of his book: "We will use as our point of departure the questions posed by the social praxis in the process of liberation as well as by the participation of the Christian community in this process within the Latin American context. The Latin American experience holds special interest for us."[1]

SOCIAL SALVATION

In the first section of his *Perspectives,* Gutiérrez deals with the theme of "faith and the new man." He begins by saying that what

1. Gustavo Gutiérrez, *A Theology of Liberation: History, Politics and Salvation*, p. 143.

motivates Christians to participate in the liberation of the oppressed "is the conviction of the radical incompatibility of evangelical demands with an unjust and alienating society. They feel keenly that they cannot claim to be Christians without a commitment to liberation."[2] The motivation, he says, is Christian, evangelical; the problem is social, and the solution has to be given on the collective plane. It is not simply a matter of the salvation of individuals, but of the transformation of society.

Gutiérrez does not deny the reality of sin; on the contrary, he affirms it emphatically. Neither does he ignore that there is personal sin, but he is interested especially in social sin:

> Therefore, sin is not only an impediment to salvation in the afterlife. Insofar as it constitutes a break with God, sin is a historical reality, it is a breach of the communion of men with each other, it is a turning in of man on himself which manifests itself in a multifaceted withdrawal from others. And because sin is a personal and social intrahistorical reality, a part of the daily events of human life, it is also, and above all, an obstacle to life's reaching the fullness we call salvation.[3]

According to José P. Miranda, the apostle Paul teaches that sin is incarnated in social structures; it is "a manifestly supraindividual force which gains control over peoples as such and increases its own power," and "which by no means is reducible to the sum of individual sins."[4] The *adikia* (injustice) in the letter to the Romans is predominantly social sin. Gutiérrez explains the sin that is the concern of liberation theology:

> But in the liberation approach sin is not considered as an individual, private, or merely interior reality—asserted just enough to necessitate a "spiritual" redemption which does not challenge the order in which we live. Sin is regarded as a social, historical fact, the absence of brotherhood and love in relationships among men, the breach of friendship with God and with other men, and, therefore, an interior,

2. Ibid., p. 145.
3. Ibid., p. 152.
4. José P. Miranda, *Marx and the Bible: A Critique of the Philosophy of Oppression*, pp. 181-82.

personal fracture. When it is considered in this way, the collective dimensions of sin are rediscovered. . . . Sin is evident in oppressive structures, in the exploitation of man by man, in the domination and slavery of peoples, races, and social classes. Sin appears, therefore, as the fundamental alienation, the root of a situation of injustice and exploitation.

Consequently, sin "demands a radical liberation, which in turn necessarily implies a political liberation. Only by participating in the historical process of liberation will it be possible to show the fundamental alienation which is present in every partial alienation."[5]

THE RELATION OF CHRISTIAN FAITH TO LIBERATING ACTION

How is the Christian faith articulated through that participation in the liberating process? The motivation can be Christian, but how does the liberating commitment relate to the evangelical faith? Gutiérrez himself asks the question without giving a clearcut answer. He says that "the form" of that relationship "belongs to the level of intuition and groping—at times in anguish." But he adds that theology as a critical reflection on praxis should help to show how the bond is established between the Christian faith and liberating action. At the same time, theology will help to correct possible deviations along the road to liberation, so that the commitment to liberation may be "more evangelical, more authentic, more concrete, and more efficacious." Theology is also necessary because what is sought beyond the struggle against misery, injustice, and exploitation is the creation of a *new man*. That objective coincides with the teaching of Vatican II and, in a sense, with the Bible. But Gutiérrez seems to be thinking also about Marxism, as indicated by a footnote where he cites the words of Marx on the men who are to live in the new world.[6]

In summary, in order to eliminate social injustice and to create a new man, the Christian has to identify himself "radically and militantly with those—the people and the social class—who bear the brunt of oppression." In that way, in less than three pages, Gutiérrez describes systematically the nature and objective of the

5. Gutiérrez, *Theology of Liberation*, pp. 175-76.
6. Ibid., pp. 145-46.

mission of the Christian in the world. The question of how to relate liberating action with the Christian faith has not yet been answered; but there is an attempt at an answer in the following part of the book.

Before getting to that, however, Gutiérrez directs his attention to three questions that follow the famous programmatic questions of Immanuel Kant in the *Critique of Pure Reason:* "What can I know? What should I do? What can I hope for?" Gutiérrez asks: "In the light of faith, charity, and hope, what then is the meaning of this struggle, this *creation*? What does this option mean to *man*? What is the significance of *novelty* in history and of an orientation towards the future?"[7] Gutiérrez says that those questions signal above all three tasks that should be carried out. Once more his interest in the priority of praxis for the theological task stands out.

THE MEANING OF SALVATION FOR GUTIÉRREZ

Gutiérrez asks, "What is the relationship between salvation and the process of the liberation of man throughout history? Or more precisely, what is the meaning of the struggle against an unjust society and the creation of a new man in the light of the Word?" Gutiérrez says that to answer those questions would imply the attempt to specifically define what is meant by salvation. This is a "complex and difficult" task that should lead us to consider three elements that offer a broad perspective on what salvation means for Gutiérrez at this stage in his theological reflection: (1) Salvation is intrahistoric and this-worldly, not ahistorical or other-worldly. It is the action of God here and now, transforming the whole of human reality and carrying it towards its fullness in Christ. (2) Salvation is for the total man and goes beyond that which is merely individual. It also has social and cosmic dimensions. (3) Salvation's center is Christ. In the words of Gutiérrez, salvation is "a concept central to the Christian mystery."[8] Consequently, it is necesssary to try to understand it if one is to discover its relationship to man's process of liberation through history.

7. Ibid., p. 146.
8. Ibid., p. 149.

UNIVERSAL SALVATION

THE QUALITATIVE EMPHASIS IN CATHOLIC SOTERIOLOGY

Why is it that Gutiérrez likes so much the step that contemporary Catholic theology has taken from the *quantitative* to the *qualitative* in the concept of salvation? It is because the qualitative emphasis eliminates numerical concerns (how many and who are saved); it puts aside the distinction between the sacred and the profane; it abandons the tendency to make out of salvation a concept that belongs to the other world, to the hereafter; it sees man in his totality; and it emphasizes the fact that salvation is universal. It is much easier now for theologians like Gutiérrez to set forth the problem of the relationship between salvation and liberation and to offer a solution that, according to them, is viable.

Gutiérrez points out that liberation theology became possible when the *theology of two planes*—profane-sacred, laity-clergy, church-state, natural-supernatural, temporal-eternal—lost its influence.[9] Dualism is being surpassed, and the way has been opened to talk about a close relationship between salvation and the process of political and social liberation which is carried out through history.

There are at least two great consequences of the qualitative concept of salvation: emphasis is given to the universality of the salvific will of God and to the historical and earthly character of salvation.

SALVATION OUTSIDE CHRISTIAN FAITH

The qualitative focus opposes the idea that there is no salvation outside the church. According to Gutiérrez, in the search for the way to extend the possibility of salvation one arrives at what he calls "the very heart of the question":

> Man is saved if he opens himself to God and to others, even if he is not clearly aware that he is doing so. This is valid for Christians and non-Christians alike—for all people. To speak about the presence of grace—whether accepted or rejected—in all people implies, on the

9. Ibid., pp. 63-77.

other hand, to value from a Christian standpoint the very roots of human activity. We can no longer speak properly of a profane world.[10]

Later Gutiérrez makes other statements that also leave themselves open to the possibility of being interpreted in universalist terms, as when he says that any man is a temple of God: "Since God has become man, humanity, every man, history, is the living temple of God. The 'profane,' that which is located outside the temple, no longer exists." However, Gutiérrez only follows the guideline that others have marked out for him. In the fourth chapter of this book I spoke about the theology of Vatican II, in which some see that the way is prepared for the teaching of universalism. Gutiérrez himself quotes the council in support of his thesis.[11]

RAHNER AND "ANONYMOUS CHRISTIANS"

The conciliar documents follow the reflection of theologians like Karl Rahner, for whom there is no such thing as a "pure nature," divested of salvific grace. There is within the nature of man—of all men—an infused grace that enables him to receive divine love. What is referred to is not merely the natural revelation that all men receive according to Rom. 1, nor the common grace of which Reformed theologians speak, but a "supernatural existential," a capacity and a determination to seek God and to receive His love.[12]

Rahner comments that "perhaps we may only have looked too superficially and with too little love at the non-Christian religions and so have not really seen them." Furthermore, the non-Christian religions contain "supernatural elements arising out of the grace which is given to men as a gratuitous gift on account of Christ," and in them the pre-Christian man was able to reach the grace of God. Rahner clarifies that that does not mean the religions outside of the Old Testament were legitimate in all their elements nor that every religion has been legitimate. However, the general thesis is that the concrete religions of pre-Christian humanity "contain

10. Ibid., p. 151.
11. Ibid., pp. 151, 194.
12. Karl Rahner, "Concerning the Relationship between Nature and Grace," in his *Theological Investigations,* vol. 1 (Baltimore: Helicon, 1961), p. 312.

quite certainly elements of a supernatural influence by grace which must make itself felt even in these objectifications." Today Christianity meets the man in non-Christian religions "as someone who can and must already be regarded in this or that respect as an anonymous Christian." Non-Christianity should be conceived by the Christian as a Christianity of an anonymous kind. The explicit preaching of Christianity is not superfluous, says Rahner, because it results in "a still greater chance of salvation [for the hearer] than someone who is merely an anonymous Christian."[13] Obviously Rahner's teaching can easily be interpreted in a universalist sense.

UNIVERSAL OPENNESS IN KÜNG AND GUTIÉRREZ

Gutiérrez recognizes that expressions such as "anonymous Christianity" and "Christianity without the name" are "equivocal and the choice of words poor" and that it is necessary "to refine them so that they will point with greater precision to a reality which is itself indisputable: all men are in Christ efficaciously called to communion with God." All men are the temple of God; but "man is saved if he opens himself to God and to others, even if he is not clearly aware that he is doing so."[14] The last words might indicate the possibility that whoever does not do such a thing is lost. The emphasis, however, does not fall on the perdition of some, but rather on the salvation of all, since that which is profane no longer exists.

Openness to universalism seems to have been amplified in post-conciliar Catholicism. The case of the theologian Hans Küng is well known. He opposes a "narrow-minded, conceited, exclusive particularism which condemns the other religions *in toto,* a prose-lytism which carries on unfair competition and takes too restricted a view not only of the religions but also of the Gospel." Küng proposes "an inclusive Christian universalism claiming for Christianity *not exclusiveness, but certainly uniqueness.*" He thinks that Christianity should not consider itself in possession of the truth, but that instead it should search for it in dialogue with the non-Christian religions. What Küng desires as a result of this dia-

13. Karl Rahner, "Christianity and the Non-Christian Religions," in his *Theological Investigations,* vol. 5 (Baltimore: Helicon, 1966), pp. 121, 130-32.
14. Gutiérrez, *Theology of Liberation,* pp. 71, 151.

logue is a Christianity "without a false, antithetic exclusiveness, but with a creative rethinking, resulting in a new, inclusive and simultaneously critical synthesis." Ecumenism, in the broad universal Christian sense, is based not on "missionary conquest of the other religions, but listening to their concerns, sharing their needs and at the same time giving a living testimony of its own faith in word and deed."[15]

SEGUNDO: THE GOSPEL IS MINORITARIAN YET UNIVERSAL

Among the Catholic theologians of liberation, Gutiérrez is not the only one to expound ideas of universalist openness. For example, Juan Luis Segundo begins his book *Masas y Minorías* by indicating that just as Adam passes on sin and death to everyone, so Christ passes on to everyone justice and life. Consequently, according to Segundo there is a contradiction in the effort to win converts to Christianity. Even if it is admitted that according to the spirit of Jesus the task of the church is to go through the world making followers, it must also be recognized, suggests Segundo, that Adam did not need to convert anyone to have all under the dominion of sin and death. "The tendency to collaborate with the saving victory of Christ through the quantitative acquisition—what other acquisition could there be?—of followers and of converts, has been terribly dangerous, if not fatal for Christianity."[16]

At the same time Segundo concludes, based on his concept of "masses and minorities," that the gospel is minoritarian and antimassive. The mass is characterized by its tendency to follow the law of least resistance. The message of Christ is essentially antimassive, although precisely at the service of the multitude, because that which is announced in the gospel of John must be carried out: "And I, if I am lifted up from the earth, will draw all men to myself" (12:32).

The victory of Christ includes all human beings, as is seen in the typological opposition of Adam-Christ; but the Christian message is minoritarian, antimassive. Segundo sees a contradiction not in his thesis that all are already included in the victory of Christ

15. Hans Küng, *On Being a Christian,* translated by Edward Quinn (Garden City, N.Y.: Doubleday, 1976), pp. 111-15.
16. Juan Luis Segundo, *Masas y minorías en la dialéctica divina de la liberación,* p. 10.

although the gospel is antimassive, but in the effort to win converts for the church. The contradiction is found in a Christianity that "permits the mechanisms of belonging to Christ to be identified with the mechanisms of belonging to the world."[17] That is a contradictory Christianity because it uses mass methods for universality. J. Andrew Kirk thinks that Segundo is trying to do the impossible when he tries to adopt a dual ecclesiology: "On the one hand he calls the church to be a minority community and, on the other, he extends salvation to cover those who reject this minority call."[18]

Segundo's emphasis with regard to salvation is *qualitative,* not *quantitative,* and it can be interpreted in a universalist sense. We must recognize, however, that he opposes the reduction of the gospel to a merchandise that can be easily acquired by the whole world. This warning is worth taking into account in our work of evangelization. But it should be obvious as well that we also need to be alert in order to not fall naively into the universalism into which liberation theology could lead us.

INTRAHISTORICAL SALVATION

The emphasis on the universality of salvation also has as its purpose to demonstrate that the salvific action of God encompasses all of humanity *here:* in the world and in the present time. The emphasis on the qualitative aspect of salvation shows the possible relationship or convergence of salvation with the human liberating process through history. Salvation is not something otherworldly, it is also given in a real and concrete way here and now; salvation "is something which embraces all human reality, transforms it, and leads it to its fullness in Christ." The focus is not on the hereafter but on this world, in order to see in that hereafter "the transformation and fulfillment of the present life."[19]

If salvation is also a reality that occurs within history, it is not hard to conclude that "there is only one human destiny, irreversibly assumed by Christ, the Lord of history." There are not two histories, one sacred and the other profane, whether parallel or

17. Ibid., p. 49.
18. J. Andrew Kirk, *Liberation Theology: An Evangelical View from the Third World,* p. 202.
19. Gutiérrez, *Theology of Liberation,* pp. 151-52.

related to each other, but only one. In his interpretation of history, Gutiérrez thinks he has ended all dualisms. As a consequence, "the historical destiny of humanity must be placed definitively in the salvific horizon" of the action of God. It is not only the history of salvation, but salvation *in* history, and the salvation *of* history itself, because history is carried to its fullness by salvation. In the words of Gutiérrez, salvation is "the communion of men with God and the communion of men among themselves."[20] He concludes his argument by saying that there is only one history, a "Christo-finalized" history. That word seems to echo Pierre Teilhard de Chardin, who sees Christ as the omega point of the evolution of all creation.

The thesis of the unity and evolution of history is vital for the argument that the liberating process of man and the salvific process of God are intimately related. If there is not a profane history different from sacred history, but rather only one history, then God and man are working together to transform it and bring it to its fulfillment. Gutiérrez thinks he has explained his thesis. He only has to support it with the Scriptures. For that he makes use of two great biblical themes: the relationship between creation and salvation, and the eschatological promises. He believes that those two themes tie together the action of God and human action in history.

CREATION AND SALVATION

Because Gutiérrez deals with the creation of a new man, the theme of original creation is unavoidable. If there is a possibility of a *new* creation, it is because there is an old creation. Moreover, earthly history has its point of departure in creation, and if history is one, then creation and salvation are mutually related.

CREATION AS THE FIRST SALVIFIC ACT

Gutiérrez is convinced that God created men so that they might be His "sons." Creation is thus the first salvific act. Creation is part of salvation, and history is a continued process in which man carries out the creative work. As Gutiérrez puts it: "Man is the

20. Ibid., pp. 152-53.

crown and center of the work of creation and is called to continue it through his labor (cf. Gen. 1:28)." In another place he says: "since man is the center of creation, it is integrated in the history which is being built by man's efforts."[21]

But if man does not contribute to his own creation but rather is merely an object of the divine fiat, Gutiérrez may be asked how creation can become integrated into history, which is constructed by the effort of man. Did God bring about creation by the help of man?

The most important questions have to do with the testimony of the Scriptures. Does the Bible teach the relationship that Gutiérrez proposes between creation and salvation? If creation is "the first slavific act," does that mean that all human beings are saved by the mere fact of having been created? What about the "dialectic" of sin in the universe? Why is a "new creation" necessary? Is it satisfactory from the point of view of the Bible to brush aside those questions and others like them by simply saying that they are the product of a quantitative focus of salvation?

Gutiérrez handles the Bible irresponsibly in trying to prove his thesis. Gutiérrez's thesis is an effort to bring back into proper focus the theme of creation and the teaching regarding the development of the purpose of God in history; it cannot be denied that the Scriptures affirm that God the creator is also the liberator of His people. That is how the Israelites thought of Him. But an objective exegesis of texts like Isa. 43:1; 44:24, and 55:4 does not prove that creation is the first salvific act of God for all human beings, but rather that Yahweh redeems His people with the same power with which He created them. And when the event of the Exodus of Israel is used as a key to interpret creation, there is another hermeneutic leap. That the God of the Exodus is the same God of Genesis does not prove that creation is the first salvific act of God for all men, even if the Israelites understood creation in the light of their departure from Egypt.

CREATION AND ELECTION

From the New Testament, Gutiérrez quotes Eph. 1:3-5, where the apostle Paul says that the heavenly Father chose us "before the

21. Ibid., pp. 154, 158.

creation of the world [NIV]." Is Paul trying to teach the philosophy of "only one history" as Gutiérrez does, or is he simply trying to demonstrate that salvific election precedes the creation of the world? There is an expression parallel to "before the creation of the world" in 1 Cor. 2:7, where the apostle affirms that God chose wisdom "before time began [NIV]." Also it is said in 2 Tim. 1:9 that grace was given to us in Christ Jesus "before the beginning of time [NIV]."

It is not necessary to delve here into a discussion of the order of the divine decrees: whether the decree of salvation precedes that of creation or vice versa, or if the order of the decrees is logical rather than chronological. What is beyond any doubt is that in Eph. 1:3-14 the apostle talks about election and predestination, concepts that contradict the thesis that creation is the first salvific act of God with a universal, or universalist, outreach. Whatever the theological school of the interpreter might be—whether Arminian or Calvinist—it is undeniable that Paul does not say that all human beings have been predestined to be sons of God by means of Jesus Christ by the simple fact of having been created by him.

The Greek words translated as "chosen" or "predestinated" indicate the action of selecting, or marking out. Even if it is said that God knew who would believe and consequently chose them, or that He chose the church corporally in Christ, the principle of selection still remains. If everyone is included, no one is "chosen." Paul has in mind only those who have heard and believed the gospel (v. 13). There is no place there for universalism.

THE EXODUS AS EVIDENCE FOR LIBERATIONISM

Gutiérrez attempts to answer the fundamental question he has raised: "What is the relationship between salvation and the process of the liberation of man throughout history? Or more precisely, what is the meaning of the struggle against an unjust society and the creation of a new man in the light of the Word?"[22]

Gutiérrez has said that salvation is tied to history even in the creative act, because creation is also of a salvific nature. Man, the crown and center of creation, takes creation forward by means of his labor throughout history. Salvation and the liberating process

22. Ibid., p. 149.

of man, then, form a single history. The other argument Gutiérrez uses to defend his thesis of the unity between creation and salvation is that of the Exodus, that is, the marvelous liberation of Israel from Egyptian slavery.

The Exodus and creation are for Gutiérrez a single salvific act; "the creative act is linked, almost identified with, the act which freed Israel from slavery in Egypt. . . . Creation and liberation from Egypt are but one salvific act."[23] Liberation theologians find in this Old Testament event a paradigm of the interaction of God and man in the liberating process that comes about in history.

THE EXODUS AS A POLITICAL EVENT

As stated by Segundo, the importance of the Exodus to liberation theology is its obvious political character:

> The Old Testament, and the Exodus event in particular, show us two central elements completely fused into one: i.e., God the liberator and the political process of liberation which leads the Israelites from bondage in Egypt to the promised land. In no other portion of Scripture does God the liberator reveal himself in such close connection with the political plane of human existence. Moreover, it is a well-known fact that from the time of the Babylonian exile on, the *sapiential* literature became more individualistic, inner-directed, and apolitical. And at first glance the New Testament would seem to deprecate or even reject any connection between liberation and politics, even though it might talk about the former.[24]

Gutiérrez considers the Exodus to be a political event. The people of Israel were socially and politically oppressed, in harsh servitude. Yahweh then raised up Moses as the liberator and called together the people not only in order for them to leave Egypt, but also, especially, to take them to a better land, a more spacious good land which was flowing with milk and honey. Gutiérrez does not deny "the religious event"; he sees it as "the deepest meaning" of the entire narrative.[25] However, his emphasis falls on the political aspect. In order to make the people a holy nation, Yahweh

23. Ibid., p. 155.
24. Juan Luis Segundo, *The Liberation of Theology*, pp. 110-11.
25. Gutiérrez, *Theology of Liberation*, pp. 155-57; see also pp. 157-60.

liberates them politically. The history of Israel is a "re-creation" in which man takes part. It is actually a matter of a "self-creation." It is interesting to note the title Gutiérrez gives to the section in which he interprets the Exodus: "Political Liberation: Self-Creation of Man."

THE PARTICIPATION OF MAN

We have already seen that liberation theologians believe man participates in creation, prolonging it by means of his labor throughout history. Now Gutiérrez appeals to the Exodus to tell us that within that history, in which salvation and the liberating process are joined together, man also participates in the creation of a just society by means of social praxis, or in other words, by means of politics:

> To work, to transform this world, is to become a man and to build the human community; it is also to save. Likewise, to struggle against misery and exploitation and to build a just society is already to be part of the saving action, which is moving towards its complete fulfillment . . . it is to become part of a saving process which embraces the whole of man and all human history.

Of course, Gutiérrez clarifies that the work of Christ "forms part of this movement and brings it to complete fulfillment."[26] Nevertheless the major emphasis is on the active participation of man in the construction of a just society, in the creation of the new man.

When Gutiérrez steps into the political realm through his interpretation of the Exodus, he seems to advance in his attempt to answer another very important question already mentioned, which he himself asks: How is the liberating commitment of the Christian to a life of faith expressed? If the meaning that liberation theologians give to the Exodus is correct, then it could be said that the narration of that liberating deed represents a biblical basis for Christians to become politically committed to the transformation of society and the creation of the new man. Consequently, it is very important to know whether the Exodus has the meaning that liberation theologians attribute to it.

26. Ibid., pp. 158-60.

EXODUS AND THE VIEW OF SCRIPTURE

Above all it must be kept in mind that in the field of biblical interpretation any conservative evangelical has difficulty entering into dialogue with the liberation theologian. That is so for several reasons: (1) The Catholic concept of the inspiration and authority of the Scriptures is not as high as that of the conservative evangelical; (2) In his approach to the Bible the Catholic theologian of liberation is open to liberal theology; (3) He does not give the necessary importance to the scientific exegesis of the Scriptures in order to determine the hermeneutical norm; (4) He may speak of a "reserve of biblical meaning," that is, a deeper meaning than that of the *sensus literalis* (literal sense). Even if the reference is not exactly to the *sensus plenior* (the full meaning), of which so much was said during preconciliar times, one cannot help recalling that concept.

The Catholic theologian Raymond E. Brown gives the following definition of the *sensus plenior:* "The [*sensus plenior*] is the deeper meaning [than the literal one] intended by God but not clearly intended by the human author, that is seen to exist in the words of Scripture when they are studied in the light of further revelation or of development in the understanding of revelation." Brown points out three problems in the theory of the *sensus plenior:* First, it "cannot be reconciled with the instrumental theory of inspiration." Brown hastens to add that "to decide from a philosophical theory of instrumentality what God could and could not have done in inspiring Scripture is risky, especially since all acknowledge that the instrumentality in the process of inspiration is unique." Second and more compelling, "when a deeper meaning of a biblical text is recognizable only in the light of further revelation, the meaning is not contained in the text itself but is acquired at the moment of the further revelation." Third, the *sensus plenior* "is seldom verified and so is of little use in justifying or explaining N[ew] T[estament], patristic, liturgical, or ecclesiastical exegesis."[27]

In spite of the difficulties of the *sensus plenior,* some liberation theologians use a modified form of it. They speak, for example, of germinal events that have a certain "reserve of meaning."[28]

27. Raymond E. Brown, "Hermeneutics," *The Jerome Biblical Commentary,* 2 vols. in 1 (Englewood Cliffs, N.J.: Prentice-Hall, 1968), 2:616-18.
28. J. Severino Croatto, *Exodus: A Hermeneutic of Freedom,* pp. 3, 8.

J. Andrew Kirk agrees that liberation theology does not refer to *sensus plenior* as such, but seems to employ a "methodology akin to that underlying the rather imprecise theory of *sensus plenior.*"[29] José Míguez Bonino affirms that the readings of the "founding and generative events of the faith," which are carried out in commitment to liberating praxis, are not "arbitrary inventions." He gives as an example of a "germinal event" the resurrection of Jesus Christ, and he concludes by asking, "Is it altogether absurd to reread the resurrection today as the death of the monopolies, the liberation from hunger, or a solidary form of ownership?"[30]

IMPOSED MEANINGS

In the specific case of the Exodus of Israel from Egypt, the effort of liberation theologians to draw out from the biblical text—or rather to impose on it—a meaning adapted to a particular ideology is evident. Thus it is not surprising that their interpretation of the Exodus encounters serious problems. For example, even a superficial reading of the biblical text reveals that the Israelites were not protagonists, active participants, or effecters of their own liberation. In reality, the Exodus is not a paradigm of the self-liberation of man. On the contrary, it is an outstanding example of the sovereign intervention of God in the liberation of those who call out to Him, precisely because they cannot liberate themselves. In fact the moment comes when they do not even want to be liberated.

Perhaps the most that can be pointed out by liberation theologians in support of their thesis is the part that Moses played as a representative of Yahweh before the Israelites and before Pharaoh. But even in that case the leader and his people did nothing more than wait for what the Lord was going to do. The action of the midwives—supposing that they were Israelites—did not have to do directly with the Exodus. The truth is that there was no popular uprising to dethrone Pharaoh by means of a violent struggle. Neither did the Israelites devise a political project to change the structures of Egyptian society. They were not supposed to remain in Egypt to transform it, but to serve Yahweh in another place.

29. Kirk, *Liberation Theology,* p. 157.
30. José Míguez Bonino, *Doing Theology in a Revolutionary Situation,* p. 101.

In the light of the serious problems that the biblical text poses for them, some liberation theologians suggest that the oldest nucleus of the narrative of the Exodus should be sought. That nucleus, they think, could reveal the process of organization and participation of the nation in the struggle for liberty.[31] Clearly such reasoning pertains to a purely speculative realm. The only objective biblical basis we have for our theological reflection concerning the victorious exit of Israel from Egypt is the narrative in the book of Exodus and the interpretation of that narrative in the rest of the Scriptures.

THE SPIRITUAL, PERSONAL MEANING OF THE EXODUS

That there was social injustice in Egypt is obvious. The Israelites were suffering from economic, social, and political oppression. As slaves, their labor was stolen from them; the Israelites were not working for their own welfare or that of their children. Pharaoh wanted to humiliate them, exploit them, and if possible exterminate them. They called out to God, and He heard them and liberated them in demonstration of His loyalty to the covenant He had made with the patriarchs.

Indeed, the covenent of Yahweh with the patriarchs of the Israelite nation can never be overemphasized when interpreting the Exodus. Before the Exodus, Israel was already a people with a long history in which their monotheistic faith, the knowledge of Yahweh the Lord, stands out. The foundation and frame of reference for the theological significance of that great liberating event are found in the covenant by which God committed Himself to His people—beginning with Abraham—to bless them and make of them a means of blessing for all the families of the earth. It was in faithfulness to that commitment that Yahweh intervened on behalf of His people, liberating them from slavery in Egypt.

It is also evident that the Exodus had economic, social, and political consequences for Israel. But, in spite of what might be said in the theology of liberation, the supreme purpose of that liberating deed was spiritual. After a meticulous study of the vocabulary of liberation in the Old Testament, the Spanish Augustinian theologian S. Sabugal, professor of New Testament exegesis and

31. Kirk, *Liberation Theology,* pp. 148-50.

history of Exegesis in the Instituto Patristico "Agustinianum" of Rome, concludes that the socio-political aspect exists in the Exodus, but that what is most important is the spiritual dimension.[32]

Speaking positively, the nation was liberated from Egypt in order to go to worship Yahweh (Ex. 3:18; 4:23; 5:1). Negatively, the purpose of the Exodus was to liberate Israel from Egyptian idolatry (Ezek. 20:5-9) and to cause the nation to trust in Yahweh, the living and true God (Deut. 4:34-35; Hos. 12:9; 13:4).

The theme of the liberation of Israel from slavery in Egypt runs through the whole of biblical revelation, all the way to the Apocalypse. It is important, therefore, to ask what kind of interpretation this great event receives in both Testaments. Sabugal chides liberation theologians for not having taken into account all of the biblical testimony concerning the Exodus, especially that of the New Testament. This is a theme that also demands the careful attention of evangelical exegetes. It is necessary to explain what the Exodus meant for the Israelites who lived after that great event and what it can mean for us today.

Juan Luis Segundo's assertion that biblical literature becomes individualistic after the Exile in Babylon, and that in the New Testament there seems to be a tendency to disregard or even discard any relationship between liberation and politics, would clearly mean a nonpolitical interpretation of the Exodus in both Testaments. Segundo also points out that it is naive to say that the Exodus holds the key for the interpretation of Scripture as a whole. Sabugal sees that the salvation effected by Christ is presented as the new and definitive Exodus throughout all of the New Testament.[33]

The results of a strict exegesis of the biblical text, then, do not allow the Exodus to be used as the paradigm for political and revolutionary struggle in the transformation of Latin American society. Yet by no means does the Exodus lack a message for us; nor do we attempt to deny the urgent need for profound social changes that will truly favor the Latin American people. Tangible results may be expected here and now from the salvation that comes from the Lord in personal, family, and social life. But we can insist on those results without violating the text of the Scriptures.

32. S. Sabugal, *¿Liberación y secularización?* p. 39.
33. Segundo, *Liberation of Theology*, p. 112; Sabugal, p. 77.

FAITH AND IDEOLOGY: SEGUNDO'S HERMENEUTIC

Juan Luis Segundo sees that the interpretation of the Exodus in biblical literature and the attitude of Jesus—both evidently non-political—present a major pastoral problem for liberation theology. Segundo does not find the solution in the *sensus plenior,* but studies the relationship between faith and ideologies. According to Segundo's thesis, there is a continuity in the whole of revelation, but revelation contains two elements: "One element is permanent and unique: *faith.* The other is changing and bound up with different historical circumstances: *ideologies.*"[34]

In the Bible, ideologies may change, but faith remains the same. Thus "we cannot appeal to the historical Jesus in order to throw out the solutions of the Old Testament."[35] For example, the circumstances in which Jesus said that we have to turn the other cheek are very different to those in which Yahweh ordered, in the Old Testament, the extermination of certain peoples. The need to destroy those peoples was the ideology that faith adopted in those circumstances. The circumstances of Jesus were very different. It follows then that Christ's pacifist commandment had to do with a different ideology, and not with the content of faith.

Segundo means that ideology is the bridge between the concepts we receive from God in revelation and the problems that arise from a history in the process of change. Faith is permanent; ideologies are provisional but necessary means to unite faith with the historical situation. Of course, "each and every ideology presented in Scripture is a human element." Segundo points out that the scientific way in which exegesis approaches the content of both Testaments is to see it "as a succession of religious ideologies, each one being bound up with its historical context and being comprehensible only in terms of that context."[36]

In the specific case of Latin America, Segundo suggests that theology has two ways to relate faith to the situation. One is to invent an ideology to fit the contemporary situation; the other is "to seek out the biblical situations most akin to those of the present day and to accept the ideology that Scripture presents in those situations as the correct response of faith." For example, the

34. Segundo, *Liberation of Theology,* p. 116.
35. Ibid.
36. Ibid., pp. 116-17.

relationship between the situation of the Exodus and ours is closer than the situation of Jesus and that of the Latin American people today. Conclusion: the Exodus and not the gospel should be the source of inspiration for finding the current ideology that will be in closest agreement with faith.[37]

Ideology may be defined by its content, but it is very difficult to do the same with faith. Is it possible then to draw out the nucleus of faith apart from any ideological trappings? According to Segundo the answer has to be negative, because he believes that the idea of God is never presented apart from ideologies, and it cannot be separated from historical contexts. Segundo tries to resolve the problem by means of a theory of learning that leads him to conclude that the ideologies present in the Scriptures "are responses learned vis-à-vis specific historical situations," whereas faith "is the total process to which man submits, a process of learning in and through ideologies how to create the ideologies needed to handle new and unforeseen situations in history."[38] According to those definitions faith is not an objective, concrete, and final revelation that has already been given to the church, but a process of learning and a creation of new ideologies.

Revelation is continuous, a process that can continue to progress "through its own proper means. And those means are nothing else but a succession of ideologies vis-à-vis the concrete problems of history." History itself is in charge of continuing the process, and it is animated by the Spirit of Christ. Faith is not an ideology, but "it has sense and meaning only insofar as it serves as the foundation stone for ideologies." Without the historical mediation provided by ideologies faith is dead, because it does not have historical relevance. Consequently, Christians cannot escape the risk of ideologies. They "cannot evade the necessity of inserting something to fill the void between their faith and their options in history."[39]

In the final analysis, Segundo cannot define the content of faith, nor does he give any clue to distinguish in the Bible itself between faith and the ideologies he believes are "a human element" in the Scriptures. His conclusion is that faith should not be considered as "a universal, atemporal, pithy body of content summing up

37. Ibid., p. 117.
38. Ibid., pp. 118,120.
39. Ibid., pp. 109, 121.

divine revelation once the latter has been divested of ideologies. On the contrary, it is maturity by way of ideologies." In another part of his work Segundo states that we are forced to have a different conception of revealed truth. "It is not a *final* truth, however absolute it may be. Instead it is a fundamental element in the search for *the truth*."[40] In other words, there is no objective, concrete, and final revelation that may serve as a norm for the Christian and the church. Faith depends on ideologies, and ideologies continually change along with the historical situations.

UTOPIA: THE BOND BETWEEN MAN'S POLITICAL ACTION AND GOD'S SALVATION

Segundo is conscious that there is a difference between *ideology* and *utopia*. Ideologies "are the situationally transcendent ideas which *never succeed de facto* in the realization of their projected contents"; utopia—in the sense in which liberation theologians use the term—tends "to shatter, either partially or wholly, the order of things prevailing at the time."[41]

Gutiérrez explains from his point of view the difference between ideology and utopia: "Ideology does not offer adequate and scientific knowledge of reality; rather, it masks it. Ideology does not rise above the empirical, irrational level. . . . Ideology tends to dogmatize. . . . Utopia, however, leads to an authentic and scientific knowledge of reality and to a praxis which transforms what exists." He gives the following definition of utopia: "The term *utopia* has been revived within the last few decades to refer to a historical plan for a qualitatively different society and to express the aspiration to establish new social relations among men."[42]

To the question of the relationship between faith and political action, Gutiérrez responds with a historical project described by the term *utopia*. In his concept of liberation there are three levels of meaning:

40. Ibid., pp. 110, 122.
41. Ibid., p. 100, quoting Karl Mannheim, *Ideology and Utopia* (New York: Harcourt, Brace, Jovanovich, 1936), p. 192.
42. Gutiérrez, *Theology of Liberation*, pp. 232, 235.

"Economic, social and political liberation"	corresponds to the level of	"scientific rationality which supports real and effective transforming political action"
"Liberation which leads to the creation of a new man in a new society of solidarity"	corresponds to the level of	"utopia, of historical projections"
"Liberation from sin and entrance into communion with God and with all men"	corresponds to the level of	"faith"[43]

The first level is political, and the third level is that of faith. Utopia is between the two, tying them both together. Utopia, or the historical project, encompasses everything and is related to the central and fundamental theme that Gutiérrez has been developing: the construction of a new society and the creation of a new man. According to Gutiérrez, creation and the Exodus show that there is only one history, and that within that history the salvific action of God and the liberating process of man are joined together. The Exodus shows also that the liberating process is a political one. How is faith related to political action for the creation of a new society and of a new man? The bond is utopia, the historical project. What is the historical project of Gutiérrez? He specifically rejects capitalism, developmentalism, and any supposed political "third alternative." The option that remains for him is a Latin American socialism.

To review: according to Gutiérrez, creation is tied to the Exodus, and that event is a political liberation. Man continues the work of creation through his work and builds a new society by means of liberating praxis. In that way the history of salvation and the process of man's liberation are united. There is no natural order of creation and supernatural order of redemption; the perspective of political liberation allows for only one, in which salvation as the self-creation of man takes place. It is man who, by means of his work and his liberating praxis in history, ties together creation with redemption, salvation with the liberation process. The connection between faith and political action for the sake of a more just society is made possible by means of the political option of the Christian in a concrete situation. In this case, it is a socialist option.

43. Ibid., p. 235.

For the conservative evangelical who does not want to be tied either to the political left or the political right, the fundamental problem of liberation theology is its tendency to exalt an ideology, or a utopia, as the criterion for interpreting the narrative of the Exodus and all the Scriptures. But the critique of the new way of doing theology should also be a warning against any attempt to "ideologize" the sacred text. It doesn't matter if the political option is from the left or from the right.

The concept of utopia takes us inevitably to the eschatological plane, the other biblical theme Gutiérrez uses to defend his thesis that history is one and that the salvific work of God and the liberating process of man transform it and take it to its fullness.

ESCHATOLOGICAL SALVATION

The theologians of liberation see the Exodus as a paradigm of total liberation, but feel the need for a historical project that can mobilize and transform history. The backward look at the Exodus demands to be complemented with eschatological vision. It is here that promise and hope come in. It is here that we also see the influence of Jürgen Moltmann's *Theology of Hope* and the influence of the Christian-Marxist dialogue regarding the future, especially in relation to the work of Ernst Bloch. In *The Hope Principle,* Bloch follows Karl Marx in the conviction that it is imperative to change the world, not only to explain it, and he presents hope as an element that becomes subversive to the present order of things. Gutiérrez himself points out that Marx exerts a certain influence on the theology of hope through the works of Bloch.[44] But again it must be said that liberation theologians accept European influence with a critical attitude.

Alves, Assmann, and Gutiérrez are not totally satisfied with the approach of Moltmann and J. B. Metz to Christian hope. Alves, for example, thinks that hope according to Moltmann is too transcendent. Gutiérrez fears that the theology of hope will become an evasion, that is, that it will merely replace a "Christianity of the beyond" with a "Christianity of the future"; whereas the former tends to forget the world, the latter "runs the risk of neglecting a miserable and unjust present and the struggle for liberation."[45]

44. Ibid., p. 220.
45. Ibid., p. 218.

Liberation theologians want a hope that will become rooted in the heart of historical praxis. In spite of such reservations, European theology comes to the aid of liberation theologians in their attempt to develop, with certain biblical justification, a historical project that will harmonize with the political option they support.

ESCHATOLOGICAL PROMISES AND EARTHLY REALITIES

Gutiérrez says that "the commitment to the creation of a just society and, ultimately, to a new man, presupposes confidence in the future." That which is yet to come is like a powerful magnet that attracts human history towards the establishment of a better world, a new man, a new humanity. History is not a remembrance, but instead is "a thrust into the future."[46]

In liberation theology Bloch's "hope principle" becomes "eschatological promise," and the concept of *utopia*, or of historical project, takes on a biblical hue. Metz had already deindividualized the eschatological promises. Gutiérrez "defuturizes" them, in the sense of underscoring the fact that they have a relationship to the present; they are slowly being fulfilled, transforming history.

Gutiérrez believes that "the Bible presents eschatology as the driving force of salvific history radically oriented toward the future." There is a fundamental promise, which is "a gift accepted in faith." That promise was made initially to Abraham, and it will reach its complete fulfillment in Christ. Meanwhile, it is developing its potential in the promises that God has made throughout history. The *promise* is not exhausted by those promises or by their fulfillment, but "is announced and is partially and progressively fulfilled in them."[47] For example, the resurrection of Christ is a fulfillment and, at the same time, the anticipation of a future. There is an *already* and a *not yet*. The promise illuminates, makes productive, and leads to its fullness the ongoing history of mankind.

The prophets, according to Gutiérrez, are interested in the *future* and in the *present*. They do not come in order to maintain the status quo, but to change it. The prophetic message is a rupture with the past and an opening to the future. The Exodus itself is a

46. Ibid., p. 213.
47. Ibid., pp. 161-62, 167.

breaking off from the past and a projection towards the future. As expected, Gutiérrez does not spiritualize the eschatological promises. On the contrary, he insists that they are partial fulfillments that are given "through liberating historical events, which are in turn new promises marking the road towards total fulfillment." He continues:

> Christ does not "spiritualize" the eschatological promises; he gives them meaning and fulfillment today (cf. Luke 4:21); but at the same time he opens new perspectives by catapulting history forward, forward towards total reconciliation. . . . it is only *in* the temporal, earthly, historical event that we can open up to the future of complete fulfillment. . . . A poorly understood spiritualization has often made us forget the human consequences of the eschatological promises and the power to transform unjust social structures which they imply. The elimination of misery and exploitation is a sign of the coming of the Kingdom.[48]

The partial and total fulfillment of eschatological promises has to do primarily with social transformation, not with individual salvation. But it is only fair to recognize that Gutiérrez does not limit that fulfillment to the achievements of a particular process or revolutionary movement. The liberating effect that the eschatological promises produce "goes far beyond the foreseeable and opens up new and unsuspected possibilities." There is an opening to the future that "is not only not suppressed by the implementations in the present, but is rather affirmed and dynamized by them." There is an *already* and a *not yet*. "The complete encounter with the Lord will mark an end to history, but it will take place in history."[49]

How will it take place in history? If the liberating process of man is incorporated in the salvific work of God in history, then in which political liberating movements is the eschatological promise being fulfilled partially today? Inevitably liberation theologians answer this question by saying that the fulfillment takes place where the cause of the oppressed is being defended. No Latin American who knows firsthand and feels the anguish of his people opposes that cause, but even on the political plane it must be

48. Ibid., p. 167.
49. Ibid., pp. 164, 168.

asked whether the option of the liberation theologians is the only valid one, since, as Juan Luis Segundo says, "There are profound differences in the way of conceiving and carrying out the revolution in favor of the oppressed."[50] Another question is whether that political option will liberate and really do justice to the oppressed, or if it will result in another dictatorship that will brutally frustrate the hope of liberation for the individual and society.

FAITH, UTOPIA, AND POLITICAL ACTION

In liberation theology *utopia* does not indicate something that cannot be attained, that does not take place in human experience. It is used rather to describe "a historical plan for a qualitatively different society and to express the aspiration to establish new social relations among men." The utopian project has a quality "of being subversive to and a driving force of history."[51]

Utopia does not belong only to the future; it is related to present historical reality. It is a *denunciation* of the existing order and a *proclamation* of a new society. It promotes transforming action; it is not limited to words. It ties together faith and political action when it offers itself as the project for the creation of a new type of man in a different society. In relation to that point, Gutiérrez quotes the words of Ernesto ("Che") Guevara as proof that political liberation in socialism "appears as a path toward the utopia of a freer, more human man, the protagonist of his own history."[52]

In order for utopia to be effective and valid it has to be verified by social praxis. What is the contribution of faith to the historical project? According to Gutiérrez, the meeting place between political liberation and the communion of all men with God is cultural revolution, that is, the permanent creation of a new man in a different and unified society. Faith reveals that sin is "the ultimate root of all injustice, all exploitation, all dissidence among men."[53] In other words, faith reveals social sin, but it also announces fraternity, which someday will be total and evident in the profound sense of the history that man himself is forging.

Gutiérrez also says that *utopia* is what gives a human face to

50. Segundo, *Masas y minorías,* p. 93.
51. Gutiérrez, *Theology of Liberation,* p. 232.
52. Ibid., p. 236.
53. Ibid., p. 237.

economic, social, and political liberation. Utopia guards liberation from falling into "idealism and evasion" or from becoming translated "into any kind of Christian ideology of political action or a politico-religious messianism." Gutiérrez then goes on to clarify that Christian hope "keeps us from any confusion of the Kingdom with any one historical stage, from any idolatry toward unavoidably ambiguous human achievement, from any absolutizing of revolution." He concludes by saying that the gospel does not provide us with a utopia, that is, a human work. But the gospel is not alien to the historical project, or utopia. The human project and the gospel "imply each other."[54] For Gutiérrez there is no other way of relating faith to the liberating process except by means of utopia, which evidently has to be the historical socialist project.

The conservative evangelical sees that the historical project can absorb and annul the gospel and that the gospel can evaporate in a supposedly liberating action that receives its inspiration from materialistic propositions. That can happen when the hermeneutical criterion comes from a utopia, not from the written Word of God.

CHRIST AND COMPLETE LIBERATION

Salvation and the struggle for a just society. Gutiérrez states that "salvation embraces all men and the whole man." Salvation is equivalent to the liberating action of Christ, and that action is "at the heart of the historical current of humanity; the struggle for a just society is in its own right very much a part of salvation history."[55] In other words, there is a close relationship between the saving work of Christ and the struggle of man for his self-liberation.

The question arises anew as to how that relationship is effected and how it can be detected in ongoing history. Gutiérrez avails himself of the theme of the kingdom of God in answering. In his theological scheme, as in that of other theologians of liberation, the kingdom of God is already inaugurated and in process. It is a matter of the "already" and the "not yet" of the kingdom. If the kingdom of God is already here in the world, it is natural for

54. Ibid., p. 238.
55. Ibid., p. 168.

Gutiérrez to state that the liberating process is incorporated in
salvific history. But he has to clarify the relationship between
human progress and the growth of the kingdom.

Catholic precedents. To do so he does not appeal to the Scriptures but to the constitution *Gaudium et spes* of Vatican II. Gutiérrez would have preferred for the council to have accepted the
preparatory document for the Constitution (the "Schema of Aric-
cia"), due to its more unified view of history; but the conciliar
fathers opted for not identifying temporal progress with the
growth of the kingdom, although they saw the two as integrally
related to each other. *Gaudium et spes* says: "Earthly progress
must be carefully distinguished from the growth of Christ's kingdom. Nevertheless, to the extent that the former can contribute
to the better ordering of human society, it is of vital concern to
the kingdom of God" (no. 39).

Gutiérrez believes that he finds more support for his thesis of
one history in Pope Paul VI than in Vatican II. The *Populorum
progressio* of Paul VI describes integral development as the transition from less human living conditions to living conditions that are
more human. Gutiérrez emphasizes that the pontiff speaks of
human conditions, not of supernatural or superhuman conditions.
That allows for "a profound integration and an ordering toward
the fullness of all that is human in the free gift of the self-commu-
nication of God."[56]

However, Gutiérrez complains that the teaching of the magisterium still views development in terms that do not radically challenge the unjust system on which society is based: "The conflictual
aspects of the political sphere are absent; or rather they have been
avoided." In order for the salvific work to be complete, political
liberation is indispensable. Structural sin, as the basic alienation,
demands a radical liberation, which is not possible apart from a
political liberation. The fundamental obstacle to the growth of the
kingdom, Gutiérrez points out, is sin, as the root of all misery,
injustice, and exploitation. Consequently "any effort to build a just
society is liberating. . . . It is a salvific work, although it is not all
of salvation."[57]

56. Ibid., p. 172.
57. Ibid., pp. 172, 177.

I do not see in the work of Gutiérrez a *total* identification between the growth of the kingdom and the self-liberation of man; but "the growth of the Kingdom is a process which occurs historically *in* liberation," without exhausting itself in it.

> This is not an identification. Without liberating historical events, there would be no growth of the Kingdom. But the process of liberation will not have conquered the very roots of oppression and the exploitation of man by man without the coming of the Kingdom, which is above all a gift. Moreover, we can say that the historical, political liberating event *is* the growth of the Kingdom and *is* a salvific event; but it is not *the* coming of the Kingdom, not *all* of salvation. It is the historical realization of the Kingdom and, therefore, it also proclaims its fullness. This is where the difference lies.[58]

Gutiérrez concludes a discussion of "Liberation and Salvation" by saying that "nothing is outside the pale of the action of Christ and the gift of the Spirit." Salvation in Christ "is a radical liberation from all misery, all despoliation, all alienation." It is "political liberation, the liberation of man throughout history, liberation from sin and admission to communion with God."[59]

Evangelical concerns. Of course the question of which events are truly and integrally liberating for the Latin American man—and thus, which events may be considered vanguards of the kingdom in our history—remains. If the kingdom of God is the exercise of His sovereignty in the world, we have the right to expect that all movements or political systems that may be contributing to the progress of the kingdom should give total liberty for the proclamation of the message of Jesus Christ the King and for obedience to His sovereign dictates. I wish to make it clear that I do not have in mind a particular political ideology, whether of the right or of the left, but am thinking of the total biblical revelation, faithfully interpreted under the ministry of the Holy Spirit, in answer to our personal and social reality.

Another concern of conservative evangelicals has to do with the sometimes disproportionate emphasis of liberation theology on the self-liberating praxis of man for the edification of the kingdom of God in the world. That concern is highlighted in the case of the premillenial theologian, whose eschatology teaches that the kingdom of universal justice and peace will not be established by man, but by the Messiah when He returns to the world in the invincible power of His Spirit. Meanwhile, the church is the community and agent of the kingdom in its present form, in conflict with the demonic powers that were conquered *de jure* at Calvary, but that will not be defeated *de facto* until the second coming of the King of Kings and Lord of Lords. In other words, it is not a matter of the kingdom of man, nor much less of the kingdom *without* God, but of the kingdom *of* God. Jesus said to Pilate: "My kingdom is not of this world" (John 18:36), meaning that His kingdom neither proceeds from this world nor adjusts to the models of the world, but it comes from above, as a celestial manifestation that radically transforms the world. It is the kingdom *of* heaven, the kingdom *of* God.

Conservative evangelicals are also concerned with the fact that liberation theology identifies the growth of the kingdom with the progress of a socio-political system in which the historical project turns its back on the God of the Scriptures, denying His sovereignty and even His existence. The politics of "the hand of friendship" that this system practices is not an affirmation of the kingdom of heaven, but a strategy of tolerance in view of the undeniable reality that the immense majority of Latin American people believe, at least, in the existence of God.

SUMMARY AND EVALUATION

I have limited my discussion of salvation in liberation theology basically to the work of Gustavo Gutiérrez, who is one of the least radical among the Catholic theologians of liberation. He has made an effort to show that salvation (a salvific act of God) and liberation (the self-liberating process of man) are closely knit together in the ongoing of a single history. In order to support his thesis biblically he makes use of the narratives of the Exodus and creation and of the eschatological promises. The theme of the Exodus and creation illustrates in Gutiérrez's thought that God and man act together, transforming history. Man continues the work of creation by means of the labor that is humanly carried out in the transformation of nature. And according to the paradigm of the Exodus, man transforms history by means of social and political praxis.

The eschatological promises push history onward, because they testify to a better future and open the way for a historical project, or utopia, which offers the creation of a new man in a different society from the present one. That which is utopian becomes real in light of eschatology. The eschatological promise is being fulfilled slowly in history by means of the self-liberating process of man, as it points out new possibilities of liberation, broadening the eschatological horizon. The kingdom of God is here, manifesting itself in human achievements of liberation, but is always moving, going beyond those achievements, towards its consummation.

Salvation for Gutiérrez is the work of God and the work of man in a synergism of faith and works. That notion is not foreign to Roman Catholic soteriology, which serves Gutiérrez very well in supporting his unitarian thesis. Salvation is social, universal, intrahistorical, eschatological, and human. Sin enters the picture, but the emphasis does not fall on individual sin but on social sin. Sin is characterized as an offense to one's neighbor, to the oppressed. There is no reference to the eternal consequences of sin, nor to the responsibility of the oppressed before the justice of God. The fact is overlooked that in the sight of God there is no one righteous, not even one—whether rich or poor, oppressor or oppressed—and that nobody attains to the measure of divine righteousness. Not enough attention is given to the redemptive significance of the sacrifice of Christ, nor to the ministry of the Holy Spirit and the Word of God in the salvation of the sinner. There is no mention of repentance towards God, nor of faith which lays hold of salvation. The doctrine of the new birth as evangelicals perceive it is noticeably absent. In his philosophy of history Gutiérrez, like other liberation theologians, does not take into account the demonic forces at work in the universe, opposing the purposes of the Creator and the best efforts of man.

In the final analysis, what stands out in liberation theology is not the action of God, but that of man. What Gutiérrez hopes for is a world "fashioned by [man's] own hands"; not so much a theophany, or manifestation of God, as an "anthropophany," or manifestation of man.[60]

---

60. Ibid., p. 213.

Nevertheless, it must be recognized that liberation theology makes us rethink the biblical theme of salvation, challenging us to study it seriously in response to the social problems of Latin America. If evangelicals have fallen into an individualism that is uninterested in collective problems, liberation theologians convert salvation into a political crusade for social transformation. We would do well to maintain our emphasis on the salvation of individuals, while at the same time bringing back into focus in our ministry the social dimension of the gospel.

8

Jesus the Liberator

In 1971 Hugo Assmann pointed out two "fundamental theological gaps" in liberation theology: the hermeneutical gap and the Christological gap.[1] His cry was for an authentic Latin American Christology. The next year Leonardo Boff, a Brazilian theologian like Assmann, published *Jesus Christ Liberator,* in which he pointed out the characteristics that a Christology produced in Latin America should have.[2] However, in the opinion of J. Andrew Kirk, Boff's work itself "does not fulfill the promise of offering a Christological focus which ties in firmly with the particular situation of the continent, although from another point of view it contains a solid and well organized Christology." Kirk bases his criticism on "the impression that the book gives of being a Christological study which could have been written in any European university by almost any European theologian."[3]

In *Jesus Christ Liberator* Boff does not deal directly with liberation theology, although he suggests it, and later he expounds and defends it in his book *Teologia desde el Cautiverio* (Theology from

1. Hugo Assmann, *Theology for a Nomad Church,* p. 103.
2. Leonardo Boff, *Jesus Christ Liberator,* pp. 43-48.
3. J. Andrew Kirk, bibliographical note on Leonardo Boff's *Jesucristo el liberador,* in *Revista Bíblica* (Buenos Aires), 161 (1976).

Captivity).[4] Still, Boff has been considered the first to respond to the lack of Christology in liberation theology.[5]

Mention should also be made of *Being and the Messiah,* by the Mexican theologian José P. Miranda, originally published in 1973, and *Christology at the Crossroads* (1976) by Jon Sobrino, a Spaniard who resides in El Salvador. Like Boff, both authors develop their Christological thought starting with the historical Jesus.[6] In contrast to a descendent Christology, that of the God who comes down to be incarnated, theirs is an ascendent Christology—Christology *from below*—focusing on the man Jesus who slowly reveals His divinity.

The Christologists of liberation are in a sense heirs of a new Christological reflection that began within Catholicism before Vatican II. Examples of that reflection are the non-radical writings of Karl Adam of Tübingen[7] and the now famous article by Karl Rahner on the Symbol of Chalcedon.[8] Walter Kasper, who writes under the influence of the school of Tübingen and particularly under that of Karl Adam, offers an outline of the fundamental tendencies of contemporary Christology and points out what he calls the "tasks of Christology today." According to Kasper, Christology should be historicaly oriented, have a universal outreach, and be determined soteriologically.[9]

Latin American theologians of liberation evaluate the Christological currents of the past and of the present critically; they assimilate that which they consider to be positive, and they reject directly any attempt to reduce Christology to that which is purely metaphysical or dogmatic. They want to go beyond progressive European theologians in their search for a Christology "designed to fit a particular ideological purpose at a particular moment . . . a historically mediating christology relevant to the basic problems of a given historical situation."[10] Boff says that "in each generation Christ knows a new parousia, because in each time he acquires a

4. Leonardo Boff, *Theología desde el cautiverio*. See also by the same author, *Jesucristo y la liberación del hombre*.
5. Jon Sobrino, *Christology at the Crossroads: A Latin American Approach,* p. xi.
6. José P. Miranda, *Being and the Messiah*.
7. Karl Adam, *The Son of God,* trans. Philip Hereford (Garden City, N.Y.: Image, 1960).
8. Karl Rahner, "Current Problems in Christology," in his *Theological Investigations,* vol. 1 (Baltimore: Helicon, 1961), pp. 149-200.
9. Walter Kasper, *Jesus the Christ* (London: Burns & Oates, 1976), pp. 20-26.
10. Assmann, *Theology,* p. 103.

new image, the product of the difficult synthesis between life and faith. Today in the experience of faith of many Latin American Christians, Jesus is seen and loved as the Liberator."[11] In other words, the Christological systems of the past have to give way to a Christology that can respond adequately to the hopes or desires of each generation. Liberation theology attempts to give a Christological answer to the spiritual, moral, and social problems of Latin America.

THE POINT OF DEPARTURE FOR A LATIN AMERICAN CHRISTOLOGY

REACTION TO OTHER THEOLOGIES

Traditionally, Catholic Christology has begun with the dogmatic formulation of the Council of Chalcedon (A.D. 451), according to which the complete humanity and true divinity of Jesus should be maintained simultaneously, without dividing the fundamental unity of His person. But that formula has come under severe criticism in some sectors of Catholicism. Karl Rahner, for example, said that the Chalcedonian symbol is not the end but the beginning of Christological reflection.[12]

Boff is of the opinion that the weakest point in the classical Christology of the theological treatises "is found exactly at the point where it believes to be strong: in its philosophical and theological systematization." Classical Christology, he says, did not lead Christians to "an ethic and a behavior which were typically Christian. . . . Orthodoxy, that is, the correct thinking about Christ, occupied the primacy over orthopraxy, the correct behavior in light of Christ." The result was that generally speaking, dogmatic Christology did not liberate, nor did it support liberation movements. It is the conviction of Boff that a Christology developed in Latin America should give primacy to the anthropological aspect over the ecclesiological, to the utopian (in the sense of a historical liberating project) over the factual, to the critical over the dogmatic, to the social over the personal, to orthopraxy over orthodoxy. Thus he chooses to begin with Jesus of Nazareth, the Jesus

11. As quoted by Sobrino in *Christology at the Crossroads,* p. 34.
12. Rahner, "Current Problems in Christology," p. 150.

theologically interpreted by the primitive Christian community of the gospels. Furthermore, one "cannot simply speak *about* Jesus as we would speak about other objects. We can only speak *with him as a starting point,* as people touched by the significance of his reality."[13]

Jon Sobrino also chooses as his point of departure not the Christ of the dogmas but the historical Jesus, that is, "the person, teaching, attitudes, and deeds of Jesus of Nazareth insofar as they are accessible, in a more or less general way, to historical and exegetical investigation."[14]

Liberal theology is also not acceptable to liberation Christologists, because it ignores the eschatological character of the mission of Jesus and tends to present Christ as if He were a good bourgeois citizen in nineteenth-century style. Nor are they in agreement with the Bultmannian Christ of uncertain history and heavy individualistic accent. Soteriological Christology seems to them to be based on the individualistic and personal interests of man, not on what should be its true interests in light of faith and the reality in which we live. They also oppose a Christology that begins with the resurrection of the Son of God, because it does not give the necessary importance to the historical Jesus, His life, His words, His deeds, and His death.

USE OF TEXTUAL CRITICISM IN FINDING THE HISTORICAL JESUS

What about a biblical Christology? Liberation theologians are keenly interested in searching for the historical Jesus in the pages of the gospels, but they accept without reservation the opinions of modern textual criticism, including, of course, form criticism, redaction criticism, and tradition history. "Form criticism" (*Formgeschichte*) studies the influence of the life situation (*Sitz im Leben*) on the production or development of the text of the gospels. With that method one tries to determine, for example, if certain sayings of Jesus were truly pronounced by Him or if they were put in His mouth by the post-resurrection Christian community. The "tradition-historical" method (*Traditionsgeschichte*) concentrates on investigating the different currents of thought

13. Boff, *Jesus Christ Liberator,* pp. 43, 46.
14. Sobrino, *Christology at the Crossroads,* p. 3.

arising from the primitive Christian community that ended up in the text of the New Testament. For example, a Judeo-Christian tradition and a Christian-Hellenistic tradition are spoken of. "Redaction criticism" (*Redaktionsgeschichte*) sees the biblical text as the final phase in the process of tradition and as the product of the theological interpretation of the writer or writers. After a brief description of "form criticism," Boff says:

> One cannot always decide in a convincing manner whether or not a particular saying did or did not come from Jesus, even though in the present elaboration in the Gospels it is uttered by Christ. Form criticism permeates this entire study. At times we have made decisions of a theological nature based on a critical reflection inspired by this method. At other times, we have interpreted a text as not being the actual words of Jesus (especially those concerning his titles) even though common tradition, having no critical preoccupations, has always interpreted it as coming directly from Jesus.[15]

According to Sobrino, what is taught biblically about the titles of Christ and the great events of His life "already embody a later process of theologizing the Jesus event. Chronologically they come after Jesus himself, introducing us to an already developed Christology." Besides, Sobrino indicates that in the New Testament there are several Christologies and that it is impossible to unify them into one.[16]

An illustration of the way Boff uses historical-critical studies is found in the ninth chapter of his book *Jesus Christ Liberator,* where he concludes that the Christology of the gospels is a product of the theological reflection of Christians who, between A.D. 75 and 85, had arrived at the conviction that Jesus had been constituted by God as the Messiah Savior, Son of God and God Himself in human form. Consequently, narratives such as that of the Nativity are not history in the usual sense of the term, but rather a theological and literary elaboration that attempts to communicate a deeper truth about the child Jesus.

That He was born in Bethlehem, that some shepherds heard the angelic announcement, that wise men came to worship the Child, that Herod decreed the killing of the children in Bethlehem, that

15. Boff, *Jesus Christ Liberator,* p. 34.
16. Sobrino, *Christology at the Crossroads,* p. 5.

Joseph, Mary, and the Child fled to Egypt and returned after a time
to Nazareth—all of that is no more than theological reflection in
the rabbinical style and a literary embellishment of the history of
Jesus' childhood. The gospel writers, says Boff, used the literary
genre known among the Jews as *haggadic midrash,* which takes a
scriptural fact or saying "and fashions it and embellishes it with
the intention of underlining some truth of faith and proclaiming it
in an unequivocal form." For Boff, if the "myths" of the New
Testament "have lost their historical factual value, perhaps now
they can begin to take on their true religious-anthropological
significance. . . . The symbol is, humanly speaking, more real and
significant than historically factual cold data."[17]

This is not the time to enter into an analysis of historical-critical
studies of the New Testament. In the field of biblical scholarship
things are not as simple as they seem. With all due respect to
modern criticism in its effort to establish the historical authenticity of the gospels, it must be said that such criticism contains a
large dose of speculation.

Edward Schillebeeckx, widely known as an avant-garde Catholic
theologian, states that "a modern theology or Christology cannot
ignore the historical and critical data. To deny this is to fail to take
seriously the historical basis of Christianity and to see its constrain-
ing power located in a purely formal *kerygma.* . . . Christianity
does then lose its historical basis and becomes a purely fortuitous
phenomenon in the life of man the religious being, liable to vanish
out of it as readily as it came."[18] Then Schillebeeckx mentions
some criteria for discerning in the biblical narrative that which is
authentically from Jesus, or that which comes directly from Him;
in other words, for differentiating that which is truly historical
regarding Jesus from the additions that would be the product of a
reflection of the Christian community after the resurrection of its
founder.

Schillebeeckx considers as valid criteria form criticism, redaction criticism, and the different traditions that converge in the
Christology of the New Testament. However, he warns that caution
is indispensable in the use of those methods, because in them is
always the presence of the subjective, of different personal view-
points, and of that which is hypothetical. Schillebeeckx assumes
an open but critical attitude towards modern exegesis without

17. Boff, *Jesus Christ Liberator,* pp. 175-77.
18. Edward Schillebeeckx, *Jesus: An Experiment in Christology,* trans. Hubert
    Hoskins (New York: Crossroad, 1981), p. 75.

coming to the point of rejecting it. In the specific case of form criticism, he says that it is "in my view a valid method as form criticism but one which has not sufficiently realized how relative and perhaps 'subordinate' to other methods its significance is." He adds that form criticism "cannot (or will not) lead us to 'Jesus of Nazareth.'"[19]

I have quoted the opinion of a theologian whose openness to new biblical and theological currents is undeniable, lest I be accused of depending only on what conservative evangelicals say with regard to modern exegesis.

In spite of the inherent limitations in the "valid criteria" for historical New Testament investigation, Schillebeeckx believes that it is possible to arrive at the historical Jesus, because in the gospels we not only have the post-resurrection theological elaboration of Christians, but also the "global image" of Jesus of Nazareth, the memory which lives on in the reflection and theological development that followed the events of the life, ministry, death, and resurrection of Jesus. There is then in the gospels not only a Christological evolution, but also a memory of the historical Jesus. According to Schillebeeckx, historical exegesis demonstrates that "in all pre-canonical and New Testament traditions of early Christianity the absolute identification of the earthly Jesus with the Christ proclaimed by the local churches is a basic assumption." Furthermore, "one could even call this identity the hermeneutic key to a right understanding of the gospels. The concrete man Jesus of Nazareth "is the one and only basis for an authentic Christology."[20] Therefore, to look for and to find the historical Jesus is the exegetical task for our time. But when Schillebeeckx carries out his search in subjection to historical criticism, the result is that for him the Christology of the New Testament is due in great part to the reflection of the Christians of the first century. There is an identification, but also an abysmal difference between Jesus of Nazareth, the concrete man, and the Christ proclaimed by the primitive Christian community.

Liberation Christologists have also chosen as their point of departure the concrete man Jesus of Nazareth. But if the assumptions of modern exegesis are accepted uncritically, then there is very little left in the gospels by which to reconstruct the figure of the

19. Ibid., p. 88.
20. Ibid., pp. 81–82.

authentic Jesus. Who is, after all, the historical Jesus, if even the "valid criteria" of which Schillebeeckx speaks are not totally trustworthy? The most that Sobrino can say is that he will attempt "to point up those traits of Jesus which are most securely guaranteed by exegesis, and which offer us a most trustworthy image of the historical Jesus."[21] The basic problem of liberationist exegesis is found in the evidently indiscriminate use of historical-critical methods and, above all, in the lack of a high view of the revelation and inspiration of the Scriptures. Fundamentally the problem has to do with the authority of the written revelation of God.[22]

THE CHRIST OF LIBERATING PRAXIS

The point of departure for liberation Christology is not only the Jesus revealed by historical-critical studies of the New Testament, but also the Christ that emerges out of liberating historical praxis. Assmann declares:

> The Christian discovers and adheres to Christ here and now, to the Christ who is present and contemporaneous in the brethren, above all in the oppressed; this should become for the Christian the first meaning of the expression "historical Christ," that is, *Christ in present history*, however much the discovery of this contemporaneity of Christ may evidently demand the confrontation with the Christ in his former life and actions.(Emphasis added.)[23]

For his part, Sobrino says:

> Even *after* the church has formulated dogmatic statements about Christ, Christian communities are not excused from the task that the first Christian communities had to undertake. They, too, must contemplate and think about Christ in terms of their own situation and praxis . . . this Christology is meant to be historical Christology. Here I do not simply mean that it is worked out on the basis of present-day history. . . . I mean that we must be historical in the very process

21. Sobrino, *Christology at the Crossroads*, p. 14.
22. Assmann, for example, has said that "the Bible itself is not a direct source of criteria," and that the usual perspectives of exegetes who "work on the sacred text" are not sufficient; he wants to work on "the reality of today." His favorite text is the social context (*Theology*, pp. 60, 105).
23. Hugo Assmann, *Teología desde la praxis de la liberación*, p. 149.

of reflecting on Christ himself and analyzing the content of Christology. . . . If the *end* of Christology is to profess that Jesus is the Christ, its *starting point* is the affirmation that this Christ is the Jesus of history.[24]

Sobrino's purpose in his *Christology at the Crossroads* is "to attain an understanding of Jesus based on a praxis that follows Jesus in proclaiming the coming of the kingdom, in denouncing injustice, and in realizing that kingdom in real life—even if only partially. That, in turn, will lead to a new round of discipleship."[25] The fundamental method of Christology is changed in liberation theology. The question now is not whether Christology is "from above" or "from below," but whether it is "from within" or "from without," because as Sobrino says, commenting on Moltmann's thought, "the indispensable critical element can only come 'from outside.'"[26] Christology does not depend so much on the written revelation of God as on the life context (*Sitz im Leben*) of the interpreter and liberating historical praxis. In the hands of liberation theology, Christology can easily be converted into an ideology.

According to Sobrino, what most influences theology today is not "the first Enlightenment"—the intellectual movement that prevailed in Europe during the eighteenth century—but the "second Enlightenment"—that of Marxism:

> The second stage of the Enlightenment also exerts an influence on Christology, however sketchy that Christology still may be. Emphasis is placed on those christological elements that serve to constitute a paradigm of liberation (e.g., the resurrection as utopia and the kingdom of God) or to highlight practical ways of understanding and realizing it (e.g., the socio-political activity of Jesus and the obligation to follow in his footsteps).[27]

The difference between the Christology of the Latin American evangelical community and that proposed by liberation theologians is very deep. The latter has to be primarily shaped by the social context, by the revolutionary ideology of the day, by the struggle

24. Sobrino, *Christology at the Crossroads,* p. xxi.
25. Ibid., p. xxv.
26. Ibid., p. 31. See also Jürgen Moltmann, *Man: Christian Anthropology in the Conflicts of the Present,* trans. John Sturdy (Philadelphia: Fortress, 1974).
27. Sobrino, *Christology at the Crossroads,* pp. 34-35.

for political, economic, and social liberation. The point of departure is a Christ who emerges not simply from the traditional text of the gospels, nor from ancient ecclesiastical dogmas, but from the liberating praxis of the people. We are urged to know Him by following Him faithfully down the revolutionary path. Inevitably, He is a changing Christ, subject to changes in the social context. His traits "which are most securely guaranteed" by modern biblical exegesis will have to become adjusted to each new situation. The point of departure for Christology will always have to be that offered at any given moment by theologians or ideologists of revolution.

We do need to study more diligently than ever the formation of the biblical text from a historical point of view; we also must formulate a biblical Christology that can respond in a meaningful way to our individual and social problems; but also we must ask whether the Christ described to us by liberation theology is not actually another Christ, different from the One revealed in Scripture.

THE PERSON OF JESUS THE LIBERATOR

CHALCEDON AND CONTEMPORARY THEOLOGY

In the year A.D. 451, the Council of Chalcedon defined the Christological dogma, affirming the true humanity and deity of Jesus Christ and explaining that in the unity of the Person of the eternal Word there subsist two distinct natures, without confusion, without change, without division or separation. Until recent times there seemed to be a consensus among Catholic theologians that the Chalcedonian creed had spoken in a definitive way for the church. However, there are now those who think that the symbols or creeds are limited to expressing the doctrinal convictions of a particular time. Karl Rahner, for one, is open to a new Christological reflection that will be pertinent to our times:

> We propose to show by means of a kind of transcendental hermeneutics starting from dogma that the Church's Christological dogma never claims to be an adequate condensation of Biblical teaching,

and so that there does remain from the viewpoint of dogma a place for further Christological Biblical theology.[28]

Rahner affirms that we will truly arrive at the Chalcedonian formula if for us that creed is not only the end, but also the beginning. One tendency of contemporary theology is that of detecting and in a sense erasing the traces of Greek philosophy in church dogmatics. Rahner says, for example, that the Council of Chalcedon "used the Greek model of comprehension, employing the words 'nature' and 'person.'"[29] Liberation theologians are reluctant to use the Christological categories of traditional dogmas. They consider that although those categories were adequate for a culture of faraway centuries, today they may prove ineffective.

The Council of Chalcedon tried to satisfy the demands of the Alexandrian theologians with regard to the unity of Jesus the Christ, as well as those of the Antiochean theologians with regard to the duality of natures in the incarnate Word, a duality that does not affect the unity of His person. Reinhold Seeberg, a Lutheran theologian, says that with the Chalcedonian formula of "one person in two natures," the historical Christ was gained, "although only in the faintest outline, as the norm and the corrective for the ideas of the dogmaticians."[30] According to Louis Berkhof, the symbol of Chalcedon "did not put an end to the Christological disputes any more than the Council of Nicaea terminated the trinitarian controversy."[31] The content of the Chalcedonia formula allows the existence of two Christological schools; one that emphasizes the divinity of Christ, and the other that underscores His humanity.

BOFF: A COSMIC CHRIST WITHOUT HISTORICAL MOORINGS

Boff points out that in the Middles Ages the Thomistic school preferred to consider Jesus on the basis of His divinity, whereas the Franciscans took as their starting point His humanity. Because

28. Rahner, "Current Problems in Christology," p. 154.
29. Boff, *Jesus Christ Liberator*, p. 191.
30. Reinhold Seeberg, *Text-book of the History of Christian Doctrine*, trans. Charles E. Hay, 2 vols. (Grand Rapids: Baker, 1956), 1: 272.
31. Louis Berkhof, *The History of Christian Doctrines* (Grand Rapids: Baker, 1976), p. 108.

of his Franciscan training and due to his radical option, Boff leans towards the second of those schools. He believes that he finds God in the total and complete humanity of Jesus.[32] His radicalism goes hand in hand, of course, with that of his colleagues in liberation theology, who give a strong emphasis to the humanity of Christ; and although they do not reject His deity, neither do they affirm it without ambiguities or limitations, as conservative evangelicals do.

Boff wants to remain "within the orienting framework" of the Chalcedonian symbol; he professes to believe in "the mystery of the incarnation of God in Jesus of Nazareth."[33] But at the same time, he suggests that Jesus was not conscious of being the Son of God. Jesus could have had, of course, a clear awareness of His liberating mission, but He did not, according to Boff, give Himself the title of Son of God, or any other title that would express the Messianic and eschatological hopes of Judaism. It was after the resurrection that the primitive church, under Greek influence, took titles and images of its cultural world and attributed them to Jesus of Nazareth. The famous conversation between Simon Peter and Jesus, when the apostle says to Him, "Thou art the Christ, the Son of the living God" (Matt. 16:16), is not historical, says Boff. It was after the resurrection that Peter expressed in that statement that which had come to be the common faith of the church.[34]

Boff does not affirm the divinity of Christ on the basis of God's revelation or because it is the testimony of a text inspired by the Holy Spirit. It is true that according to Matt. 16:17 Jesus said to Peter that Christological faith comes by revelation from the heavenly Father; but, as Boff sees it, we cannot be sure that Jesus pronounced those words. Belief in the deity of Christ is, in the opinion of Boff, a product of the post-resurrection Christological reflection of Christians in the first century. In the various Christological traditions of the New Testament, Jesus is the Christ, the Son of Man for the Palestinian Christian community; the new Adam and the Lord for the Judaeo-Christians in the diaspora, and the only begotten of God and God Himself for the Hellenistic Christians, who reached the climactic point in the process of Christological reflection and elaboration. Boff says:

32. Leonardo Boff, *Jesus Christ Liberator,* pp. 285-86.
33. Ibid., pp. 286, 300.
34. Ibid., p. 168.

The Gentiles also knew many sons of gods (*theios aner*) born of virgins: e.g., emperors (Alexander the Great), wonder-workers (Apollonius of Tyana), and philosophers (Plato). The Son of God pertains to the divine sphere. The Gentiles began to understand the biblical title attributed to Christ, "Son of God," no longer in its juridical but in its physical meaning. . . . If then he is the Son of God, the next step was to reflect on him as being at the side of God. . . . Being preexistent, he also possesses a participation in the creative act of God. . . . This interpretation occurred in about A.D. 90, outside Palestine, and was certainly a great contribution of Hellenist Christians to the Christological process.[35]

Thus when the New Testament speaks of the deity of Christ it reflects a belief of the Hellenistic Christians, not necessarily that of the other traditions that appear on the pages of the New Testament. It is not so much a matter of revelation and divine inspiration as of human reflection.

Boff's notion of a cosmic Christ reflects the influence of Teilhard de Chardin, who viewed the totality of created things in a process of evolution and unification en route towards a culminating point, the "omega point" which is Christ. Boff says that "Jesus' human being is the result of a long process of cosmic evolution."[36] Upon rising from the dead, Christ did not abandon the world and the body; on the contrary, He assumed them fully and profoundly. Now He lives in the spirit, that is to say, in a new mode of existence that allows Him to overcome all temporal and spatial limitations and to make Himself present, in a pneumatic form, in all things and to reveal in Himself the anticipated end of the world. The resurrected Christ gives radical and transcendent unity to the cosmos and to all creation.

Boff warns that this is only metaphysical speculation, but he defends it and draws from it consequences of a practical sort. For example, if Christ is present in all creation, He also has to be present in a very special way in every human being, especially in the poor. Man is the greatest sacrament of Christ, "the greatest manifestation not only of God, but also of Christ resurrected in our world." Therefore, "without the sacrament of brother and sister no one can be saved." It must be concluded, furthermore,

35. Ibid., pp. 153-55.
36. Ibid., p. 209.

that the resurrected Christ is present for salvation in anonymous as well as in latent Christians:

> This is independent of their ideological coloring or adhesion to some religion or Christian belief. Wherever people seek the good, justice, humanitarian love, solidarity, communion, and understanding between people, wherever they dedicate themselves to overcoming their own egoism, making this world more human and fraternal, and opening themselves to the normative Transcendent for their lives, there we can say, with all certainty, that the resurrected one is present, because the cause for which he lived, suffered, was tried and executed is being carried forward.[37]

At the same time, Boff shows his ecclesiastical loyalty by clarifying that the resurrected Jesus is present in a deeper way in explicit and declared Christians and that the Roman Catholic church is the primary sacrament for the presence of the Lord. But he has left the door open for latitudinarianism and—why not say it—also for neo-universalism. The latter theme has already been discussed in the chapter on salvation and liberation.

SOBRINO: THE "UNFOLDING" OF JESUS' DIVINITY IN HUMAN PERCEPTION

Six years ago, in an article titled "New Debate over Jesus' Divinity," *Time* magazine dedicated a few paragraphs to Jon Sobrino, the Jesuit theologian of Basque origin who has an evolutionist idea of Jesus as the Son of God. Jesus of Nazareth came to be the Son of God by means of His obedience to the will of the heavenly Father. Sobrino admits that that can sound like adoptionism, but he insists that his Christological thought is in harmony with the dogmatic formulas.[38]

Discussing the theme of the consciousness of Jesus regarding the kingdom of God, Sobrino opposes the idea that the man Jesus in His earthly life "was aware that he was the Son of God in the strict, metaphysical sense of the term," and he insists that some biblical quotes such as John 10:30, 36, 38 and Matthew 11:27 are not authentically of Jesus. He also questions the practice of using

37. Ibid., pp. 218-19.
38. "New Debate over Jesus' Divinity," *Time,* 27 February 1978.

the titles of Christ to support the thesis that He had a Messianic consciousness.[39]

Sobrino sees development and change in the faith of Jesus. In the first stage of His ministry Jesus believed that the coming of the kingdom was near in time. Then He realized that He had "failed in his mission as he had previously understood it" and began to talk about His future passion. It should be accepted, therefore, that Jesus was ignorant of some things in the process of the development of His intelligence. He was wrong with respect to the day of the coming of the kingdom and "did not envision the existence of a 'church' as it appeared after his resurrection."[40] What about His divinity? Sobrino answers:

> It is his *relationship* to the Father that constitutes the essence of his person. Thus the category of relationship is important in trying to describe the total reality of Christ, and it may serve as a better basis for trying to understand what goes to make up his divinity. Here we propose to reformulate in relational categories what Chalcedon affirmed in ontic categories. The divinity of Jesus consists of his concrete relationship to the Father. This unique, peculiar, and unrepeatable way of being in relationship with the Father is what constitutes his concrete way of participating in divinity. . . . Thus we can say that Jesus *becomes* the Son of God rather than that he simply *is* the Son of God. . . . It should be noted that Jesus, strictly speaking, does not reveal the Father. . . . What Jesus reveals to us is the way of the Son, the way one becomes Son of God. Jesus does not, then, reveal the absolute mystery.[41]

Sobrino contrasts his Christology with the "Christologies of descent," which state that the Son comes and becomes man. In those Christologies Sobrino sees an implicit downward evolution, whereas in the one that he proposes the evolution is upward: Jesus of Nazareth becomes slowly the Son of God. But is there not in that thesis a certain type of adoptionism, condemned as a heresy by the ancient church? Sobrino answers that in the Christology of descent as well as in that of ascent "there is an element of mystery that cannot be satisfactorily explained, due to the limitation of the

39. Sobrino, *Christology at the Crossroads*, pp. 67-68.
40. Ibid., pp. 93, 101.
41. Ibid., p. 105.

human mind to understand what 'becoming' might mean in God."[42]

After stating that both explanations are evolutionistic and possess this element of mystery, Sobrino insists that the Christology of ascent, or "from below," does justice to the history of Jesus in the New Testament, where it is said that He reached perfection by means of obedience.[43] He does not mention, as does Walter Kasper, those texts that support the Christology of descent such as those that speak of the fact that Jesus has come from the Father, that He has been sent, and that He has come from without, or from above, in obedience to the Father.[44]

Sobrino prefers to believe that the Christology of descent is only a reflection of the Hellenistic Christian community. The texts that express in some way the idea that the Son of God becomes man would belong to that particular reflection. It is in that way that the Christology "from below" tries to find support in the historical-critical studies of the New Testament. But as I have already suggested, those studies, although they might be respectable and even necessary, can become very subjective and even arbitrary in their approach to the Scriptures. With regard to those who use scientific exegesis of the New Testament to stubbornly support a particular thesis, Oscar Cullmann says:

> One assigns all too often today the role of scapegoat, so to speak, to the believing community, a role which once was ascribed to Paul by viewing him as the one who distorted the gospel of Jesus. Now it is not at all my intention to discredit in principle that duty which is incumbent upon every serious exegete, and which, as form criticism teaches us, consists in considering the role of the community in the formation of the Gospels. Rather I am opposing exclusively the *arbitrary*, naive, unrestrained application of a method which is in and of itself legitimate. It is simply not justifiable, with the help of this method (distinguishing between authentic words of Jesus and "community formations"), to push aside all that speaks against one of our favorite assertions. The exegete should impose upon himself in this respect an extremely strict self-discipline.[45]

42. Ibid., p. 338.
43. Ibid.
44. Walter Kasper, *Jesus the Christ,* pp. 172-73.
45. Oscar Cullmann, *Jesus and the Revolutionaries,* translated from the German by Gareth Putnam (New York: Harper & Row, 1970), pp. 11-12.

The most important thing for Sobrino seems to be that for the Christian "the divinity of Jesus unfolds historically in the experience of fashioning history together with Jesus. . . . We can say that we only know that Jesus is the Son in brotherly communion with him, in following the path of his faith."[46] Hence the subtitle of his book in Spanish: "Esbozo a partir del seguimiento del Jesús histórico" (A sketch from the following of the historical Jesus). It is in the praxis of following Him that Jesus is revealed to us in His divinity.

In his book *Jesús en América Latina* (Jesus in Latin America), Sobrino makes an effort to answer the criticisms that have been made of his *Christology at the Crossroads*. He asserts that liberation theology does not deny the divinity of Christ and that it accepts the New Testament affirmations and the conciliar teachings to the effect that Jesus of Nazareth is the eternal Son of the Father. But he also suggests that it is necessary to clarify "the relationship between historical and transcendent affirmations, between that which is the plane of our knowledge about Christ and the plane of the reality of Christ himself."[47] Based on that difference he reiterates and defends the following theses with regard to the divinity of Christ:

> After the resurrection, Christians deepened in the reality of the person of Christ. . . . In this believing process, Jesus was confessed as the son of God. . . . By affirming the reality of Christ as a divine filiation an attempt was made to manifest the absolute and unrepeatable relationship of Jesus with God and, on the other hand, the absolute and unrepeatable manifestation of God in Jesus. This relationship came to be conceived in such a profound way, that centuries later and in the language of the Greek world, it came to be affirmed that Christ is consubstantial with the Father, of the same nature as the Father, that is, a divine reality.[48]

Once again, the emphasis falls not on "the reality of Christ himself," but on that which He becomes in the consciousness of the church throughout time. It is still a Christology based more on human reflection than on divine revelation.

46. Sobrino, *Christology at the Crossroads*, pp. 107-8.
47. Jon Sobrino, *Jesús en América Latina*, pp. 47, 80.
48. Ibid., p. 41.

THE WORK OF JESUS THE LIBERATOR

It is a fact that liberation theology is more interested in the words and deeds of Jesus than in discussions about His person. It offers a Christology that is not so much ontological as it is functional; it gives more importance to what Jesus said and did than to who He is. The humanity of Christ dominates the scene. His deity is, according to liberation Christologists, an element that was introduced into the New Testament by the Hellenistic Christian tradition and which must somehow be explained. Evidently, even without that tradition Jesus would still be the Liberator.

In view of the social problems of Latin America, the Christological controversies of antiquity do not make any sense for liberation theologians. They think that the philosophical categories of traditional Christology should give way to a liberating language that, according to their criteria, is more relevant to our Latin American reality. What they are saying about the person of Christ leaves much to be desired from the point of view of conservative evangelicals. We might ask, then, if the liberationist's concept of the work of Christ is more satisfactory than their concept of His person.

THE EARTHLY MINISTRY OF JESUS

Not overtly political, but having political implications. It is natural that a "Christology from below" should be more interested in the so-called "historical Jesus" than in the preexistent Christ who is now exalted at the right hand of the Father in the heavenlies. Gustavo Gutiérrez does not take time in *A Theology of Liberation* to develop the concept of the person and natures of Christ. He does state that in the man Jesus of Nazareth, God became flesh; but he makes that statement in passing in a paragraph that insists that the truly urgent task is that of approaching Jesus of Nazareth "to penetrate not only in his teaching, but also in his life, what it is that gives his word an immediate, concrete context."[49]

Gutiérrez takes a special interest in the attitude of Jesus toward the political situation of His time. He does not believe in the alleged apolitical attitude of Jesus and suggests that that suppos-

49. Gutiérrez, *A Theology of Liberation*, p. 226.

ition should be revised with a respect for the historical Jesus, that is, without betraying the authentic Jesus. It is incorrect, according to Gutiérrez, to want to "discover in Jesus the least characteristic of a contemporary political militant," but he suggests that the ministry of Christ had a political aspect. Jesus was crucified by the Romans as a Zealot chief, but to say that he was not a Zealot is not enough. There are differences and areas of agreement between Jesus and the Zealots; the matter is not simple. Jesus opposed politically powerful Jews, and the reasons of the Sanhedrin for condemning Him were both religious and political. Gutiérrez does not believe that Jesus would have called the people to a purely personal conversion, which would be opposed in a sense to the need for transforming social structures. He concludes that "the life and preaching of Jesus postulate the unceasing search for a new kind of man in a qualitatively different society."[50]

It was of course inevitable, sooner or later, for the presence, message, and attitude of Jesus to have political implications. For example, the very person of Jesus was a sort of contradiction or reproach to the established order. His preaching condemned the concept of power prevalent in that culture, and in all cultures. Jesus contrasted the conduct of humility and service which should characterize His disciples with that of the governors who were lords of the nations (Mark 10:35-45). Jesus did not hide His opposition to Herod, whom He called a "fox" (Luke 13:32).

It should also be recognized that the relationship between religious leadership and political power in Palestine during the time of Christ was different from that of the western world at the end of the twentieth century. At that time the Jews were under the Roman Empire, but their religious leaders had certain political powers. When Jesus publicly criticized and censured them, they felt they were in danger of losing both their religious and political control. That is why they tried to destroy Him by accusing Him of political crimes. They even threatened Pontius Pilate when they told him that if he did not crucify Jesus he would become an enemy of Caesar. Jesus was thus crucified as a subversive, although He was really far from being such a thing. But that is another example of the political implications of His life and ministry.

50. Ibid., pp. 226-29, 231.

The kingdom of God and political change. The theme of the kingdom of God was also very important in the preaching of Jesus. Both Sobrino and Boff insist that He did not come to preach concerning Himself, nor to speak only about the Father, but to announce the kingdom of God. He taught not only about God but about the kingdom of God. That is of great importance in liberation theology. Without a doubt the announcement of the kingdom of heaven could have been interpreted as a challenge to the power of the empire. The word "kingdom" is loaded with political meaning.

According to Sobrino, there was a "Galilean crisis" which divided the ministry of Jesus into two stages. In the first stage He presented Himself as an orthodox Jew announcing that the kingdom of God was near. He thus placed Himself in a Jewish apocalyptic tradition, which nurtured the hope of a theocratic, geopolitical kingdom. But then came the "Galilean crisis," in which Jesus realized that He had failed in His mission as He had previously understood it: "The crowds are abandoning him, the religious leaders of the Jewish people will not accept him, and God is not getting any closer with power to renovate reality." It is then that "the implanting of the kingdom took on the features of the work attributed to the Servant of Jehovah," and the concept of following Jesus took on a new dimension: "Instead of being sent out with power, His followers would now have to follow the suffering-laden pathway of Christ himself, with all the perilous social, personal, and political implications involved."[51]

At the same time, the kingdom of God became universal and radical. There was a break with Jewish orthodoxy. The norm of the kingdom became Jesus Himself. His kingdom would be entered not by means of orthodoxy but by "orthopraxis," that is, by following Jesus. "Only in the *praxis* of following him do we glimpse the mental categories that will enable us to understand the real nature of the kingdom of God and formulate it in a meaningful way."[52]

Evangelical response. The idea that Jesus was a failure and that He was forced by circumstances to modify His concept of the kingdom does not sound too convincing to conservative evangeli-

51. Sobrino, *Jesús en América Latina,* pp. 58, 93.
52. Ibid., p. 60.

cals, whose Christology holds a high concept of the Son of God and emphasizes His deity as well as His humanity. The New Testament passages that might seem to teach a change in the plans of Jesus need to be balanced by those texts that speak of the eternal and sovereign purpose of God (e.g., Luke 24:45-46; 1 Pet. 1:19-20; Acts 4:27-28). Of course, Sobrino and Boff would say that those texts, and others like them, arose out of the theological reflection of the church after the resurrection of Christ; they do not belong to the oldest New Testament tradition. Thus we come back to the problem of the relative authenticity and validity of the New Testament writings. Is it possible to have a true theological dialogue if each of the participants accepts without discussion only that biblical testimony which he needs to support his thesis?

With regard to the things Jesus did to promote the kingdom of God, it is significant that in spite of the political implications of His ministry, He did not behave as those who pretend to use His name as a symbol of radical and even violent transformation of social structures in Latin America wish He would have behaved. Jesus did not enter into the party struggles for political power in Palestine. He did not ally Himself with any of the factions that were making efforts in one way or another to maintain, or reach, political control. He did not become a Pharisee, or a Sadducee, or a Herodian, or a Zealot. He did not identify Himself with any of these groups; rather, He was willing to receive all who would believe in Him. The circle of His closest disciples included at least one Zealot, but there was also a publican, a tax collector at the service of the Roman Empire. Both had decided to follow and serve the Messiah.

Jesus did not come to establish another religious group or a political party. His purpose was to establish a new community, the community of the kingdom of God, sustained and characterized by love, humility, justice, peace, service, and harmony between men of good will. The contrast could not be greater between that new community and the different groups that were seeking to attain or preserve political and social power in Palestinian society. The followers of Jesus were not called to lord it over their people; their mission was not to seek to be served, but to serve. The greatest example of what it means to live for the sake of others, and, if it is necessary, to die for them, is given by Jesus Christ Himself (Mark 10:35-45). Even Boff says:

Jesus does not present himself as a revolutionary bent on modifying
the current relationships of power, as Bar Kokba did; nor does he
emerge as a preacher only interested in the conversion of consciences, as John the Baptist. . . . Jesus does not announce a particular,
political, economic or religious scheme, but an absolute scheme
which encompasses everything, and at the same time, surpasses
everything. The key word by which this radical scheme, opposed to
the present, is expressed, is the kingdom of God.[53]

Nonviolence and love. It is obvious that Jesus never appealed to
violence in order to promote His kingdom. He did not show His
love to enemies by fighting them, as some claim should be done
today in the name of liberation. Boff sounds moderate on this topic
when he states that Jesus did not shun communication with His
enemies, but rather condemned the attitudes which enslaved them
and made them enemies. "To desist from the scheme of hatred is
not the same thing as to desist from opposition. Jesus opposed,
contradicted, argued, not, however, with violence, but with deep
personal commitment. To desist from opposition would be to
desist from the good of our fellow-man and the defense of his
rights, and to add fuel to the fire of domination."[54]

In the concept of Sobrino, the universal love of Jesus is political
and is manifested in various ways according to the situation: "He
manifests his love for the oppressed by being *with* them, by offering them something that might restore their dignity and make
them truly human. He manifests his love for the oppressors by
being *against* them, by trying to strip away all that is making them
less than human."[55] Gutiérrez seems to be more explicit when he
says:

> To love all men does not mean avoiding confrontations; it does not
> mean preserving a fictitious harmony. . . . One loves the oppressors
> by liberating them from their inhuman condition as oppressors, by
> liberating them from themselves. But this cannot be achieved except
> by resolutely opting for the oppressed, that is, by combating the
> oppressive class. It must be a real and effective combat, not hate. This
> is the challenge, as new as the Gospel: to love our enemies. . . . But

53. Leonardo Boff, *Jesucristo y la liberación del hombre,* p. 304.
54. Ibid., p. 311.
55. Sobrino, *Jesús en América Latina,* p. 214.

love does not mean that the oppressors are no longer enemies, nor does it eliminate the radicalness of the combat against them. "Love of enemies" does not ease tensions; rather it challenges the whole system and becomes a subversive formula.[56]

The important question is whether Jesus really loved His enemies that way. One does not have to be a radical pacifist to seriously question the idea that Jesus teaches us to love our enemies by fighting them and converting our love for them into a subversive formula against the established order. No matter how many exegetical acrobatics are done with the biblical text, the fact remains that Jesus did not love His enemies in that way, although on the other hand it cannot be denied that He reprimanded them harshly for the sins of which they were guilty. But His love was not seditious in the political sense that some want to give it today; He did not try to change the structures of power in the society of His time by means of violence.

It should be made clear that to reject violence does not mean to oppose active non-violence, the attitude that does not want to keep a guilty silence in the face of injustice or close its eyes to causes of injustice at the national and international levels.

THE DEATH OF JESUS

Liberation Christologists give great importance to the death of Christ because it is part of the experience of the historical Jesus. I have already mentioned that they do not agree with a Christology that begins only with the resurrected and ascended Christ. They consider that to be a post-resurrection Christology which does not give proper place to the earthly life of Jesus nor to His death at Calvary.

Sobrino: The scandal of the cross. Sobrino's reflection on the cross of Christ is very interesting in more than one way. It is impossible here to discuss in detail everything that he says on the subject; we have to limit ourselves to a few comments. According to Sobrino, in the New Testament itself "it was hard for people to preserve the scandal of the cross, though the cross typifies Chris-

56. Gutiérrez, *Theology of Liberation*, pp. 275-76.

tianity." That scandal, he says, represents the fact that Jesus, being the Son of God, had to die, and that the Father was passive at the cross. After the resurrection the affirmation was made that Jesus is the Son of God, and titles that point more to His resurrection than to His death were attributed to Him. One way of detracting from the cross in the New Testament, according to Sobrino, was to interpret it soteriologically—that is, to point out only its salvific consequences for men. In contrast to the soteriological meaning of the cross, liberation theology emphasizes that suffering is a way of being God, that God was at the cross and suffered there the death of the Son. At the same time, by means of that death He manifested His divine power in the presence of so much death, "whether physical and definitive death or the death that people experience in the toils of oppression, injustice, and sinfulness."[57] The cross of Christ is the answer to the many crosses that humanity suffers. In a similar vein, José P. Miranda states that "Christ died so that we might know that not everything is permitted."[58]

Sobrino insists that the theology of the cross should be historical; in other words, we should not see the cross as "an arbitrary design on God's part, we must see it as the outcome of God's primordial option: the incarnation." Sobrino also explains that what is typical of the death of Christ, in contrast to the death of other religious or political martyrs, is that "Jesus dies in complete rupture with his cause," feeling Himself abandoned by the very God whose approach in grace He had been preaching. The cross is also a criticism against any attempt at knowing God on the basis of natural theology. The true knowledge of God is achieved by remaining with Him at the cross: "the systematic importance of this point for any historical theology of liberation lies in the fact that the privileged mediation of God ever continues to be the real cross of the oppressed. . . . It is when service is rendered to the oppressed, that we 'stand by God in his hour of grieving.'"[59]

Sobrino finishes his discussion of the death of Jesus by stating that the cross "is not the last word on Jesus because God raised him from the dead. But neither is the resurrection the last word on history because God is not yet 'all in all.'" Furthermore, "it is the cross that makes Jesus' resurrection *Christian*. It is by main-

57. Sobrino, *Jesús en América Latina*, pp. 184, 192, 196.
58. José P. Miranda, *Being and the Messiah*, p. ix.
59. Sobrino, *Jesús en América Latina*, pp. 201-2, 217, 222-23.

taining the scandal of the cross that we can conceive of a Christian God, of the Father of Jesus."[60]

As noted earlier, Sobrino's point of departure in Christological reflection is the historical Jesus, and his approach to the New Testament is made from the perspective of historical critical exegesis. For evangelicals, however, it is evident that the Christian community of those times gave no signs of wanting to avoid the scandal of the cross; on the contrary, it frequently testified in a verbal and symbolical manner (the Lord's Supper) concerning the death of Christ. The gospel that Paul had received was based on two great historical facts: the death and the resurrection of Christ. New Testament scholars believe that the text of 1 Cor. 15:3-5 was a declaration of faith that was used as a liturgical formula in the Christian communities of the first century. The apostle Paul gloried in the cross of Christ (Gal. 6:14) and purposed to know nothing among the Corinthians except Jesus Christ, and Him crucified (1 Cor. 2:1-2). It was the Judaizers who tried to take away "the stumbling block of the cross" (Gal. 5:11). Paul calls them "enemies of the cross of Christ" (Phil. 3:18).

In Pauline theology the scandal of the cross consists not only in the fact that Jesus, being the Son of God, died feeling abandoned by the Father. The cross is a stumbling block, or foolishness, to all those who are perishing, whether Jews or Gentiles (1 Cor. 1:18). The Jews asked for "signs" (*semeia*), that is, manifestations of divine power. They did not believe in a crucified Messiah. They demanded miracles, but Christ "was crucified in weakness" (2 Cor. 13:4, NIV); He did not liberate Himself from the cross (Matt. 27:42). The Greeks demanded "knowledge" (*sophia*), that is, philosophy; but the wisdom of God announced by Paul was precisely the fact that Jesus had died crucified (1 Cor. 1:21-25).

The scandal of the cross is not avoided when one proclaims the soteriological significance of the death of Christ. On the contrary, those to whom the message of the cross was a stumbling block were the people who refused to accept that their salvation depended on a Jew who died crucified as a subversive. Of course the soteriological significance of the death of Jesus is not limited to merely individual salvation. He died for all sin, for all sins, including those that plague society.

60. Ibid., pp. 229, 233-34.

Boff: Jesus dies as a prophet. What most interests Christologists of liberation is "the concrete man, Jesus of Nazareth," who acts and dies within a specific social context, amid economic, religious, and political forces that are contrary to Him and that in great part shape His life and ministry. From this Jesus, they suggest we can receive the teaching and example to confront in an effective way Latin American social problems.

Leonardo Boff sees the significance of the death of Christ in "the condemnation of oppressive practices and in the denunciation of mechanisms which produce suffering and death."[61] How does he arrive at this conclusion and similar ones? By taking as his point of departure the historical context and content of the cross of Christ, rather than the theological context and formulations of first-century Christians. By "theological context" Boff understands the process of reflection by which the Christian community came to interpret the death of Christ as a sacrifice for sin.

Boff emphasizes that Jesus died for the same reasons for which the prophets of all times have died. He died because He upset the religious and political situation. He opposed Jewish orthodoxy and suffered martyrdom. Christians saw the need of explaining why their Messiah suffered death in such a shameful way, by crucifixion. They went to the Old Testament and in an interpretative and theological effort—better yet, apologetic—attributed to that death a transcendent and salvific significance.[62]

Like Sobrino, Boff studies the New Testament text on the basis of historical-critical exegesis. He believes that the procedures of that exegesis are "not as arbitrary as they might seem," but he admits that there are different opinions about the passages and that "there is not any exegesis which is totally neutral." His exegetical method then leads him to conclude that the New Testament contains different interpretations concerning the suffering and death of Christ; that some details are historically correct, whereas others are only the product of theological development. Therefore there is much legend in those accounts. "The historically true events are the crucifixion, the condemnation by Pilate and the inscription on the cross in three languages known by the Jews. The rest of the events are theologized or are pure theology

61. Boff, *Jesucristo y la liberación del hombre*, p. 292.
62. Ibid., pp. 313-15.

developed in light of the resurrection and of the reflection upon the Old Testament."[63]

According to Boff, Jesus Himself did not think about dying at the beginning of His ministry. He did not want death, He did not seek it, although He was willing to obey the Father in everything and was aware of the tragic end which a faithful prophet might expect. He slowly began to warn that what was coming was not the kingdom, but the death of Messiah upon the cross. Then He began to consider Himself as the suffering Just One of the Old Testament. Boff goes as far as to say that it was not until Christ was on the cross that He realized that His death was something that the Father wanted.[64]

According to Boff, Jesus did not consider Himself to be the suffering servant of Isa. 53.[65] The passages that seem to indicate something different than that are a development that came after the resurrection. Christians put words on the lips of Jesus that give a vicarious and expiatory meaning to His death. Even the prophecies of Jesus Himself regarding His death and resurrection are not authentic from a purely historical point of view. Thus the explanation of Isa. 53 as a prophecy of the expiatory sacrifice of Christ is of a later origin than the resurrection.

It is impossible to comment here on all the explanations Boff offers of the development of the theology of the cross in the early Christian community. He concedes, by the way, that in all the reflective process of those Christians there is revelation, under the action of the Holy Spirit.[66] Boff's emphasis, however, does not fall on the supernatural, but on the human effort to interpret the death of Jesus of Nazareth in answer to a specific situation. The result is inevitable: the transcendent meaning of that death (expiation, propitiation, justification, etc.) is a product more of human reflection than of divine revelation. With the use that Boff makes of historical-critical exegesis, he rejects any other interpretation.

Boff does not deny outright the transcendent meaning of the death of Christ, but neither does he give it all the importance it deserves. He admits that in the accounts of the crucifixion it seems clear that the cause of Christ's death was our sin, in fulfillment of

63. Ibid., pp. 317, 330.
64. Ibid., pp. 350-51.
65. Ibid., p. 357.
66. Ibid., p. 376.

the Old Testament prophecies; but he adds that this type of interpretation, however valid it might be, "tends to create—if the
reader does not keep alert—an image of the crucifixion as if it
were a suprahistorical drama in which the actors, Jesus, the Jews,
Judas, Pilate, seem like puppets at the service of a previously drawn
out plan, and exempt from responsibility."[67]

Boff's desire to restore the historical situation in which Jesus
lived and the historical causes of His death is certainly proper, so
long as our own life context does not become the norm, or
dominant and determining factor, in the process of interpretation.
That, however, is precisely what occurs in Boff's thought.

Boff points out that we meditate theologically on the death of
Christ from a very different angle from that of the first Christians.
Their social problems and ours are not the same.

> We discover a new meaning to the suffering and death of the Lord
> beginning from political commitment, within a liberating praxis. Our
> "life context" is, therefore, different. And this difference has to be
> taken seriously into account, since it allows us to contemplate reality
> with other eyes and make a different reading. The sources, however,
> are the same, the gospels, written with other interests and in a
> different life context. If the gospel writers had written with a liber-
> ating political interest they would have written the gospels in a
> different way and they would have emphasized other aspects of the
> passion of Christ.[68]

In other words, what the gospel writers did not do, we have to
supply by a "new reading" of our reality and of the gospel.

But relativism is inevitable if we base our Christology on a free
and even arbitrary use of the biblical text, if the point of departure
is our political commitment (even if that commitment is opting
for the poor), and if we formulate our own Christological thought
within a supposedly liberating praxis, the development and final
destiny of which are uncertain. To say it in a different way, if the
source, that is the gospels, are of uncertain origin, and if our
reading of them has to be done in subjection to a changing "life
context" such as ours, all that is left to us is a Christology of the
road, following whatever direction the winds may blow. In the
final analysis we know neither what Jesus was like nor what it was

67. Ibid., p. 313.
68. Ibid., p. 296.

that He really did; we know neither what He will be like nor what He will do for us and for the world in future years.

On the other hand, I must reiterate my respect for the kind of biblical exegesis that seriously tries to establish, with a greater degree of accuracy than has been achieved in the past, the historicity and meaning of the biblical text we now possess, and reaffirm my conviction that we need an eminently biblical Christology that will be able to provide an adequate answer to the questions and hopes of the Latin American people. But I do not believe that it is necessary to sacrifice on the altar of mere exegetical speculation profound convictions regarding the inspiration and divine authority of the Scriptures. Nor do I believe that we should sacrifice on the altar of relevance the identity of the Christ revealed in Scripture.

SUMMARY AND EVALUATION: THE CHALLENGE TO EVANGELICALS

The liberation theologians quoted in this work have serious discrepancies with conservative evangelicals regarding doctrines fundamental to the Christian faith. The chasm that separates the two groups is much more than a mere difference of opinion about the causes of Latin American social problems and the way of solving them. The discrepancy goes far beyond the political and ecclesial; it transcends the conflict between capitalism and socialism and touches the very foundations of our faith, as can be seen in the case of Christology.

Liberation theology questions not only the way in which the post-apostolic church formulated its Christological creed; it puts in doubt the authenticity of various portions of the New Testament and prefers to interpret biblical Christology in terms of theological evolution. That means that New Testament Christology is largely the product of the reflection of the first Christians after the resurrection of the Master. It is more a Christology of human devising than of divine revelation. It does not give enough importance to the inspiration and divine authority of the Scriptures.

Liberation Christology is "from below," a Christology of ascent, not of descent. Jesus of Nazareth, it claims, slowly became the Son of God; and the idea of the preexistent, eternal Word who came down from the Father to become a man in order to be the mediator between God and man is the product of theological development that took place after the resurrection of Christ. Those who see in that teaching a form of the old adoptionism now decked out in revolutionary garb do not lack a basis for their conclusion.

Among the liberation theologians we have been studying there is no clear-cut, unambiguous confession that Jesus is God grounded in the fact that written revelation affirms it by the inspiration of the Holy Spirit. In contrast to Christology of descent, liberation theologians prefer to exalt the figure of the concrete man, Jesus of Nazareth. They emphasize His humanity and His earthly life.

In a sense, this new emphasis on the humanity of Christ is a reaction to the lack of balance in a Christology that magnifies the deity of the Word incarnate at the expense of His humanity. Many of us Latin American evangelicals are the heirs of an Anglo-Saxon Christology formulated in answer to Protestant liberalism, which questioned or openly denied the deity of Jesus Christ. Thus what was emphasized in evangelical conservative Christology was necessarily the deity of the Logos, without denying His humanity. We were presented with a divine-human Christ in the theological formula; but in practice He was far removed from the stage of this world, aloof to our social problems.

For Roman Catholics, He was the Christ nailed to the cross or shut up in His funerary casket; He was the Christ exalted to glory on the altars, but silent and immobile before the painful drama of injustice that millions of Latin Americans were living. He was not the man Christ, powerful in word and deed, who identified Himself fully with the people, who experienced their anguish and heartaches as one of them, among them and on their behalf, announcing the kingdom of God and its liberating power.

The Christ proclaimed to many of us evangelical Christians gave the impression of being confined to the heavenly heights, from which He dealt with each of us as individuals, preparing us for our journey to glory and promising us that He would come back to the world to solve all the problems of humanity. For the present He had nothing to say about social problems; nor should we become interested in them, because our mission was only to rescue the greatest possible number of souls from the sinking boat of the world. That may seem like a caricature, but it is not. At least it is the way in which many of us who came to the evangelical church in the years of the Second World War perceived Christ. Unfortunately, even today there are those who claim that we should continue to perceive Him that way. A great number of evangelical Christians hold to a Christ who remained immobile and silent before the painful social panorama of Latin America.[69] Sociologically speaking, the great difference between the evangelical Christ and the Christ of popular Catholic religiosity was that the former was seen resurrected and exalted at the right hand of the Father in the heavenly heights, not nailed to the cross or shut up, lying still, in a crystal casket. But He was still far removed from social conflicts. He was the Christ whom His followers guarded diligently so that He might not be identified with liberal preachers such as Harry Emerson Fosdick or with Walter Rauschenbusch, champion of "the social gospel." The purpose was noble and the effort was necessary in a time of great doctrinal controversies; but at some point the balance was lost, and in practice, evangelical Christology has run the risk of becoming docetic.

In past years we evangelicals have not given great importance to the Christ of the gospels, the One who set up His tabernacle among human beings in order to live among them in fullness of grace and truth. We saw Him in the glory of the heavens, not so much in the glory of the manger and of the carpenter's shop of Nazareth. We gave very little or no attention to the social and political implications of the conflict between Jesus and the religious leaders of His country. Nor did we emphasize as we should have that Jesus Himself was a sign of contradiction for those who were hungry for earthly power and who were ready to go to any length, even physical, brutal violence, to achieve or maintain it. We did not dare to say that although Christ came to save that which was lost, and in His loving and saving search made no distinction among persons or social classes, at the same time He undeniably was born, lived, and died in deep poverty and took on the cause of the poor—the poor in spirit and the poor materially. Neither did we insist on the fact that the teachings of Jesus contain potentially powerful seeds capable of producing great social transformations here and now. Generally speaking, our Christ was a disembodied Christ for disembodied souls. We were seeking the

69. See Emilio Antonio Núñez, C., *El Cristo de Hispanoamérica*.

salvation of souls apart from bodies, without considering that the word *soul* can also mean the totality of the human being.

Then the attack of liberation Christology came. The pendulum swung in the opposite direction, evidently with the intention of remaining there for a long time. Now the Christ who bordered on doceticism is rejected, and adoptionistic notions prevail. Instead of being considered only divine in the faith and praxis of the church, He is thought to be primarily human. He is seen as the Nazarene who became the Son of God, who died as a prophet, as a martyr. His death has been given historical and political significance by virtue of the fact that He confronted the dominant powers of the Palestinian society of his time. The transcendent meaning of His death, it is said, was attributed to Him by His disciples after the resurrection to justify or vindicate the fact that the Messiah had such a shameful end as death on the cross. His person and work must, we are told, be interpreted by each generation according to its "life context," in a new political reading of the gospel.

The Christ of liberation theology has decided to break His silence of centuries in the face of the social problems of underdeveloped countries. He has decided to speak in contemporary political language. He uses expressions such as "alienation of labor" and "surplus value," imperialism and underdevelopment, exploitation and dependence, capitalism and socialism, class struggle, option on behalf of the poor, political and violent love, liberating historical praxis. He is the Christ who uses revolutionary jargon and leads us to understand that Christian authenticity is only possible in unreserved political commitment to a leftist ideology.

The liberation theologians want to take their Christ out from the shadows of the colonial cathedrals and carry Him, not in a peaceful and solemn religious procession, but in a revolutionary march to churches, theological seminaries and universities, to factories and offices, to the fields, to the streets, to the market places, and to high government spheres with the demand for social change. The procession passes in front of the evangelical church, before our astonished or fearful eyes. This Christ is a stranger to us; He is different from the one we preach. But He pretends to be the authentic one, the one whom the gospels reveal and whom the reality of our Latin American countries acclaim.

The challenge is here. It is not possible to avoid it. No evangelical who considers himself a theologian can give himself the luxury of underestimating it. It is not enough to close one's eyes and yield to the illusion that liberation theology is just a passing fad that will soon die as the "death of God" theology did. Liberation Christology is making an impact, directly or indirectly, on Latin American evangelical thought. In a sense that is positive. It is pushing us to study with diligence and enthusiasm the person and work of Christ, not only in traditional systematic theologies, but especially in the sacred Scriptures. It has also caused us to think with greater interest than before on the urgent need of formulating a Christology that corresponds in the first place to our cultural and social reality.

We already have indications of a Christological awakening in the Latin American evangelical community. It seems clear that, since the appearance of liberation theology, our Christology cannot be the same in its emphasis as the Christology that was to some degree a product of evangelical reaction to Protestant liberalism of the nineteenth century. Without isolating ourselves from our life context, we must continue to study the sacred Scriptures diligently, because they are what give the fundamental and authentic testimony concerning the person and work of the Son of God.

9

The Ecclesiology of Liberation

In a dialogue concerning liberation theology sponsored by the Latin American Episcopal Council (CELAM) in Bogotá, Colombia (1973), Monsignor Alfonso López Trujillo said, "We are conscious that there are enormous voids and gaps in liberation theology. There aren't even outlines of a serious Christology. . . . We are working with an implicit ecclesiology, but I think that one of the failures in some elaborations is precisely in their ecclesiological approach."[1] It is not surprising that the distinguished South American prelate should express such a concern, especially if one takes into account the fact that Gustavo Gutiérrez and other liberation theologians demand a profound social change that would not leave the ecclesiastical structures intact. But the concern of Monsignor López Trujillo was also of a theological order. For example, he was concerned about the unity of the church. Liberation ecclesiology is also disquieting for the conservative evangelical, who studies it in the light of the written revelation of God.

That the church—whether Catholic or Protestant—needs constant renovation nobody denies. The question is whether the renovation proposed by liberation theologians is in line with the ecclesiological principles established in the Scriptures. Gustavo Gutiérrez is convinced that there is need for a "radical revision of

1. Alfonso López Trujillo, "Diálogo," in *Liberción: Diálogos en el CELAM,* p. 99.

what the Church has been and what it now is." In practice that
revision would mean a "substantial transformation" in the nature
of the church itself and of its mission:

> But what is called for is not simply a renewal and adaptation of
> pastoral methods. It is rather a question of a new ecclesiastical
> consciousness and a redefinition of the task of the Church in a world
> in which it is not only *present,* but of which it *forms a part* more
> than it suspected in the past. In this new consciousness and redefini-
> tion, intraecclesial problems take a second place.[2]

The main interest of liberation theologians is not so much in
defining what the church *is* in accordance with the lucubrations
of traditional theology, as in reflecting upon *what it means to be
a church* today in a revolutionary context, a context of extreme
poverty and social injustice. In the liberationist view the church is
defined by what it does in the fulfillment of its prophetic mission
in the midst of the social whirlwind. Therefore, in the scheme of
liberation ecclesiology the nature and mission of the church go
hand in hand. I do not intend to ignore that relationship, but for
practical reasons I will give attention first to the nature of the
church and then to its mission.

THE NATURE OF THE CHURCH

Liberation ecclesiologists are particularly interested in what the
church is in its missionary praxis. I will focus here on its universality and its unity. Gustavo Gutiérrez and Leonardo Boff speak to
both topics at length.

THE UNIVERSALITY OF THE CHURCH

The universal sacrament of salvation. In chapter four I mentioned that according to the Second Vatican Council the church is
the sacrament of salvation for the whole world.[3] I also pointed out

2. Gustavo Gutiérrez, *Theology of Liberation: History, Politics and Salvation,* pp.
   251, 255.
3. *Dogmatic Constitution on the Church,* arts. 1, 9, 48.

that that idea had already appeared in preconciliar Catholic theology.

In ordinary usage, the word *sacrament* immediately evokes the seven sacraments of the Roman Catholic salvific system. In that system, a sacrament is "a thing perceptible to the senses, which upon the ground of divine institution possesses the power both of effecting and signifying sanctity and righteousness."[4] The theologian Miguel Nicolau explains that a sacrament is "an *efficacious sign* to produce that which it signifies."[5] In other words, the sacrament is much more than a visible sign of sanctifying grace; it also confers that grace on the one who believes in what the Catholic church teaches.

The *Dogmatic Constitution on the Church* of Vatican II (*Lumen Gentium*) neither defines the sacrament nor explains the exact way in which the church should be given a sacramental character, although the council affirms that the church is a means of salvation for the whole world. Commenting on the ecclesiology of the council, Aloys Grillmeier says that the notion of the church as a sacrament of salvation "forms a close link with patristic and modern ecclesiology." He goes on to explain the sacramental nature of the church on the basis of the biblical word *mystery, (musterion)* which the Latin versions translate as *sacrament (sacramentum)*. In its use in *Lumen Gentium,* Grillmeier explains, "mystery" or "sacrament" means "the whole economy of salvation, that is, the eternal plan and decree of God to bring the world into the fellowship of salvation with himself in Christ." He also clarifies that the intention of the council was to ascribe to the church the value of "a sacramental symbolism and instrumentality" in relation to the saving purpose of God for all mankind.[6]

Gutiérrez points out that Vatican II gave the guidelines for a new ecclesiological perspective when it spoke of the church as a sacrament. Although the council was not able to free itself totally from an "ecclesiocentric perspective,"[7] it made it possible to reject the ecclesiocentric attitude of the medieval church, which pro-

---

4. Ludwig Ott, *Fundamentals of Catholic Dogma,* ed. James Canon Bastable, trans. Patrick Lynch (St. Louis: Herder, 1958), p. 326.

5. Miguel Nicolau, *La Iglesia del Concilio,* p. 48.

6. Aloys Grillmeier, "The Mystery of the Church," translated by Kevin Smith, in *Commentary on the Documents of Vatican II,* vol. 1, ed. Herbert Vorgrimler (New York: Herder and Herder, 1967), pp. 139-40.

7. Gutiérrez, *Theology of Liberation,* pp. 258-59.

claimed that outside of the church there was no salvation. In
alliance with the state, the church considered itself to be the only
depository of saving truth for humanity. There were, according to
Catholicism, no elements of that truth outside of the limits of the
Roman Catholic church, and consequently the papal hierarchy
opposed religious liberty. Gutiérrez sees that in the documents of
Vatican II that ecclesiological perspective is changed.

On the basis of the teaching of the council, Gutiérrez insists that
the church is "a universal sacrament of salvation." He interprets
the sacramentality of the church in the sense of an "uncentering"
of the church, by which it "must cease considering itself as the
exclusive place of salvation and orient itself towards a new and
radical service of people." We have already seen that in Gutiérrez's
opinion "man is saved if he opens himself to God and others, even
if he is not clearly aware that he is doing so. This is valid for
Christians and non-Christians alike—for all people." Divine
grace—whether accepted or rejected—is in all men. It is no longer
possible to speak properly of a "profane world." There is no
distinction between a profane world and a sacred world. Salvation
therefore is also found outside the church. It is not just the Christian who is a temple of God; every man is. "The 'pro-fane,' that
which is located outside the temple, no longer exists." Consequently, we find God in our encounter with human beings, especially with the poor. Christ is in our fellow man.[8] In his new book
We Drink from Our Own Well, Gutiérrez insists that "the other is
our way for reaching God," but he also clarifies that "our relationship with God is a precondition for encounter and true communion with the other."[9] Such thinking recalls Leonardo Boff's
concept of man as "the main sacrament of Christ" and his assertion
that "without the sacrament of the brother, no one can save
himself,"[10] as well as Rahner's "anonymous Christianity."

The conversion of the church to the world. Gutiérrez is opposed
to the separation of the natural order from the supernatural order,
or the sacred from the profane. For him there are not two histories;
there is only one history in which the salvific purpose of God for

8. Ibid., pp. 151, 194, 196-203, 256.
9. Gutiérrez, *We Drink from Our Own Well: The Spiritual Journey of a People,*
   p. 112.
10. Leonardo Boff, *Jesus Christ Liberator,* p. 219.

all mankind is fulfilled. Neither does he accept the ecclesiocentrism that makes a separation between the church and the world. The church is not only present in the world; it is part of the world. It is not "a non-world; it is humanity itself attentive to the Word. It is the People of God which lives in history and is orientated toward the future promised by the Lord." Consequently "the Church must turn to the world, in which Christ and his Spirit are present and active; the Church must allow itself to be inhabited and evangelized by the world." Gutiérrez recognizes that there are those who do not accept the Word in an explicit way, but he wants to avoid any dualism between the sacred and the profane; he sees that the focus on the church as a sacrament implies a dialectical relationship between it and the world, to the point that "a theology of the church in the world should be complemented by 'a theology of the world in the Church.'"[11]

The dividing line between the church and the world vanishes in the attempt to go beyond traditional "ecclesiocentrism." In a paper presented to the International Theological Commission in Rome, 1976, the Catholic theologian Karl Lehmann said regarding liberation ecclesiology: "The frontiers between the Church and the world become blurry or disappear completely."[12] The emphasis of liberation ecclesiology is not on the conversion of the world to the church, but on the conversion of the church to the world. It should be evangelized by the world, especially by the poor. Its sources of renewal are found not so much in the Word of God and in the Holy Spirit as in the world.

Universality beginning with the poor. Leonardo Boff also views the church from a sacramental perspective. To the criticism that choosing on behalf of the poor is classist and would lead the church to renounce its universality, Boff responds that there is a link between universal mission and concrete liberation, because "the way of fulfilling the mission and universality of the Church should go through the mediation of the particular and the concrete,"[13] which in the case of Latin America is the liberation of the

11. Gutiérrez, *Theology of Liberation*, pp. 260-61.
12. Karl Lehmann, "Problemas Metodológicos y hermenéuticos de le teología de la liberación," p. 13.
13. Leonardo Boff, *La Fe en la periferia del mundo*, p. 145.

exploited. Otherwise universality would be no more than an abstraction, and mission would lack content.

Boff defines the universality of the church "starting from the understanding of its mission as the process of a liberating incarnation, within a historically defined situation. That is: when confronting universal causes, the Church also becomes universal." Actually "the Church as a whole is having a spiritual and political experience which confers upon it a new universality."[14] There have been three ways, according to Boff, in which the bond between mission and universality has been manifested:

(1) The church projected itself *from outside of the world* as a *sacrament-instrument* necessary for salvation. The church believed that it had a monopoly on truth, and it made an effort to implant its ecclesiastical system in the whole world. It had a colonialist religious mentality. It tried to export and impose European Christianity with its doctrinal, liturgical, and ethical uniformity. The church, inevitably, was characterized by its intolerance towards other ways of thinking and acting.[15]

(2) In the second stage, encouraged by Vatican II, the church fulfills its mission from *inside the world,* as a *sacrament-sign* of universal salvation. The church makes visible not only the grace it communicates, but also the grace that is already present in the world.

> Its mission is not to mold everyone into its historical model but to defend and deepen that which is good and legitimate in all human manifestations. . . . That's why this church can show itself flexible in cooperation with all movements which seek a truly human development and favor openness towards others and towards God. . . . The great Church, the grand Church is made up of all those who anonymously live in the realization of truth and good in all human dimensions.[16]

However, Boff explains that in the *sacrament-sign* model, universality is not really "universal" yet. The council sees the church

14. Ibid., p. 148.
15. Ibid., pp. 148-49. See also by the same author, *Teología desde el cautiverio,* pp. 188-95.
16. Boff, *Teología desde el Cautiverio,* pp. 194-95.

within the world, but universality has as its point of departure modern man, "the illuminated bourgeois class."[17]

(3) Consequently it is necessary for liberation ecclesiology to establish the bond between universality and mission within the *sub-world,* that is, the world of the poor, of the non-men, those who live in subhuman conditions due to social injustice.

How does the church become universal inside the sub-world? Boff answers that in order to fulfill its mission and its universality the church "should go through the mediation of the particular and the concrete (in this case, the liberation of the exploited)." By taking up the cause of the poor, the church opts for justice, which is justice for all; it proclaims rights that are for all without distinction. "If the cause is a true one, then it enjoys an intrinsic universality. It is true for all and, *a fortiori,* for the Church. By making this cause its own, the Church becomes truly universal."[18]

But the option for the poor, according to Boff, implies commitment to and participation in the liberating struggle: "The presence of the Church and its evangelization assume in this way a political dimension in the struggle against the situation of dependence and oppression. In such a situation, to evangelize means to bring crisis and conflict to the creators of dependence and oppression."[19] The church becomes universal by struggling against the oppressors. Boff does not seem to have really answered in a convincing way the criticism that a class option presupposes "a rejection of universality and the pastoral care which the Church should have towards all men, independent of its social involvement."[20]

Lack of biblical support. The idea of universality in liberation ecclesiology reveals, in addition to a serious threat of universalism, a lamentable lack of biblical evidence. The absence of a New Testament balance regarding the relationship of the church to the world is evident. The gospels teach that the church was drawn out from the world and given to Christ, that the church is in the world but does not belong to the world, and that it has been sent to the world to be the salt of the earth and the light of the world (John

17. Boff, *La Fe en la periferia del mundo,* p. 151; cf. *Teología desde el cautiverio,* pp. 195-97.
18. Boff, *La Fe en la periferia del mundo,* pp. 145, 154.
19. Boff, *Teología desde el cautiverio,* p. 199.
20. Boff, *La Fe en la periferia del mundo,* p. 145.

17; Matt. 5:13-16). The New Testament also teaches that the church should maintain its identity in the world (1 Pet. 2:9-10). We conservative evangelicals also reject the idea that outside of the institutional church there is no salvation. We condemn intolerance and advocate the practice of religious liberty. But we also repudiate any universalist tendency and insist on the fact that salvation is found only in Christ as He is revealed in the Scriptures. In order to be saved, the sinner has to come personally, in faith and repentance, to the Son of the living God. The gospel traces a deep dividing line between those who receive Christ and those who reject Him (John 3:36; 14:6; Acts 4:12; 2 Thess. 1:3-10; I Tim. 2:5). The church is both a sign of saving grace and a sign of divine judgment upon the impenitent. The message of the church is good news of salvation yet at the same time a solemn warning of eternal condemnation for every sinner.

THE UNITY OF THE CHURCH

In liberation ecclesiology the idea of universality of the church leads inevitably to the idea of the unity of the church. The church is the sacrament of salvation for the world in a concrete and active form when it expresses human brotherhood in fulfillment of its mission. That happens especially in the celebration of the Eucharist, which is a testimony to the work "which creates a profound human brotherhood." Gutiérrez presents three realities that are signified by the New Testament term *koinonia* (communion, community), based on the thought of the Catholic ecclesiologist Y. M. Congar: (1) "the common ownership of the goods necessary for earthly existence"; (2) "the union of the faithful with Christ through the Eucharist," and (3) "the union of Christians with the Father," with the Son, and with the Holy Spirit. Thus human brotherhood has a trinitarian base.[21]

Unity through working for justice. Gutiérrez and other liberation theologians do not see the unity of the church apart from social reality. The Christian community "is in a world divided into antagonistic social classes, on a universal scale as well as at the

21. Gutiérrez, *Theology of Liberation*, pp. 263-65.

local level."[22] Class struggle is a reality that divides the church itself. Therefore, liberation ecclesiologists conclude that it is impossible to manifest the true unity of the church without taking the side of the oppressed class for the achievement of a more just society in which authentic brotherhood may reign. Otherwise, according to Gutiérrez, the church may take sides with the dominant class in the name of a fictitious unity and help to perpetuate the unjust and oppressive social system.

In view of the fact that the church itself lives within that unjust system, its unity cannot truly be achieved without the unity of the world, and "the unity of men is only possible in the exercise of justice for all."[23] Consequently, the function of the Christian community is "to struggle against the profound causes of the division among men."[24] That is the only way in which the church can be an authentic sign of unity.

The desire to participate in the unification of the world by means of liberating praxis has brought about a new type of ecumenism that goes beyond merely ecclesiastical concerns.[25] It is a *secular ecumenism* that tries to bind Christians and non-Christians together in order to change the social structures in Latin America and the world. The teaching of Vatican II and Popes John XXIII and Paul VI have opened the door for the cooperation of the Catholic church with movements of a non-Christian or anti-Christian philosophy in the struggle for social transformation.

In an evaluation of liberation ecclesiology the question immediately arises whether the social divisions that now exist in the church would not become even deeper than they are if the church were to take sides with "the oppressed class" in their struggle against the "oppressors." Boff explains:

> The mission of the church, as also that of Christ, consists of reconciliation. However, there cannot be any true reconciliation as long as the motives which lead to social rupture and class struggle persist. Consequently, reconciliation is only possible through the conversion of those who crush men for impoverishment with injustices.[26]

22. Ibid., p. 276.
23. Episcopado Peruano, as quoted by Gutiérrez in the Spanish edition of *Teología de la liberación*, p. 360.
24. Gutiérrez, *Theology of Liberation*, p. 278.
25. Ibid., pp. 278-79.
26. Boff, *Teología desde el cautiverio*, p. 199.

Boff has said before that "to evangelize means to bring crisis and conflict to the creators of dependence and oppression."

In the opinion of Gutiérrez, "the Church itself will become more and more unified in this historical process and commitment to the liberation of the marginated and exploited." By opting for the exploited in society and opposing the dominant class, the church "can free itself from that which now prevents it from being a clear and true sign of brotherhood."[27] At least that is what Gutiérrez hopes. Is Gutiérrez dreaming of a church without classes for the present? Without a doubt, social conflicts are reflected in one way or another in the Christian community. In not a few cases social conflicts among the members of the church are an obstacle to the practice of unity.

Working for unity while ignoring God's Word. But is the solution really the option and the struggle that Gutiérrez proposes? Where does the answer of Gutiérrez and other liberation theologians come from? From the New Testament or from a political ideology? Do concepts such as "class struggle" and "liberating praxis of the poor" come from the New Testament? Did Jesus and the apostles establish violent struggle against oppressors as a requirement for the cultivation and expression of authentic Christian unity? Those questions, and others that could be asked, are not intended in any way to close our eyes to the dehumanizing reality in which millions of Latin Americans live. Much less are they meant to condone social injustice in Latin America. Rather they focus attention on the basis and methods that liberation ecclesiology proposes for the practice of Christian unity.

It greatly troubles me and other evangelicals that Gutiérrez and his colleagues do not make use of serious biblical exegesis in discussing a subject of such great importance as the unity of the church. We know that in the primitive Christian community there were members of different social classes. It is possible that in some congregations the number of slaves was very great, perhaps greater than the number of free people. However, whether we like it or not, Jesus and His apostles never emphasized class struggle (although they recognized its existence); much less did they encourage an uprising of the slaves against their masters in a rebellion

27. Gutiérrez, *Theology of Liberation*, p. 278.

that would have turned out to be useless for Christianity, for society, and for the disciples involved in such a conflict.

Jesus of Nazareth was neither a subversive like Judas the Galilean (Acts 5:37), nor a Bar Kokba, who led the Jewish revolt against the Romans in A.D. 132. Christianity was not destined to be just one more revolutionary movement among the many recorded in history. Its enormous potential for social changes has to be devoloped in other ways, by other means, not as the world and liberation theology suggest. The message of the gospel contains powerful seeds of liberation; but they do not germinate in the way of the world, in soil fertilized by anti-human or anti-Christian ideologies (whether of the right or of the left). That Onesimus the slave should return voluntarily to his master, and that Philemon should forgive and receive him, no longer as a slave but as a brother in Christ, was the result of the grace and power of God, not of a violent praxis against oppressors. That may be considered pure lyricism, but that is how the word of the cross seems to the world. It is a word that "is to those who are perishing foolishness but to us who are being saved it is the power of God" (I Cor. 1:18). Such is the true scandal of the cross.

Gutiérrez has told us that the unity of the church cannot really be achieved without the unity of the world, and that as a consequence Christians should struggle for the sake of universal brotherhood. That struggle has to be carried out, of course, not only in the theological realm, nor only in a purely pastoral ministry of a traditional type. Political commitment is demanded. Liberating praxis is indispensible and unavoidable. But what guarantee do we have that the church would contribute to the establishment of universal brotherhood by involving itself as a church in a violent struggle against the oppressors? Would it preach peace at the international level and violence in the local scene? Would it oppose tenaciously the use of nuclear weapons by the world powers but support and encourage kidnapping, physical and mental torture, and killing in underdeveloped countries? Aren't those who die as a result of violence human beings also, whether their deaths are the result of institutionalized violence or that of "liberating praxis"?

The unity of Christ. Turning our eyes from that grim perspective and putting aside all political considerations—for example, that the church as a church may stop catering to one ideology in order to cater to another that may be more oppressive than the preceding one—we still have the impression that according to liberation ecclesiology it is the church which must produce unity. Furthermore, that unity has to be of a social and political nature. Nobody denies that Christian unity is experienced in concrete situations. In that sense it is historical, earthly, and not otherworldly. But what is its true nature? What is its origin? What is its purpose? Are Latin Americans going to be united in a *Christian* sense by the simple fact that the church actively supports a particular political system? How is *Christian* unity revealed in the New Testament? Jesus of Nazareth gives the answer in His high priestly prayer (John 17). As He converses with His Father, He reveals the nature and purpose of the unity which He desires for His own in the world. In the first place this unity is possible for human beings. The disciples were human, belonging to a race, a geography, a cultural and social system; they were earthlings, not heavenly beings. Jesus calls them "those whom you gave me out of the world" (v. 6, NIV). They were of the Father ("they were yours," v.6); now they are of the Father and of the Son (vv. 9-10). They have entered voluntarily into unity with the Father and the Son, believing that Jesus came from the Father and was sent by the Father (v. 8). Christianity, then, is a unity of persons who believe that Jesus is the preexistent Son of God. They believe that He is God.

The unity for which Christ prays includes and excludes. It excludes those who reject Him; it includes those who receive Him. Jesus does not ask for the unity of the world, but for the unity of those whom the Father has given Him (v. 9). Whether we like it or not, there is a non-world and there is a non-church. The dividing line is drawn by Jesus Christ in His prayer to the Father. That is a matter decided in the council of the Trinity.

The desire of Christ is that believers in Him might be *one;* that they may be one not apart from the world, but in the world, yet kept from the world, being sanctified by the word of the Father (vv. 11-17). They come out of the world (v. 6) and they are sent into the world, as the Father sent His Son into the world (v. 18).

Jesus develops even further the theme of Christian unity when He prays that this unity may be similar to the one that exists between Himself and the Father; "that they may be one as we are one" (vv. 11, 22, NIV). Christian unity is much more than an ecclesiastical organization—intraecclesiastical or interecclesiastical; it is much more than a social and political organization.

This unity—real, deep, spiritual, and practical—is experienced only in the personal relationship of human beings with the Father and the Son: "may they also be in us" (v. 21, NIV). Apart from personal faith in the Lord Jesus Christ it is impossible for human beings to share in the unity for which He prays. It is at the cross that the "dividing wall of hostility" is torn down; there Christ makes peace between man and God and between man and man, destroying enmities (Eph. 2:14-15). Authentic Christian unity does not come as a result of human efforts for peace; it comes from God by means of the person and work of His Son and by means of the ministry of the Spirit, who comes to baptize into one body—the Body of Christ—all who believe the gospel (1 Cor. 12:13; Gal. 3:27-28).

We as believers in Christ do not have to make unity; we are already united in Him by His saving grace. But we have to keep this unity and express it (Eph. 4:1-16) in mutual fellowship and cooperation in the service of the kingdom of God. It is sad that although we already have unity in Christ, we become more and more divided at the level of ecclesiastical structures. Before a world that is deeply divided, we offer the painful spectacle of a church that we ourselves have fragmented in practice.

The fundamental and supreme purpose for expressing Christian unity is that the world may believe that Jesus Christ was with the Father in His glory before the world was created (John 17:5), that the Father loved Him from before the foundation of the world (v. 24), and that being one with the Father, He came from the Father (v. 8), being sent by the Father to the world (v. 18). Without a doubt, those are affirmations of the preexistence of the Son, of His unity with the Father, of His deity. It is a Christology "from above," a Christology "of descent," not of "ascent." The purpose of Christian unity is that the world may believe that Christology. And Christian unity becomes visible, concrete, and historical in the communion of believers in Christ, in the *koinonia* that includes much more than liturgical communion; the unity is also expressed in service to the brethren and the civil community.

Fundamental biblical truths like those expressed in the high priestly prayer of Christ are what we miss in the ecclesiology of liberation.

THE MISSION OF THE CHURCH

In the ecclesiology of liberation the nature and mission of the church are closely related to each other: the church is not seen apart from its mission. Thus without being able to avoid it we have, in our discussion about the nature of the church, touched on some concepts that pertain to its mission. That way of dividing the subject, however, is only a practical convenience. The theme of the mission of the church is so important that it is preferable to treat it separately as well.

Gutiérrez says emphatically that the purpose of the church is not to save in the sense of "guaranteeing heaven." Rather, "salvation embraces all men and the whole man; the liberating action of Christ—made man in this history and not in a history marginal to the real life of man—is at the heart of the historical current of humanity; the struggle for a just society is in its own right very much a part of salvation history."[28] According to those words, the mission of the church is not limited to what we call spiritual and eternal, and it should not be defined in abstract terms. Salvation is not ahistorical; it does not have to do only with life after the tomb. It encompasses the present aspect of existence without excluding the struggle for economic, social, and political liberation.

THE PREFERENCE FOR THE POOR

In liberation ecclesiology the point of departure for fulfilling the mission of the church is the recognition that class struggle exists and that it is indispensible for the church, in order to be the church, to take sides with the poor against the oppressors. The main missionary motivation is not that the glory of God might be manifested in the fulfillment of His salvific purpose in history. Nor is it the fact that every human being is lost and that "God so loved the world, that He have His only begotten Son, that whoever believes in Him should not perish, but have everlasting life" (John 3:16). Nor is the main missionary incentive the command of Christ that we should make disciples of all nations (Matt. 28:18-20).

Solidarity with the poor. The thing that most concerns liberation theologians is class struggle provoked, according to them, by

28. Ibid., pp. 168, 255.

those who oppress the poor. Consequently, the mission of the church consists of becoming conscious of social injustice, taking the side of the poor, and assuming a posture of serious and irrevocable commitment in the revolutionary process to liberate them.

> In Latin America to be the Church today means to take a clear position regarding both the present state of social injustice and the revolutionary process which is attempting to abolish that injustice and build a more human order. The first step is to recognize that in reality a stand has already been taken: the Church is tied to the prevailing social system. In many places the Church contributes to creating "a Christian order" and to giving a kind of sacred character to a situation which is not only alienating but is the worst kind of violence—a situation which pits the powerful against the weak.[29]

In support of the option for the oppressed class, liberation theologians point out that in the Old Testament Yahweh has preference for the poor and defends them from the oppressors. They add that in the New Testament the Son of God incarnate identifies Himself with all of humanity, but He does so in a special way with the poor. Gutiérrez says: "In terms of justice, God is partial: he takes sides. . . . One cannot be *on the side of the poor* if one is not *against* everything that produces the exploitation of man by man."[30]

Regarding statements of the Third Conference of Latin American Bishops held in Puebla, Mexico, in 1979, Gutiérrez comments:

> The option for the poor, as Puebla says more than once, is preferential and not exclusive. . . . The gospel is not anyone's private property, to do with as one might wish. *Preference* for the poor is written into the gospel message itself. . . . No, the gospel is addressed to every human being; only it has a predilection for the poor, and therefore makes its proclamation from a position of solidarity with the oppressed.[31]

In view of the attitude of God towards the poor, the church should become converted to them and become poor in order to speak

29. Ibid., p. 265.
30. Gustavo Gutiérrez, "Liberation, Theology, and Proclamation," p. 60, as quoted by J.G. Davies in *Christians, Politics, and Violent Revolution,* p. 100.
31. Gustavo Gutiérrez, *The Power of the Poor in History,* pp. 127-28.

from the situation of those who suffer social injustice. Only in solidarity with the exploited classes can we understand the gospel and make it understood.

The biblical view. We conservative evangelicals do not see God having a political prejudice of a Marxist type in His attitude towards social classes in biblical times. We recognize, of course, that in the Old Testament He is the defender of the orphans, of widows, of strangers, and of all the poor, whether those who live in material poverty or those who represent spiritual poverty. No exegetical manipulation can silence the prophetic outcry for social justice. No hermeneutical escape is valid in order to say that that outcry, which is also a cry of protest against the injustice that the poor were suffering, has no application to our time. If it does not have an application for us, why was it included in the Bible, seeing that "whatever was written in earlier times was written for our instruction" (Rom. 15:4)?

Evangelicals also recognize that the Messiah identified Himself with all of humanity, but He did so in a very special way with the poor. He was born poor, and He lived poor among the poor, serving the poor. He made Himself accessible to the masses; He gave priority to the poor; He suffered with them and for them; and He announced to them first of all the good news of the kingdom of God. He was not the Christ of an elite class, of a select, exclusive group in Palestinian society. He is universal in his saving offer: "Come to Me, all," "the one who comes to Me I will certainly not cast out" (Matt. 11:28; John 6:37). He did not issue that call from high social spheres, but from the reality of the poor to whose class He belonged. He visited the home of Zacchaeus, the rich chief tax collector; but He was not only a *visitor* among the poor, He was one of them; He experienced with them the sorrows and joys of life.

It is imperative, however, to consider the preference of the Lord for the poor within "the whole counsel of God," not only on the basis of certain biblical passages. Definitely, the universality (not universalism) of Christ tears to shreds any classist scheme. He came to the world because it was lost and under condemnation and because He wanted to save it. All human beings are sinners, but all of them are redeemable, if through faith they receive saving grace. In that sense Jesus is not partial or classist. He demonstrated that in the incarnation, identifying Himself with the whole human race. He demonstrated it in His earthly ministry, breaking down racial, cultural, social, and especially religious barriers. He demonstrated it on the cross, where He died for all. He demonstrated it after the resurrection when He ordered His disciples to preach the gospel to every human being, in all nations, in the whole world.

The preference of the Lord for the poor is of a salvific nature, with all the meaning that the biblical word *salvation* entails. The gospel is preached to the poor not only because they are a class of people deprived of material wealth and oppressed by the powerful in an injust social situation, but also because as individuals they suffer the oppression of sin within themselves. The fact of being poor does not exempt them from being sinners.

The sin of the oppressors exists—and so does the sin of the oppressed. "For all have sinned and fall short of the glory of God" (Rom. 3:23). The sin of structures and the sin of individuals exists. Segundo Galilea says: "I do not want to fall into a populism which mythifies the people and the poor. The poor are also sinners."[32] So liberation theologians are for the poor and against poverty, which they do not wish to glorify. They do well in assuming that attitude, which should also be ours, as long as they do not glorify the poor, as some liberationist theologians seem to do at times.

Finding a balance. According to liberation ecclesiology the option in favor of the poor implies the responsibility of becoming poor. The exhortation to practice so-called evangelical poverty has positive aspects, especially for those of us who live and work for the sake of God's kingdom in underdeveloped countries. Christ did not have the purpose of establishing an opulent church, rich in this world's goods but poor in spirit, removed from the masses, and powerless to answer the great challenges of a society such as ours in the process of change. We are tempted to want to become a church for the rich, or else to become a "church of the people," without realizing that in both cases we can be manipulated by an ideology. There is no basis in the New Testament for organizing a "classist" church, whether for the poor or for the rich. We have to be careful to not discard the biblical content of words such as

32. Segundo Galilea, *¿Los pobres nos evangelizan?* p. 53.

"poor" and "people" in order to impose on them an ideological or political meaning. We need to depend, for the renovation of the church, not on Marxist concepts of class struggle, but on the teachings of the New Testament and the ministry of the Holy Spirit. I do not intend, by these considerations, to underestimate the emphasis given in both Testaments to the poor, those who do not have what is necessary to subsist. We Latin American evangelicals would do poorly if we forgot that Jesus became poor and that the great majorities in our subcontinent are poor, in need of the liberation that the gospel brings. What we wish to do is to find and maintain a biblical balance in our attitude towards the poor and towards other social classes.

PROPHETIC DENUNCIATION

Once one has opted for the poor, one is obligated under the liberationist scheme to publicly denounce their oppressors.

In the opinion of Gutiérrez, the first task of the church is the eucharistic *celebration,* which implies the creation of human brotherhood. It is a celebration of the salvific action of God in history. Then comes the *proclamation* which is made from the point of view of the commitment to the cause of the oppressed. The Eucharist celebrates brotherhood, but before society the church has to "take a clear position regarding both the present state of social injustice and the revolutionary process which is attempting to abolish that injustice and build a more human order."[33] That is what it means "to be Church today."

Above all, says Gutiérrez, the church has to recognize that it is already bound to the current social system and that in many places it has helped to give a certain sacred character to the violence of the powerful against the weak. Now the church has to decide whether it will continue favoring the established order in order to conserve its social prestige before the dominating groups, or whether it will break with those groups in order to dedicate itself to really serving the oppressed. According to Gutiérrez, the oppressive and alienating situation already exists; the church has been part of it and has to do everything possible to modify it, beginning with modifying itself.[34]

33. Gutiérrez, *Theology of Liberation,* p. 265.
34. Ibid., pp. 265-67.

Characteristics of prophetic denunciation. Gutiérrez suggests three traits of prophetic denunciation. First, prophetic denunciation is global. It includes "every dehumanizing situation, which is contrary to brotherhood, justice, and liberty, . . . every sacralization of oppressive structures to which the Church itself might have contributed."[35] Second, prophetic denunciation is radical. It is not satisfied with pointing out some of the symptoms or consequences of the prevailing situation. It goes to the very causes of injustice and oppression. It is "a radical critique of the present order." "The Gospel message reveals, without any evasions, what is at the root of social injustice." The church has to be on guard against the danger of allowing itself to be assimilated into a society that seeks to carry out only some reforms, without bringing about deep changes. "Reformism" and "developmentalism" are not enough. A radical, revolutionary change is necessary.[36] Third, prophetic denunciation is "praxiological." It does not remain on the merely verbal level. It is made "from within the heart of the struggle for a more human world. The truth of the Gospel, it has been said, is a truth which must be done." The denunciation "is not only a 'word' or a 'text'; it is an action, a stand."[37] Inevitably, this denunciation, made from revolutionary commitment, can destabilize the prevailing order and set into motion new forces for social change.

The church's choice. In his exposition of prophetic denunciation, Gutiérrez makes us think of inescapable realities. It is true that there is social injustice in Latin America and that as a result of that injustice millions of Latin Americans suffer a "scandalous state of poverty." It is also true that the church participates in that situation; at least the church has tolerated poverty and many times has contributed to maintaining it, taking advantage of it. There is no doubt that the church has to decide in this hour of great social transformations whether it will continue to accommodate itself to the status quo or choose to be faithful to its prophetic vocation.

On the other hand, we see that the church should not allow itself to be manipulated by ideologies that also advocate social

35. Ibid., p. 267.
36. Ibid., pp. 267, 269.
37. Ibid., p. 268.

change. It can very easily leave a "Constantinianism of the right" to fall into a "Constantinianism of the left." Gutiérrez thinks that the option in favor of the oppressed is the answer to that problem;[38] but if one's choice is guided by the Marxist concept of "class struggle" the result is, inevitably, a leftist option.

The biblical concept of denunciation. Some evangelical theologians say that the word *denunciation* means to expose in front of a third party the sins of others even when the accused party is not present; but the biblical prophets confronted the guilty ones. That was the approach, for example, of Nathan before David and of John the Baptist before Herod. But did Amos preach his messages to each oppressor in private, or did he also preach them publicly when there was a good number of Israelites congregated? Did Jonah preach only to each Ninevite in particular, or did he announce his message publicly throughout the whole city? In fact, the Bible gives examples of both methods of communication when it deals with the exposure of individual and social sins. It is possible that the word *denunciation* may not be the most appropriate for this ministry, but God's people are still responsible, at all times and in all places, to not be indifferent to the sins that surround them. In one way or another it should be evident today that the church repudiates and condemns those sins and that it does not participate in them.

Some evangelicals also argue that the biblical prophets did not demand a transformation of the political system in their nation or in any other nation. They did not struggle in Israel or Judah in order to change the theocracy into another system of government. Moses did not try to transform Egypt socially or politically. The same can be said about Jonah in Nineveh and Daniel in Babylon. Jesus of Nazareth did not begin a political and violent revolution in order to dethrone Caesar and to change the Roman Empire into a biblical theocracy. Moreover, the prophets had a specific message for specific people, the people of the covenant with Yahweh. Therefore, it could be said that we should use neither the example nor the message of the prophets to denounce the sins of our society.

38. Ibid., pp. 266-67. See also Hugo Assmann, *Theology for a Nomad Church*, pp. 100-01.

There certainly is a great distance between the times of the prophets and ours. There is a great difference between the life context of those servants of God and ours today. It would not be proper to impose our cultural and social system upon the biblical world or to try to reproduce in our environment the political and religious situation of that far-away age. But the Scriptures have been given to us because they include teachings and examples that we should follow in some way (Rom. 15:4). It is very easy to try to avoid our social responsibility by chaining the biblical message to the remote past, or limiting it to a future fulfillment, instead of applying it here and now.

Application to Latin America. Having made those clarifications, a very important question arises: how should we use the biblical message in answer to Latin American social problems? History and contemporary reality tell us that the church has always been in danger of falling either into a complacent and cowardly accommodation or into a naive and senseless audacity. History and experience also teach that it is not fair to demand the church of a particular country to act in a certain way in answer to social and political problems.

There are evangelical brethren who, from outside, judge the evangelical churches in countries torn by violence for not taking sides with the political left. The evangelical church has been strongly criticized from afar for failing in a country governed by "capitalists" to denounce the violation of human rights by the civil and military authorities. It is very easy to talk about prophetic denunciation when one lives in the security and comfort of a country where the free interplay of ideas is permitted. The situation is very different for the evangelical Christian who daily experiences the drama of violence in his own country, running the risk of losing altogether his freedom to serve people in the name of Jesus Christ. The situation is very different in a country where the citizens have been condemned to silence without regard to their own human rights.

In addition, critics of the church often give the impression that it is only in countries governed by the right that there is no freedom of speech, oral or written. They ignore what takes place in leftist regimes.

What is evident is that under both rightist and leftist regimes, there are evangelical brethren who do not feel called to be martyrs and have chosen to give their lives "by working, not by dying," to use the words of the Jesuit priest Luis Espinal, who was assassinated in Bolivia in 1982.[39]

I am sure, however, that many of those brethren who have not provoked martyrdom would be ready to give their lives in the name of Christ if God's will should demand it. For the time being they have decided that the best thing to do is to subsist in order to serve. This happens in countries belonging to the capitalist orbit as well as in countries of a hard socialist line. Gutiérrez says that the church should not be anxious to subsist; that the issue is not to survive but to serve.[40] Can the church serve without surviving? The negative answer to that question explains the option of the churches that are consciously not making a "prophetic denunciation" as some people insist that they should do.

Every Christian and every church has its own life context and its own moment of ethical decision in the face of personal and social problems. It is a moment to exercise inner liberty and to remember that each one "shall give account of himself to God" (Rom. 14:12). The Christian is not called to seek martyrdom, much less to provoke it, but neither should he reject it if the Lord so demands. However, who are we, those of us who are not risking our lives daily for Christ, to judge and condemn our brethren who live and labor for the kingdom of God, in either capitalist or socialist countries, under the continuous threat of "imprisonment, exile or burial?"

ANNOUNCEMENT OF THE KINGDOM OF GOD

Prophetic denunciation should be accompanied by the announcement of "the love of the Father which calls all men in Christ and through the action of the Spirit to union among themselves and communion with him."[41] The denunciation has to do with social injustice and its causes; the announcement with its remedy.

A "conscientizing" announcement. The message of the kingdom is not simply spiritual and futuristic. As they listen to it,

39. As quoted by Gustavo Gutiérrez in *We Drink from Our Own Wells,* p. 117.
40. Gutiérrez, *Theology of Liberation,* p. 262.
41. Ibid., p. 268.

people become conscious of their historical existence, of their liberating potential, of their responsibility to forge here and now a world different from the present one. It is an announcement that can clearly expose the fact that a situation of injustice and exploitation is incompatible with the advent of the kingdom. As they listen to this message, the people who live in such a situation come to perceive themselves as oppressed, and they feel motivated to seek their own liberation.[42]

A "politicizing" announcement. Inevitably, the "conscientized" people look for political avenues to liberate themselves. Gutiérrez says that the church "politicizes by evangelizing." Commenting on liberation theology, Edward Norman interprets politicizing as "the transformation of the faith itself, in such a way that it comes to be defined in terms of political values." Gutiérrez says that the role of the gospel should be reduced to creating in men a political consciousness; what is meant is that the gospel "has an inescapable political dimension."[43]

Gutiérrez docs not close his eyes to the danger of "oversimplifying the Gospel message and making it a 'revolutionary ideology'—which would definitely obscure reality." He thinks that it is possible to avoid that danger by means of "the reflection, the spirituality, and the new preaching of a Christian message which is incarnated—not lost—in our here and now."[44] However, the threat still remains. The political discourse is so strong in liberation theology that it becomes difficult to hear the content of the gospel.

The concrete ways in which the denunciation and the announcement should be made are not known beforehand. "Some chapters of theology can be written only afterwards." But this uncertainty should not keep the church from taking a position in favor of the oppressed, recognizing "the incomplete and provisional character of any and every human achievement."[45] The church should not "sacralize" an ideology. That which is definitive is yet to come. There is an "already" and a "not yet" of the

42. Ibid., p. 269.
43. Ibid., pp. 269-70; Edward Norman, *Christianity and the World Order* (Oxford: Oxford U., 1979), p. 2.
44. Gutiérrez, *Theology of Liberation,* p. 271.
45. Ibid., p. 272.

kingdom. This is not only future or otherworldly. Hugo Assmann explains: "The Kingdom of God is never identified with the structures of the world, but is inserted and developed in them as a process."[46] In chapter seven, "Salvation and Liberation," I alluded to Gutiérrez's concept of the kingdom as a historical process. That process, according to Gutiérrez, takes place in liberation but is not exhausted in it. Without liberating historical events there is no growth of the kingdom. The historical, political, liberating event is the growth of the kingdom, "but is not *the* coming of the Kingdom, not *all* of salvation."[47] It is hard to know in practice whether a particular historical event will turn out to be truly liberating, whether it will be pro-kingdom or anti-kingdom. As long as evil exists in the human heart any revolution can be perverted.

In liberation theology the kingdom is a gift of God and the work of man, although one sometimes gets the impression that in this theology the kingdom is more a human achievement than a divine one. More is said of the historical process of the kingdom than of its consummation, but both Gutiérrez and Assmann make an effort not to identify it with any political system in particular. Assmann sees the kingdom in "constant futurization, even in its victorious steps."[48] In spite of that, as we will see in the next section, liberation theology requires a political choice.

THE POLITICAL OPTION

In the ecclesiology of liberation the mission of the church means much more than to take sides with the poor, to denounce the social injustice that they suffer, and to announce the kingdom. All of that should lead to a commitment on the part of the church in liberating praxis. In other words, the church has to enter the political arena in order to fulfill its mission.

No "third option." Liberating praxis is not carried out in a political vacuum; it is impossible to live the gospel as one should apart from political involvement, because its message has an inev-

46. Hugo Assmann, *Teología desde la praxis de la liberación*, p. 154.
47. Gutiérrez, *Theology of Liberation*, p. 177.
48. Assmann, *Teología desde la praxis de la liberación*, p. 156.

itable political dimension. Moreover, the situation of injustice that afflicts millions of Latin Americans demands that Christians opt for liberation in all its forms.

> The annunciation of the Gospel thus has a conscienticizing function, or in other words, a politicizing function. But this is made real and meaningful only by living and announcing the Gospel from within a commitment to liberation, only in concrete, effective solidarity with people and exploited social classes. Only by participating in their struggles can we understand the implications of the Gospel message and make it have an impact on history. The preaching of the Word will be empty and ahistorical if it tries to avoid this dimension.[49]

There is no place for apoliticity in liberationist thought:

> Any claim to noninvolvement in politics—a banner recently acquired by conservative sectors—is nothing but a subterfuge to keep things as they are. . . . Every attempt to evade the struggle against alienation and the violence of the powerful and for a more just and more human world is the greatest infidelity to God. To know him is to work for justice. There is no other path to reach him.[50]

Liberating praxis inevitably implies a political option, and liberation theologians close the way to a third route. They do not believe that neutrality exists, and they reject any supposed third alternative. Either we are in the struggle for the poor against the established order, or we are party to the oppressors. If we are not active in the political left we are supporting in one way or another the political right. If we want to be faithful to God we have to be affiliated with the left and struggle "against alienation and violence of the powerful." And it should be noted that liberation theologians make no distinction between the church as an entity and its members as individuals with regard to political decisions and actions. The church as a church should be committed to liberating praxis if it truly desires to fulfill its mission.

Edward Norman comments that "Christianity today is, in this sense, being reinterpreted as a scheme of social and political action, dependent, it is true, upon supernatural authority for its

49. Gutiérrez, *Theology of Liberation,* p. 269.
50. Ibid., pp. 266, 272.

ultimate claims to attention, but rendered in categories that are derived from the political theories and practices of contemporary societies."[51]

What kind of socialism? Gutiérrez and other theologians of liberation have opted for socialism as a political channel for their faith. But is it the "Latin American socialism" of the third-world priest in Argentina, or the "democratic socialism" of Bishop Méndez Arceo of Mexico, or another type of socialism? Is Gutiérrez hoping that the revolutionary movements in Latin America will produce a unique type of socialism inspired by liberation theology?

What is evident is that Gutiérrez has rejected reformism and developmentalism and maintains the thesis that Latin America "will never come out of its calamitous state unless it experiences a radical transformation, a social revolution which would change present conditions."[52] For him class struggle is a reality that cannot be avoided: "we must see clearly that to deny the fact of class struggle is really to put oneself on the side of the dominant sectors. Neutrality is impossible. . . . When the Church rejects the class struggle, it is objectively operating as a part of the prevailing system." For Gutiérrez, to defend class struggle is to desire to abolish the causes that unleash that struggle, to strive for a society without classes, "to eliminate the appropriation by a few of the wealth created by the work of the many . . . to build a socialist society, more just, free, and human, and not a society of superficial and false reconciliation and equality."[53]

Even without considering what guarantees there are that such a society will not be like the type of socialism that has been established in countries where there is not more justice, liberty, or humanization for the people, the idea that the church as a church should promote class struggle continues to be a cause for concern. The fact that the church has been implicitly involved in class struggle by tolerating and even supporting the violence of the dominant groups does not justify the demand that it simply change sides so that the killing may continue. Is that the Christian way to

51. Norman, *Christianity and the World Order,* p. 2.
52. Gustavo Gutiérrez, "Notes for a Theology of Liberation," *Theology Digest* (1971); as quoted by Robert McAfee Brown in *Religion and Violence* (Philadelphia: Westminster, 1973), p. 95.
53. Gutiérrez, *Theology of Liberation,* pp. 274-75.

repent, by simply changing sides in the war between man and man? Is that the way in which the church is to be renewed? Is that the way in which Christ orders the church to fulfill its mission? Or should the church repent of its past and overcome, by the power of the Word and of the Spirit, the temptation of continuing to be a "classist" church?

A "CHRISTIAN" VIOLENCE?

It is evident that in Latin America Christians cannot enter into the struggle that liberation theology suggests without becoming involved, directly or indirectly, in brutal violence. That is what recent history teaches. Liberation theologians are conscious of that fact when they fan the fire of class struggle. They know that violence is a necessary part of what they call "liberating praxis," and they try in one way or another to justify it. This serious problem warrants at least a brief look.

Ellacuria: Justifying violence against unjust violence. Ignacio Ellacuria, a Spanish Jesuit who has worked for more than twenty-five years in Central America, especially in El Salvador, approaches the subject of violence from the psychological and theological point of view. One of his theses is that there is sinful violence and non-sinful violence. Injustice is what gives violence its sinful character. All injustice is violent. Therefore one cannot speak of violence in the strict sense of the term when no injustice is present. A violent struggle against a violence that is the fruit of injustice cannot be considered in itself as sinful.[54]

Ellacuria clarifies that he is not preaching the use of violence to combat violence. He distinguishes between theology and ethics; but he maintains his other thesis: the violence that prevails in our midst is unjust and cries out for extreme remedies. With regard to that violence, the use of whatever force may be necessary to redeem it is not only allowed but required. But in the struggle against violence one should not lose sight of the essense of Christianity, remembering that Christian redemption derives its power not from hatred but from love.[55]

54. Ignacio Ellacuria, *Freedom Made Flesh, The Mission of Christ and His Church*, pp. 228-29, 225-26.
55. Ibid., pp. 227, 229-30.

There is more than one way in which Christians have attempted to redeem violence. Ellacuria gives three examples: (1) The pietist Charles de Faucauld, who with his brethren lived among those who suffered violence, but did not fight on their behalf; he limited himself to giving them an example of love, of meekness and service; (2) Martin Luther King, whose motive was Christian love and whose method of combating injustice was non-violence; (3) Camilo Torres, the guerrilla priest.

According to Ellacuria, those are three examples of Christian ways of dealing with the problem of violence in a redemptive spirit. In none of those examples is there a denial of Christian values. No Christian can express all the richness of Christianity. Different groups of Christians should cultivate different important aspects of the gospel message and of the example of Christ. Charles de Faucauld expresses the transcendent aspect of the gospel, and Martin Luther King the social aspect. We might ask what aspect does Camilo Torres represent when he has the machine gun in his hand? Ellacuria tries to get out of the problem by saying that the case of Camilo should be considered and evaluated in terms of his situation, which was desperate.[56]

But it is impossible to find in the example of Jesus of Nazareth justification for destruction of an enemy. That is illustrated by the fact that Ellacuria tries to explain the conduct of Camilo Torres not on the basis of the example of Christ, but on the basis of "the desperate situation" in which the Colombian priest had to struggle.

Furthermore, the distinction between sinful violence and non-sinful violence (force, coercive force, etc.) can be too subjective. For Ellacuria, the violence that is unleashed by the established order is "the worst form of violence."[57] It is to that institutionalized violence, he says, that the people should direct their attention. But if the established violence is "the worst," that means that there are other kinds of sinful violence that can be manifested in the very process of combating the violence of social injustice. Ellacuria himself recognizes, on the basis of biology and psychology, that violence is a phenomenon typical of the human being. We all have a tendency to be violent, as the Bible observed nearly two thousand years ago. We all can be violent in an unjust way. "There is

56. Ibid., pp. 218-25.
57. Ibid., p. 199.

none righteous, not even one. . . . their feet are swift to shed blood . . . the path of peace have they not known" (Rom. 3:10-18).

These brief reflections are not aimed at justifying established violence. They are not an attempt to hide or to deny, much less to approve, the social injustice that originates and encourages such violence. What we desire is that the problem be approached from a biblical perspective, especially in the light of the example of Jesus of Nazareth in His life, ministry, and death on the cross.

Gutiérrez and Bonino: Love and liberating praxis. Jesus' teaching about love is also problematic for those who wish to Christianize violence in the name of liberation. Gustavo Gutiérrez faces the difficulty by admitting first of all that "the class struggle poses problems to the universality of Christian love and to the unity of the Church." But he adds that any consideration of that fact should take into account that the class struggle is a reality and that neutrality in the matter is impossible. Later on he explains:

> One loves the oppressors by liberating them from their inhuman condition as oppressors; by liberating them from themselves. But this cannot be achieved except by resolutely opting for the oppressed, that is, by combating the oppressive class. It must be a real and effective combat; not hate. This is the challenge, as new as the Gospel: to love our enemies.[58]

When that "love" is carried to its final consequences it can mean the feelings that James H. Cone describes in these following words:

> The power of the black experience cannot be overestimated. It is the power to love oneself precisely because one is black and a readiness to die if white people try to make one behave otherwise. . . . The black experience is the feeling one has when he strikes against the enemy of black humanity by throwing a live Molotov cocktail into a white-owned building and watching it go up in flames. We know, of course, that there is more to getting rid of evil than burning buildings, but one must start somewhere.[59]

58. Gutiérrez, *Theology of Liberation*, pp. 273, 276.
59. James H. Cone, *A Black Theology of Liberation*, pp. 56-57.

If one adopts the conviction of Gutiérrez, he will not hate the enemy but will combat the enemy loving him. Love will then be an antithesis of hatred, but not of the violence he will cause the enemy to suffer.

Did Jesus of Nazareth establish this difference in His teaching and in His example? Did Paul establish it before those who hated him to death? Is the mission of the church, and of the Christian individually, to show love to the enemies of the gospel by combating them?

From an ethical perspective, José Míguez Bonino also distinguishes between love and hatred for liberating praxis: "In the mind and conscience of the Latin Americans committed to liberation, we are engaged in a project of love, not of hatred." Then he gives a few guidelines that should be followed in order to explain that love. In the first place, Míguez Bonino sees that a militant liberationist establishes his identity not in the enemy considered as a threat, but in love towards his brethren, towards his comrades in life and struggle for whom he should be ready to die. In the second place it should be recognized, says Míguez Bonino, that in every conflict there is always the dialectic of love towards the brother and hatred towards the enemy. But there is the possibility that hatred towards the enemy may be subordinated to love for the brethren. Then the struggle becomes "functional" and the possibility of affirming the humanity of the enemy during and after the conflict is opened up. "This is the kind of ethics of liberation which many—Christians and non-Christians—are trying to develop within the project of liberation."[60]

Míguez Bonino recognizes the difference between theory and practice when dealing with ethical problems. Political praxis does not lend itself to abstractions or ethical generalizations; but that does not excuse the theologian from his responsibility to develop ethical theories. The dialectic that arises in the midst of social conflict cannot be avoided. In the final analysis the leaders and the people are the ones who should decide what is correct at a particular moment, but the theoretical work can influence those decisions. "We are dealing here not with universal norms but with tentative ethical formulations that are offered as resources in the struggle."[61]

60. José Míguez Bonino, *Toward a Christian Political Ethic,* pp. 112-13.
61. Ibid., p. 109.

The explanations of Míguez Bonino may certainly seem satisfactory at a theoretical level. But questions still remain. For example, is it possible to subordinate hatred for the enemy to love for the brethren in the midst of the heat of the struggle against the enemy himself? Can a Christian manifest love to the enemy by torturing him or killing him? Is the love that Christ orders us to have towards our enemies simply the subordination of hatred to another feeling—love to those who love us—or is it a virtue—the fruit of the Spirit—that moves us to forgive the enemy and to serve him?

Another option: active non-violence. I do not deny that it should also be asked whether an oppressor who professes to believe the gospel can demonstrate true Christian love to the oppressed while he slowly kills them by starvation. But what we are talking about at this point is love and ethics in liberating praxis. If the institutionalized violence of the oppressors justifies the use of violence by the disciples of the Lord Jesus, then what is so unique about Christian love? Did Jesus love His enemies by putting them to death, or did He give Himself up on the cross to save them? Does He order us to love our enemies by killing them? Doesn't liberation theology run the risk of establishing or institutionalizing another type of violence with the name of "Christian?" Aren't we returning to the concept of "holy war?"

The fact that through the centuries not a few Christians have participated in wars and revolutions by shedding human blood does not give the church grounds for accepting and propagating a theology that approves violence.

If the church is to respond to violence with violence, how can it speak against the violence that generates greater violence? How can it break the spiral of violence? If the church opts for violence, there will be others who will struggle against violence by suffering it. Jesus was not a passive, non-violent person. On the contrary, His death on the cross was an act of personal, voluntary self-giving against violence, for the sake of justice, peace, and liberty. In the words of Leonardo Boff: "That suffering is true suffering because it was born out of the struggle against suffering. . . . This suffering is not a fatality, but rather it is assumed together with the liberating project."[62]

62. Leonardo Boff, *Jesucristo y la liberación del hombre*, p. 428.

The Christian who speaks or acts in any way against violence—
of whatever sort it might be—without arriving at violence is an
active non-violent Christian. He is not indifferent to the problem
of violence; neither does he simply observe it; he wants to do
something to solve it within the limits of human possibilities.
Active non-violence can also have its high cost: suffering violence
because of being against violence without practicing it. But the
one who suffers in that way is on the road of authentic Christian
discipleship: following Jesus.

SUMMARY AND EVALUATION

There does not yet seem to be a systematization of ecclesiological thought in liberation theology. For the time being we have
had to glean here and there among different liberationist works in
order to form at least a general idea of what they teach about the
church. The emphasis of liberation ecclesiology is definitely on
what it means *to be a church* in a revolutionary context of extreme
poverty and social injustice. And the outstanding proposal is that
the church should radically revise its nature and mission and
become converted to the cause of the poor in the liberating
struggle.

We notice immediately that liberation ecclesiology is supported
more by the sociological and theological reflection of its exponents than by a serious, careful exegesis of biblical ecclesiological
texts. There is no exposition of well-known passages like Matthew
16:16-18; 1 Corinthians 12-14; Ephesians 1-4; Colossians 1; or
1 Peter 2:1-10, to mention just a few examples. There is abundant
ecclesiological material in the New Testament, but liberation theologians do not take advantage of it as they should to give a biblical
foundation and content to their thought regarding the nature and
mission of the church.

They want to be freed of dogmatic ecclesiology, which to them
seems inadequate and unworkable for the social and political
reality of Latin America. They cry out for a true *aggiornamento,*
that is, a bringing up to date that implies a profound renewal in
the life and task of the church. They turn their backs on traditional
ecclesiocentrism that, according to them, alienates the masses of
the church and puts the church at the unconditional service of the
dominant classes. But they lean towards the political left, and their

ecclesiology does not always correspond to what the Lord of the church said about it in His written revelation. At the same time it is obvious that liberation theologians do not have a high concept of the inspiration and authority of the Scriptures, and their ecclesiology is one of the results of "the new way of doing theology."

Liberationists say that the church is a universal sacrament of salvation, that every human being is a temple of God, that the difference between the sacred and the profane no longer exists, that the church is not a non-world but "humanity itself alert to the Word," and that Christ is to be found in our fellow man and not apart from our fellow man because he is the principal sacrament of salvation. Those and many other concepts result in a secular ecumenism that encompasses not only ecclesiastical bodies but all who are concerned for social change, regardless of the possibility that they support an atheistic philosophy. The differentiating line drawn in the New Testament between the church and the world becomes more and more blurred in liberation ecclesiology.

With regard to the mission of the church we have seen that according to liberation ecclesiology the purpose of the church is not "to guarantee heaven," but to opt for the cause of the poor, to denounce the injustice of the oppressors, to announce the kingdom of God in order to "conscientize" and "politicize" the oppressed, and to participate directly in liberating praxis with a view toward establishing a socialist society that is "more just, free, and human." Liberation theologians recognize that that struggle can reach the point of physical violence, but they do not see a contradiction between the universal love of God and the violent struggle against oppressors who must be loved by fighting yet not hating them. But the contradiction continues to stand, in spite of the theological, psychological, and ethical lucubrations of the apologists concerning the use of violence by Christians in the class struggle. The example and the teachings of Jesus of Nazareth in His earthly ministry present a very difficult problem for those who advocate a "Christian violence."

As might be expected in an ecclesiology that professes to be Christian, there are several positive points in the thought of liberation theologians. For example, the teaching of neo-Catholicism regarding the possibility of salvation outside the institutional, hierarchical church is underscored; clerical arrogance is put aside by recognizing that the church is the totality of the people of God;

strong emphasis is given to the church as a community or fraternal body; it is recognized that in the past the church was allied with the powerful and became rich in the midst of a people steeped in poverty; there is a call for a profound renovation of the church; there is a demand for Christians to live a life of authentic love and total commitment to the service of one's neighbor. The Catholic theologians of liberation speak seriously of renunciation and sacrifice for the sake of the liberating cause. Their attitude moves us to ask whether we are not simply playing at being Christians, unwilling to leave our religious comfort in order to walk an extra mile for the sake of the gospel.

It is legitimate to be concerned about the enormous responsibility of the church to respond in word and deed to the cries of a society such as Latin America's, tormented by economic, political, moral, and spiritual problems. It cannot be denied that liberation theology challenges us to reevaluate our ecclesiological reflection, study its foundations, analyze the theological, historical, and cultural influences that converge on it, and bring to the fore those biblical elements that, due to those influences, we have relegated to a second or last place in our ecclesiology.

It is evident that many of us Latin American evangelicals have been satisfied with repeating an ecclesiology formulated in other latitudes, in a cultural and social context very different from that of Latin America, in a time far from our own. It is now our turn to answer the challenge of liberation theology by producing an ecclesiology that is rooted in the Scriptures and responds to the particular needs of the church and the Latin American people.

Conclusion

10

Evangelical Theology and Praxis for Latin America

In this book I have attempted to give a broad description of Latin American liberation theology and to provide a general evaluation of it. We have seen the historical and social context from which it has emerged, the currents of European thought that have stimulated it, the Protestant and neo-Catholic contributions to its development, the methodology it has employed, and some of its more important themes.

Although liberation theology is essentially political and clearly reflects a Marxist influence, I have attempted to maintain a biblical and theological emphasis in my evaluation of it. I have not been able to avoid, of course, some references to that which is social and political.

Liberation theology is a new way of doing theology. Its point of departure and hermeneutical norm is not the written revelation of God, but the social context of Latin America and the revolutionary praxis striving to create there a "new man" and a "new society" within a socialist system as a supposed manifestation of the kingdom of God.

Naturally this theology comes into conflict with capitalism and neo-colonialism; but it also differs sharply with conservative evangelical thought in the matter of biblical interpretation of the Christian faith. We have seen that liberation theologians do not have a high view of the inspiration and authority of the Scriptures. They accept modern exegesis uncritically and subject the biblical text to an ideology; as a result of that hermeneutical conditioning they give to fundamental doctrines such as Christology and ecclesiology an interpretation that is far from satisfactory for those of us who feel seriously committed to the gospel.

It is worth noting that the Vatican continues to react against liberation theology without opposing its aspirations for social justice. A recent document prepared under the direction of John Paul II and published five days before the interrogation of Leonardo Boff states:

> The "error of liberation theologians" consists in the identification of "scientific analysis" with "Marxist analysis" without critical examination. They do not take into account the fact that this analysis depends on ideological premises which are incompatible with the Christian faith and which carry a logic that leads to the "perversion of Christianity."[1]

Joseph Ratzinger, principal author of the document, has stated that it was not particularly directed at Boff and the "conversation" he was about to hold in Rome "to verify the ecclesiastical meaning of his writings."

On our part, although we reject the non-biblical foundations of liberation theology, we need to recognize that this theological system gives us conservative evangelicals a warning with regard to our social responsibility and a challenge to study the Scriptures to see what they have to say to us about Latin American social problems. Even if liberation theology goes out of style as a system or is condemned by the Vatican, its impact on the theological consciousness of Latin American Christianity may be lasting.

We conservative evangelicals can no longer afford the luxury of doing theology in social isolation. We must not answer the challenge of liberation theology by simply repeating the political arguments of its enemies in other latitudes. The hour in which we live is crucial for our society and for the church which the Lord redeemed with His blood. We need the wise counsel of our brethren in the world-wide evangelical community. But more than

1. *Prensa Libre* (Guatemala), 4 September 1984.

anything we need to lay hold of the written word of God, depend as never before on the power and guidance of the Holy Spirit, and truly live the gospel.

The evangelical response to liberation theology has to be both theological and "praxiological." It is not enough for us to become entrenched in a conservatism that closes its eyes to social reality and limits itself to repeating dogmatic formulas without explaining them or applying them to the new situation that confronts us in Latin America. We need to faithfully proclaim the gospel in terms that are relevant to that situation and live it to its final consequences. If we fulfill those conditions, we will be responding positively—much more than to liberation theology—to the teachings and exhortations of the written word of God and to the ministry of the Holy Spirit in our new life. After all, that is what is most important.

THE THEOLOGICAL RESPONSE

In the preceding chapters I have suggested some biblical elements that Latin American evangelical theology needs to emphasize or recover in order to be both faithful to the Word of God and relevant to the social situation. Here I wish to discuss in more detail some of the characteristics such a theology should have.

For the evangelical Christian there is on the one hand a theology that does not admit change because it is the word of the Lord which "abides forever" (1 Pet. 1:25). On the other hand, we are engaged in a theological task the product of which can be modified with the passage of time. It is imperative to maintain the difference between the merely human word and that which the Holy Spirit inspired, availing Himself of godly men who lived, thought, felt, and acted in close relationship with their cultural and social environment (2 Pet. 1:21; 2 Tim. 3:14-17).

Whoever studies carefully the history of theological thought knows that theology as human reflection is to a great extent the result, directly or indirectly, of the cultural and social circumstances of the different periods in which particular theologians have lived and labored. Evangelical theology is not exempt, as human reflection, from the influence of its social context. It is very difficult, therefore, to predict what Latin American theology will be like in ten or twenty years. Latin America is torn by transforming forces that could destabilize its countries and create a new social order before the end of this century. We don't exactly know where Latin America is headed if the Lord does not come soon. But we are sure that it is possible to deepen our theological roots now and suggest guidelines that should be followed in the ministry of communicating the word of God to the new Latin American society which is in gestation before our very eyes.

The evangelical theology of the future will definitely have to be *biblical* in its foundations, *ecclesiastical* in its close relationship to the community of faith, *pastoral* in its attempt to be an orientating voice for the people of God, *contextualized* with regard to that which is social and cultural, and *missionary* in its purpose to reach with the gospel those who are not Christians.

A BIBLICAL THEOLOGY

Authentically evangelical theology seeks to become grounded in the written revelation of God. Therefore, the Bible must be the main source of knowledge for the evangelical theologian and his maximum authority as well. The basis for genuine evangelical thought is not what a particular theologian says, but what the Lord says in His written Word.

It is obvious that in order to formulate a biblical theology, an effort must made to draw out the meaning of the Scriptures. Exegesis is necessary; but exegesis demands preparation, dedication, intense work, perseverance, and above all, submission to the Holy Spirit in order to be illuminated by Him. It is very easy to impose upon the Scriptures a theological scheme, whichever it might be, instead of patiently and conscientiously studying the sacred text to discover in its words both what the sacred writers wanted to express under the inspiration of the Holy Spirit and what the original readers were able to understand.

We Latin American evangelicals boast that we are people of one book: the Bible. But in reality we have not studied that book as we should in order to evaluate and improve our theological activity. In general, our theology has only been an echo of that which has been forged in other cultures. We have lacked the interest, preparation, time, and financial backing for the theological task. Besides, the conservative evangelical community has shown a preference for men of action and a certain disdain for men of reflection. There are even those in theological education who defend a functional-ism that has little esteem for academic progress: "it doesn't matter if the quality of theological training for leaders goes down as long as they are able to function." As the Latin American evangelical theologian Samuel Escobar has well stated, in some evangelical sectors "theological reflection as a form of obedience to the Word of God disappears, enslaved by an enthusiastic and effective but uncritical activism that has no time to think about the faith."[2]

It is high time for us to sit down to study the Word of God exegetically, not only in order to prove or defend our theology, but especially to discover what the biblical text has to say to us about the critical situation in which we all live. We have to go beyond systematic theologies that simply quote biblical texts in support of a particular theological system to an exegetical theology that grows directly out of the Word of God.

On the other hand it is very easy to run from our social problems by taking refuge in a meticulous exegetical exercise that does not produce a theology for the here and now of our people. We can feel very comfortable wrapped up in the study of remote biblical cultures while we turn our backs to the crude reality surrounding us. We may also take refuge in the future and become eschatolo-gists who say little or nothing about the present reality that trou-bles the Latin American people. By escaping to the past or to the future, we draw a theological arch over the distressing problems of Latin America. If there is a reference to those problems it is superficial, not deep.

We need, therefore, a greater number of *evangelical* Latin Amer-ican theologians who are rigorously trained in the biblical and theological sciences and are able to interpret the signs of the times in the light of written revelation, to adequately instruct the future pastors and teachers of God's people, and to stimulate Latin Amer-ican evangelical thought.

AN ECCLESIASTICAL THEOLOGY

What has just been said does not mean in any way that we should throw overboard everything that has been produced in the

2. Samuel Escobar, "Identidad, misión y futuro del protestantismo Latinoameri-cano."

field of theology throughout almost twenty centuries of Christianity. It would be presumptuous to believe that the Holy Spirit has kept silence during all that time and that He will not begin to speak except through us—in other words, to think that no Christian before us has had the assistance of the Paraclete in the study and exposition of the Scriptures. There is a whole doctrinal heritage, a tradition—in the best sense of the term—that we should neither despise nor exalt above the written revelation of God. The evangelical theologian should not be a stranger to any of the centuries-long process of doctrinal reflection of the church. Exegetical theology should be accompanied by historical theology.

It would be foolish to ignore the wealth of teaching in the primitive Fathers, to underestimate the great creeds of the universal church, or to take lightly the hard work of biblical exegetes of more recent times in order to gain the approval of iconoclasts who only destroy without building anything positive from a biblical point of view.

It is also necessary to be up to date with regard to what is happening in the theological world and to take advantage especially of the contributions that others make to the advance of evangelical theology in Latin America. We are indebted to the past and to the present for our theological task in Latin America.

By ecclesiastical theology we also understand a theology formed in close relationship with the community of faith. It is one thing to talk about *ecclesiological* theology, and something very different to refer to an *ecclesiastical* theology. Ecclesiological theology can remain on a purely theoretical plane, analyzing the doctrine of the church in the Scriptures and in the reflective work of theologians. That theology can be produced in isolation, apart from the community of faith. In his ivory tower the theologian thinks about the church, and from there he sends his message without seriously committing himself to any ecclesiastical group. He speaks about the church and talks to the church from outside, as a stranger.

We need the communion and the advice of our brethren in the faith, especially the advice of our colleagues in the ministry of the gospel. Evangelical theology should arise from the warmth of that fellowship and under the light of that counsel. The academic theologian should also be an ecclesiastical theologian, fully identified with the people of God.

A PASTORAL THEOLOGY

If theology is produced within the community of faith it will necessarily be pastoral because it will emerge in answer to the questions and needs of the Christian people. It will be a theology carried out from the written word of God to the concrete situation of Latin American evangelicals. This theology will not be aloof to human existence, occupied only with technicalities that are interesting to academic theologians but not to the rest of the evangelical people. An esoteric theology produced for experts is useless from the point of view of the interests of the kingdom of God if it does not come down from its highly academic pedestal in order to spiritually edify the people who occupy the pews in the churches.

The subjects that pastoral theology should treat in the context of the Latin American evangelical church are many. Among them are those related to the nature and mission of the church itself and the duties of Christians in their daily relationships with the family, the church, and society.

All of the fundamental elements of the evangelical creed should be expounded biblically with special reference to the Latin American church. Even the theological basis of our evangelical liturgy will have to be evaluated by means of a careful and objective exegesis of the biblical text. We will need to ask, for example, whether in our public worship we ought to simply imitate the liturgy of other cultures or whether there is freedom in the gospel to worship the Lord in ways that will better respond to the feelings of our own people. One of the more important questions that pastoral theology has to answer on the basis of biblical exegesis is what it means to be the church of the Lord in countries troubled by the process of social change.

A CONTEXTUALIZED THEOLOGY

Contextualization may be understood as the effort we must make in order for theology to be relevant to our own culture. This relevance cannot be achieved apart from dialogue between theology and our social and cultural context.

In the case of evangelical theology and its emphasis on biblical exegesis it must be remembered that exegetical work can fulfill

the requirement of investigating what the sacred writer communicated to his original readers. But the bridge must still be laid
between the culture of biblical times and our own. That is true
cross-culturalization. We have to investigate what the biblical text
meant for those readers and determine what the meaning of that
text teaches us at the end of the twentieth century in the Latin
American context.

The report of the Willowbank Consultation on the Gospel and
Culture (January 1978) states that for a contemporary understanding of the Word of God it is necessary to go beyond the popular
method that approaches the words of the biblical text "without
any awareness that the writer's cultural context differs from the
reader's," and to go beyond the historical method which "takes
with due seriousness the original historical and cultural context."
The contextual method of approaching the Scriptures that the
report recommends "takes seriously the cultural context of the
contemporary readers as well as of the biblical text, and recognizes
that a dialogue must develop between the two."[3]

In Latin America we need to ask the biblical text not only the
traditional questions related to the needs of the individual and to
the hereafter. We also have to ask the questions of a social nature
that are heard outside the church. There are fundamental questions that concern every human being, in any time and place; but
each generation and each social group also has its own questions
which must be answered. It may be that some of the questions of
yesterday do not have the same importance today, and that the
questions of a particular society are not the most important ones
for another social group.

Latin American evangelical theology should represent at least an
attempt to answer questions troubling Latin Americans. The biblical meaning should be studied in interaction with those questions,
but it will not be replaced by them or by an answer that might
violate the sacred text. The dialogue between Scripture and the
social context should not have the purpose of injecting meaning
into the biblical text. That text already has a meaning of its own
which we have to relate to our own Latin American situation.

The goal is not to attribute to the text a meaning foreign to it,
but to draw out the meaning it already possesses and to relate it,

3. *The Willowbank Report: Report of a Consultation on Gospel and Culture,* pp.
10-11.

without distortions, to the needs of the individual and society. If it could be modified by the whim of the interpreter or in response to social transformations, Scripture would cease to be the supreme and abiding norm for the faith and conduct of the church in every time and place. Biblical meaning would be at the mercy of different moods of the interpreter and different situations in society. We would not have a stable meaning on which we could depend in order to make the right choices and live in this changing world in a way that is pleasing to God.

It should also be pointed out that by "the biblical text" we mean "the whole counsel of God." One of the main problems in traditional evangelical theology has been its tendency to use only certain biblical sections and to limit the meaning of the Scriptures to the sphere of the individual and to "spiritual" things. Thus, for example, prominence has been given to the New Testament to the detriment of the Old Testament, and only the spiritual, individual, ecclesiastical, and eternal aspects of the salvation of Christ have been emphasized. In some cases even the sense of community that the New Testament teaches with regard to the church has been lost.

Two decades ago the majority of Latin American evangelicals gave no importance to "the social implications of the gospel." Meanwhile, a new theology was taking form on the continent with a pendular movement towards the political left. Theological liberationism offered to fill the void that the preconciliar Catholic church and traditional evangelical hermeneutics had left in Latin American Christianity. Deluded by the splendor of an ideology robed in theological pronouncements, liberation theologians urge people to take refuge in a hermeneutic that ends up distorting the meaning of the biblical text.

There is no need to distort the Scripture in order to answer the questions of our countrymen. But we must bring back into focus those biblical elements that we have forgotten. The Bible abounds with teachings about the dignity of the human being (including both sexes); liberty and slavery; personal and social justice; private property; wealth and poverty; labor relations; peace and war; family responsibilities and privileges; the origin and nature of the State; the duties and limitations of civil power; civic duties of the Christian; Christian philanthropy ("good works" as a fruit of salvation);

and human relationships within the family, in the community of faith, in the civil order, and on the international scene.

The Scriptures contain great ethical principles which the Christian community should follow and proclaim in order to truly be the salt and light of the earth. It is worth noting that non-Christian leaders have emerged as spokesmen for those biblical principles that the church has not communicated. Contemporary movements of social vindication have borrowed from the Bible some of their teachings about the dignity and freedom of men. While the church has kept silence, others have raised their voices. All we have to do to remedy the situation is restore the teachings of the Bible, "announcing the whole counsel of God."

A MISSIONARY THEOLOGY

Theology has to enter into dialogue with the cultural and social context in order to communicate the gospel effectively. In other words, it has to become a missionary theology. That should be the purpose of contextualization. Otherwise, as C. René Padilla says, theology loses the balance between faithfulness to "the faith which was once for all delivered to the saints" (Jude 3) and the relevance to the social situation. It either becomes merely an effort to preserve a theological tradition, or it accomodates itself to the social context, thus losing its Christian identity. "If theology in the Two-thirds World is to be both relevant and faithful, it must be based on a missiological hermeneutic."[4] We have to contextualize the gospel in oder to fulfill the mission that the Master has given us (Matt. 28:18-20).

Everything said here about a Latin American theology suggests that our task will not be to add something to the gospel or to take something away from it, but rather to emphasize those biblical elements that have not received enough attention in our theological task or to recover those that we have forgotten. Our task will be to provide a biblical answer for the questions and needs of the Latin American people.

THE ANSWER OF CHRISTIAN PRAXIS

In Chapter Eight I said that Jesus did not come to establish another religious group or another political party, but to establish

---

4. C. René Padilla, "Toward a Biblical Foundation for a Two-Thirds World Evangelical Theology," p. 35.

a new community, the community of the kingdom of God, sustained and characterized by love, humility, justice, peace, service, and harmony among men of good will. We understand as evangelicals that that community is made up of all those who have been born again by the power of the Word and the Holy Spirit. It is the community of those who have become sons of God by believing in the name of the Lord Jesus (John 1:11-13). This is the church, the Body of Christ, called to live and proclaim the gospel in the midst of society, not apart from the world but in the world, yet without letting itself be contaminated by the world.

The church is the people of God in this era, between the two advents of the Lord Jesus on earth (1 Pet. 2:9-10). The church is the community of the kingdom of God in the midst of "the kingdoms of this world." The apostle Paul says that believers in Jesus Christ have been liberated from the power of darkness and "transferred . . . to the kingdom of His beloved Son" (Col. 1:13). We also read in Revelation 1:6 that Christ has made us "a kingdom, priests to His God and Father." The church is the agent of the present kingdom of God. At the same time, it is called to proclaim and exemplify the virtues of the kingdom to come. If that kingdom is to be characterized by the outpouring of the Holy Spirit upon all humanity, by universal justice, peace, and brotherhood, the world should see here and now, in the conduct of each individual Christian and of the church in its totality, an anticipation of those and other blessings that Messiah will bring in fullness for all the peoples of earth.

How can we talk of that future outpouring of the Spirit and not allow Him to fill us now so that we may be able to live authentically the Christian life in the home, in the congregation, and in society? How can we talk of a justice that will reign among all peoples of the world and not be just today in our personal, family, and social life in order to support the cause of justice in society with God-given authority? How can we talk of the peace that all human beings will enjoy and not follow today peace and holiness in our personal, family, and social life? How can we talk about future universal brotherhood and love and not love each other today as the Master has commanded us?

The church is the agent of the present kingdom of God and the standard-bearer of the kingdom to come. All of that places on us a serious ethical responsibility before God and before society. We have a heavenly calling to fulfill on this planet: to live and proclaim the kingdom of God. That is what it means to be the church today in the midst of social whirlwinds. The world should *hear* the gospel, but it should also *see it* incarnated in the life of those of us who proclaim it.

Our theological response to the Word of God and to the great problems of Latin American society should be backed up by an authentically Christian praxis. We have to be Christians like the disciples who were deservingly given that glorious name in apostolic days (Acts 11). In the Latin American evangelical community many of us run the risk of becoming accommodated to the prevailing situation and playing at being Christians on Sunday mornings in servile imitation of a middle class Christianity that comes to us from affluent western societies, strangers to the painful drama that millions of Latin Americans are living.

That kind of Christianity can easily convert the churches into "self-edification clubs," as a professor of Christian education said in a North American theological seminary. It can also become the Christianity of "cheap grace," of which the young German theologian Dietrich Bonhoeffer spoke. It is sad to confess it, but there has been much of "cheap grace" in our evangelizing efforts in Latin America. We have frequently preached a gospel of "supply" without "demands," motivated in some cases by the desire to get "decisions" and to publish statistics that in the final analysis promote a personality cult. The search for a church growth that is no more than numerical is also expressed in preaching that offers personal happiness, peace in the home, physical health, professional success, economic prosperity, and the solution to all the problems of this life. It is a preaching that does not insist as it should on the fact that the Lord calls us primarily to solve the problem of our sin by means of faith in Him and His redemptive work, and that He is searching for *sinners* who are ready to become His *followers* in whatever circumstances of life may be theirs in this world.

The gospel is being so cheapened in our environment that there are those who prefer, in order to win converts, not to point out the abysmal difference that exists between the way of authentic Christian discipleship and those "Christianities" that in their doctrinal schemes deny the foundations of New Testament faith. In that way an attempt is being made to soften the gospel so that a greater number of persons may accept it without difficulty. That is not what Jesus preached. He said: "If any one wishes to come after Me, let him deny himself, and take up his cross, and follow Me" (Matt. 16:24).

Juan Luis Segundo has more than enough reason to say that the gospel is not "cheap merchandise." Genuine Christian discipleship has a cost that can be very high, according to the Lord's will. We are saved by the grace of God, by means of faith, to serve Him; and if the Master so demands it, we may also have to suffer and even die for His name. That is very strange language for those people who seek an evangelical church in order to be happy according to the world's idea of happiness.

Jürgen Moltmann quotes the Catholic theologian J. B. Metz, who describes the bourgeois church as a supermarket where products for all tastes are offered at very low prices. Moltmann says that in the New World there are so many varieties of denominations and so many churches that nobody has to worry about any problem that might emerge in his own congregation; it is very easy to go to another one that might be better suited to his taste. In the competition on the religious market, "the winner—as in other markets too—will be whoever has the cheapest and most entertaining offer." Finally, the church easily falls victim to the seduction of "class" churches, in which "social 'like' is drawn to 'like': birds of a feather flock together."[5]

In Latin America there are evangelical churches that run the risk of becoming classists, indifferent to the great majorities who suffer the most deplorable results of our social and economic underdevelopment. It seems that the middle class, which has struggled to reach that height, easily becomes devoted to preserving its achievements and even to improving them by climbing one more step up the social ladder, all the while turning its back on the less privileged classes. The churches that emerge from that social mobility can easily forget the demands of Christian discipleship and the example of the Lord Jesus, who had compassion on the multitudes who were scattered and mistreated like sheep without a shepherd.

A North American evangelical pastor from the middle class noticed that his church was bound to itself, to its traditions in

5. Jürgen Moltmann, *The Power of the Powerless*, pp. 160-61.

liturgy and work methods, to its social class, to its way of being a church in a great urban center. Having a new perception of the city itself as a mission field, he encouraged the members of his congregation to take an interest also in the neglected groups, including hobos, drug addicts, and even homosexuals. His emphasis is more spiritual that social, but he had broken chains in the area of life and mission of an urban church that had not taken an interest in other social classes. His congregation is scattered throughout the city, serving the neediest sectors. The sanctuary can accomodate only 275 people, but the number of members came to more than one thousand in 1982, up from only one hundred in 1970.[6] But the most important thing is not the numerical growth but the new type of ministry that the pastor and his church are carrying out.

Without a doubt many of our churches in Latin America have to be freed from their chains in order to serve other social segments. We must add that the challenge goes beyond the merely spiritual. It also includes the millions who cry out for social justice. The church cannot become deaf to that cry. We are told that we should not only see the effects of our social problems but also their causes, and then do something about them, in order to be consistent with our Christian faith.

This great challenge is unavoidable, and it has resulted in an awakening of social consciousness among evangelicals at the level of world consultations and congresses. The proof of that statement is seen in documents such as the Wheaton Declaration (1966), the Lausanne Covenant (1974), the Declaration on Evangelism and Social Responsibility (Grand Rapids, Michigan, 1982), and the Documents of Group III, Wheaton Conference (1983). It appears that the process of reflection and conscientization on the social responsibility of the evangelical church is irreversible. It has been a good step to begin with biblical and theological reflection on so controversial an issue. What many of us Latin American evangelicals hope is that those who are the most serene and stable in the biblical faith will participate, so that the evangelical church may fully assume its social responsibility without straying from the path marked out by the written revelation of God. May our *action* be motivated and directed, always and everywhere, by that *revelation*.

6. Frank R. Tillapaugh, *The Church Unleashed* (Ventura, Cal.: Regal, 1982).

Bibliography

Abbott, Walter M., ed. *Documents of Vatican II*. New York: Guild, 1966.
Alves, Rubem. *A Theology of Human Hope*. New York: World, 1969; reprint ed., St. Meinrad, Ind.: Abbey, 1975.
—Spanish edition, *Religión: ¿Opio o instrumento de liberación?* Montevideo: Tierra Nueva, 1970.
América hoy. (See ISAL.)
América Latina: Movilización popular y fe cristiana. (See ISAL.)
Anderson, Gerald H., and Stransky, Thomas F., eds. *Mission Trends No. 4: Liberation Theologies in North America and Europe.* New York: Paulist; Grand Rapids: Eerdman's, 1979.
Arana Quiroz, Pedro. *Providencia y revolución.* Lima: El Estandarte de la Verdad, 1970.
———. "La Revelación de Dios y la teología en Latinoamérica." In *El debate contemporaneo sobre la Biblia.* Barcelona: Ediciones Evangélicas Europeas, 1972.
Assmann, Hugo. *Opresión-Liberación: Desafío a los cristianos.* Montevideo: Tierra Nueva, 1971.
———. *Theology for a Nomad Church.* Translated by Paul Burns. Maryknoll, N.Y.: Orbis, 1975.
—Spanish edition, *Teología desde la praxis de la liberación.* Salamanca: Ediciones Sígueme, 1973. Includes Part 2: "Ejercicios políticos de la fe" not included in the English edition.
———, ed. *Pueblo Oprimido, Señor de la historia.* Montevideo: Tierra Nueva, 1972. Papers from the ISAL symposium at Buenos Aires, June 1971.

Assmann, Hugo, Jose Blanes, and Luis Bach. "Exigencias de una opción." *Cristianismo y Sociedad*, no. especial, 3a. & 4a. entregas (1972).

Blazquez, Feliciano. *Helder Camara: El grito del pobre.* Salamanca: Ediciones Sígueme, 1972.

Boff, Leonardo. *La Fe en la periferia del mundo.* Santander, Spain: Sal Terrae, 1981.

——. *Jesucristo y la liberación del hombre.* Translated from the Portuguese by F. Cantalapiedra. Madrid: Ediciones Cristiandad, 1981. Includes the contents of *Jesucristo el liberador.*

——. *Jesus Christ Liberator.* Translated by Patrick Hughes. Maryknoll, N.Y.: Orbis, 1979.

——. *Teología desde el cautiverio.* Bogotá: Indo-American Press Service, 1975.

Camara, Helder. *Espiral de violencia.* Salamanca: Ediciones Sígueme, 1970.

"Camilo Torres: ¿Sacerdote o guerrillero?" *Protesta* (Caracas: EPLA), no. 20.

Cardenal, Ernesto. *The Gospel in Solentiname.* Translated by Donald D. Walsh. 4 vols. Maryknoll, N.Y.: Orbis, 1976-1982. Spanish edition, *El Evangelio de Solentiname.* 2 vols. Salamanca: Ediciones Sígueme, 1975-1977.

Castro, Emilio. "La Creciente presencia de criterios de interpretación histórica en la evolución de la hermenéutica biblica." In *Pueblo Oprimido, Señor de la historia.* Edited by Hugo Assmann. Montevideo: Tierra Nueva, 1972.

CELAM [Consejo Episcopal Latinoamericano]. *Conflicto social y compromiso cristiano en América Latina.* Bogotá: Consejo Episcopal Latinoaméricano—CELAM, 1976.

CELAM. *Exegésis, evangelización y pastoral.* Bogotá: Secretariado General del Consejo Episcopal Latinoaméricano, 1976.

——. *La Iglesia en la actual transformación de América Latina a la luz del Concilio.* 2 vols. Bogotá: CELAM, 1969. Documents of the Second Latin American Conference of Bishops, Medellín, 1968.

——. *Liberación: Diálogos en el CELAM.* Bogotá: Secretariado General del CELAM, 1974.

Chaponay, Henryanne de. "¿A dondé va la acción ecuménica en América Latina?" *Cristianismo y Sociedad*, nos. 24-25, 3a. & 4a. entregas (1970).

Comblin, José [Joseph]. *Cristianismo y desarrollo. Colección IPLA, 5.* Quito: Don Bosco, 1970.

Cone, James H. *Black Theology and Black Power.* New York: Seabury, 1969.

——. *A Black Theology of Liberation.* Philadelphia: Lippincott, 1970.

Costas, Orlando. *A Theology of the Crossroads in Contemporary Latin America: Missiology in Mainline Protestantism, 1969-1974.* Amsterdam: Rodopi, 1976.

Cristianismo y Sociedad. Montevideo: ISAL. Publication of Iglesia y Sociedad en América Latina (Church and Society in Latin America).

Croatto, J. Severino. *Exodus: A Hermeneutic of Freedom*. Translated by Salvator Attanasio. Maryknoll, N.Y.: Orbis, 1981.

Davies, J. G. *Christians, Politics, and Violent Revolution*. Maryknoll, N.Y.: Orbis, 1976.

El debate contemporaneo sobre la Biblia. By Peter Savage et al. Barcelona: Ediciones Evangélicas Europeas, 1972. Papers presented at the First Continental Consultation of the Latin American Theological Fraternity.

Duquesne, Jacques. *La Izquierda de Cristo*. Translated from the French by Manuel Vasquez. Barcelona: Plaza & Janes, 1973.

Dussel, Enrique. "De Medellín a Puebla: Un análisis contextual de la Iglesia Católica en América Latina (1968-1969)." *Pastoralia* (San Jose, Costa Rica) 2, 3 (September 1979): 31-81.

———. *History and the Theology of Liberation: A Latin American Perspective*. Translated by John Drury. Maryknoll, N.Y.: Orbis, 1976.

———. *A History of the Church in Latin America: Colonialism to Liberation (1492-1979)*. translated by Alan Neeley. Grand Rapids: Eerdmans, 1971.

"Educación para un despertar de la conciencia: una charla con Paulo Freire." *Cristianismo y sociedad*, nos. 29-30, la. entrega (1972).

Ellacuria, Ignacio. *Freedom Made Flesh: The Mission of Christ and His Church*. Maryknoll, N.Y.: Obris, 1976.

—translation of *Teología política*. San Salvador: Ediciones del Secretariado Social Interdiodesano, 1973.

Encuentro y desafío. (See ISAL.)

Enriquez, Jose Ramon. "Ernesto Cardenal: Nuestro delito es anunciar el paraiso." *La Hora Dominical* (Guatemala), May 23, 1976.

Escobar, Samuel. "Beyond Liberation Theology: Evangelical Missiology in Latin America." *International Bulletin of Missionary Research* 6 (July 1982): 108-114.

———. "Identidad, misión y futuro del protestanismo Latinoaméricano." *Diálogo Teológico* 13 (April 1979).

Fe cristiana y cambio social en América Latina. (See Instituto Fe y Secularidad.)

Freire, Paulo. "Carta a un joven teólogo." *Selecciones de teología* (Barcelona) 13, 50 (April-June 1974).

———. *La educación como practica de la libertad*. Montevideo: Tierra Nueva, 1970.

———. *Pedagogy of the Oppressed*. Translated by Myra Bergman Ramos. New York: Herder & Herder, 1970. Spanish edition, *Pedagogía del oprimido*. Lima, 1971. This edition includes "Bibliografia de y sobre Paulo Freire," by Hugo Assmann, pp. 247-50.

Freixedo, S. *Mi Iglesia duerme*. Rio Piedras, Puerto Rico: Isla, 1969.

Galilea, Segundo. *¿Los pobres nos evangelizan?* Bogotá: Indo-American Press Service, 1976.

———. *Teología de la liberación: ensayo de síntesis*. Bogotá: Indo-American Press Service, 1976.

Garland, Alfredo. *Como lobos rapaces*. Lima: SAPEI, 1978.

Gonzalez Faus, J. I. "La teología Latinoaméricano de la liberación." *Actualidad Bibliografica* (Barcelona) (1973).

Gutiérrez, Gustavo. *Hacia una teología de la liberación.* Montevideo, 1969; Bogotá: Indo-American Press Service, 1971.

———. *Liberación, opción de la iglesia en la decada del 70.* Bogotá, 1970.

———. "Liberation, Theology, and Proclamation." In *The Mystical and Political Dimension of the Christian Faith,* pp. 57-77. Edited by Claude Geffre and Gustavo Gutiérrez. Concilium, 96 (N. S. 6, 10). New York: Herder & Herder, 1974.

———. "Notes for a Theology of Liberation." *Theological Studies,* 31 (1970): 243-61. Translation of "Apuntes para una teología de la liberación." *Cristianismo y Sociedad* 24-25 (1970): 6-22. Also condensed in *Theology Digest* 19 (1971): 141-47.

———. *La pastoral de le iglesia en América Latina.* Montevideo: Centro de Documentacion, 1968.

———. *The Power of the Poor in History.* Translated by Robert E. Barr. Maryknoll, N.Y.: Orbis, 1983. Spanish edition, *La fuerza historica de los pobres.* Lima: Centro de Estudios y Publicaciones, 1979.

———. *A Theology of Liberation: History, Politics and Salvation.* Translated and edited by Caridad Inda and John Eagleson. Maryknoll, N.Y.: Orbis, 1973.

———. *We Drink from Our Own Well: The Spiritual Journey of a People.* Translated by Matthew J. O'Connell. Maryknoll, N.Y.: Orbis, 1984. Spanish edition, *Beber en su proprio pozo.* Lima: Centro de Estudios y Publicaciones, 1983.

Gutiérrez, Juan. *The New Libertarian Gospel: Pitfalls of the Theology of Liberation.* Translated by Paul Burns. Chicago: Franciscan Herald Press, 1977.

—translation of *Teología de la liberación: Evaporación de la teología.* Mexico City: Ediciones Jus, 1975.

Guzman Campos, German. *El Padre Camilo Torres.* Mexico City: Siglo XXI, 1969.

Herring, Herbert. *A History of Latin America.* New York: Knopf, 1962.

La Iglesia en la actual transformación de América Latina a la luz del Concilio. (See CELAM.)

Instituto Fe y Secularidad. *Fe cristiana y cambio social en América Latina.* Edited by J. Alvarez Bolado. Salamanca: Ediciones Sígueme, 1973. Documents of the Encounter at El Escorial, Spain, 1972.

Interdonato, Francisco. *Teología Latinoaméricana: ¿Teología de la liberación?* Bogotá: Ediciones Paulinas, 1978.

ISAL [Iglesia y Sociedad en America Latina]. *América hoy.* Montevideo: ISAL, 1966. Documents from the Second Latin American Consultation on Church and Society, El Tabo, Chile, January 12-21, 1966.

———. *América Latina: Movilización popular y fe cristiana.* Monteviedo: ISAL, 1971. Documents of the Fourth Continental Assembly, Ñaña, Peru, July 1971.

———. *Encuentro y desafío.* Buenos Aires: La Aurora, 1961. Documents of the First Latin American Consultation, Huampani, Peru, July 1961.

———. *Pueblo oprimido.* (See Assmann, Hugo, ed.)

———. *La responsibilidad social del cristiano.* Montevideo: ISAL, 1964.

Kirk, J. Andrew. "La Biblia y su hermenéutica en relación con la teología protestante en América Latina." In *El debate contemporaneo sobre la Biblia.* Barcelona: Ediciones Evangélicas Euporeas, 1972.

———. "Exegésis técnica y anuncio de la fe." In *Exegésis, evangelización y pastoral.* Bogotá: Secretariado General del Consejo Episcopal Latinoamericano, 1976.

———. *Liberation Theology: An Evangelical View from the Third World.* Atlanta: John Knox Press, 1979.

———. *Theology Encounters Revolution.* Leicester, England: Inter-Varsity Press, 1980.

Kloppenberg, Bonaventura. "Cuestiones pendientes en la acción cristiana para la liberación." In *Conflicto social y compromisa cristiano en América Latina.* Bogota: Consejo Episcopal Latinoaméricano—CELAM, 1976.

Lehmann, Karl. "Problemas metodológicos y hermenéuticos de la teología de la liberación." In *Teología de la liberación: Documentos de la Comision Teológica Internacional.* Madrid: Biblioteca de Autores Cristianos, 1978.

Liberación: Dialogos en el CELAM. (See CELAM.)

Lopez Trujillo, Alfonso. "Medellín: una mirada global." in *Medellín: Reflexiones en el CELAM.* Madrid: Biblioteca de Autores Cristianos, 1977.

Lorscheider, Aloisio. "Que es el CELAM? (What is CELAM?)." In *Medellín: Reflexiones en el CELAM.* Madrid: Biblioteca de Autores Cristianos, 1977.

MacKay, John A. *The Other Spanish Christ.* New York: Macmillan, 1932.

Maldonado, Luis. *El menester de la prédicación.* Salamanca: Ediciones Sígueme, 1972.

Marx, Karl. *Sobre la religion.* Edited by Hugo Assmann and Reyes Mate. Salamanca: Ediciones Sígueme, 1974.

McCann, Dennis. *Christian Realism and Liberation Theology: Practical Theologies in Creative Conflict.* Maryknoll, N.Y.: Orbis, 1981.

Medellín: Reflexiones en el CELAM. Madrid: Biblioteca de Autores Cristianos, 1977.

Metz, J. B. *Antropocentrismo cristiano.* Salamanca: Ediciones Sígueme, 1972.

———. *Theology of the World.* Translated by William Glen-Doepel. New York: Herder & Herder, 1969.

Miguelez, Xosé. *La teología de la liberación y su método.* Barcelona: Herder, 1976.

Míguez Bonino, José. *Doing Theology in a Revolutionary Situation.* Philadelphia: Fortress Press, 1975.

—Spanish edition, *La fe en busca de eficacia.* Salamanca: Ediciones Sígueme, 1977. Contains additional material not included in English edition.

Miguez Bonino, José. "¿Partidismo o solidaridad?" *Cristianismo y Sociedad,* no. especial, 3a. & 4a. entregas (1972).

———. "Prologue." In Spanish edition of *Religión: Opio o instrumento de liberación*, pp. vii-ix. By Rubem Alves. Montevideo: Tierra Nueva, 1970.
———. *Toward a Christian Political Ethic.* Philadelphia: Fortress Press, 1983.
———. "Vision del cambio social y sus tareas desde las iglesias cristianas no-catolicas." In *Fe cristiana y cambio social en América Latina.* Salamanca: Ediciones Sígueme, 1973.
Miranda, José P. *Being and the Messiah.* Translated by John Eagleson. Maryknoll, N.Y.: Orbis, 1974.
———. *Communism in the Bible.* Maryknoll, N.Y.: Orbis, 1982.
———. *Marx Against the Marxists.* Translated by John Drury. Maryknoll, N.Y.: Orbis,1980.
———. *Marx and the Bible: A Critique of the Philosophy of Oppression.* Translated by John Eagleson. Maryknoll, N.Y.: Orbis, 1974.
Moltmann, Jürgen. *The Crucified God.* New York: Harper & Row, 1974.
———. "An Open Letter to José Míguez Bonino." *Christianity and Crisis,* 36, 5 (March 29, 1976): 57-63; reprinted in *Mission Trends No. 4,* pp. 57-70. Edited by Gerald H. Anderson and Thomas F. Stransky. New York: Paulist; Grand Rapids: Eerdmans, 1979.
———. *The Power of the Powerless.* San Francisco: Harper & Row, 1983.
———. "El Principio esperanza y teología de la esperanza." In his *Teología de la esperanza,* pp. 437-66. Salamanca: Ediciones Sígueme, 1969. Appendix to Spanish edition only.
Moltmann, Jürgen. *Theology of Hope.* New York: Harper & Row, 1967.
Nicolau, Miguel, et al.*La iglesia del Concilio.*Bilboa, Spain: El Mensajero del Corazón de Jesús, 1966.
Nunez, E. A. *El Cristo de Hispanoamérica.* Puebla, Mexico: Ediciones Las Americas, 1979.
———."The Church in the Liberation Theology of Gustavo Gutiérrez: Description and Hermeneutical Analysis." In *Biblical Interpretation and the Church. Text and Context,* edited by D. A. Carson. Exeter, England: Paternoster, 1984.
Oliveros Maqueo, Roberto. *Liberación y teología.* Mexico City: Ediciones Centro de Reflexion Teologica, 1977.
Padilla, C. René. "Iglesia y Sociedad en América Latina." In *Fe cristiana y Latinoamérica hoy,* pp. 119-47. Edited by C. René Padilla. Buenos Aires; Ediciones Certeza, 1974.
———. "Mensaje Biblico y revolución." *Certeza* (Buenos Aires), 10, 39 (January-March 1970): 196-201.
———. "La teología de la liberación: una evaluación crítica." *Mision* (Buenos Aires), 1, 2 (July-September 1982): 16-21.
———. "Toward a Biblical Foundation for a Two-thirds World Evangelical Theology." *Theolgical Fraternity Bulletin,* no. 4 (1982), no. 1 (1983): 29-36.
———. "¿Un nuevo Gustavo Gutiérrez?" *Mision,* 2, 2 (April-June 1983): 21.
———. "Una nueva manera de hacer teología." *Mision,* 1, 1 (March-June 1982): 20-23.

Padilla, C. René, ed. *Fe cristiana y Latinoamérica hoy.* Buenos Aires: Ediciones Certeza, 1974.

Pastoral Team of Bambamarca, Peru. *Vamos caminando.* Lima: Centro de Estudios y Publicaciones, 1977.

Perez, Pablo. *Misión y liberación.* Mexico City: Publicaciones El Faro, 1976.

"Primer Encuentro Latinoamericano de Cristianos por el Socialismo." *Cristianismo y Sociedad,* nos. 29-30, la. entrega (1972).

Sabugal, S. *¿Liberación y secularización?* Barcelona: Herder, 1978.

Santa Ana, Julio de. "Algunas referencias teológicas actuales al sentido de la acción social." In *La responsabilidad social del cristiano.* Montevideo: ISAL, 1964.

———. "ISAL, un movimiento en marcha." *Cuadernos en Marcha,* no. 29 (September 1969).

———. *Protestantismo, cultura y sociedad.* Buenos Aires: La Aurora, 1970.

Segundo, Juan Luis. "Capitalism-Socialism." In *La nueva frontera de la teología en América Latina.* Salamanca: Ediciones Sígueme, 1977.

———. *De la sociedad a la teología.* Buenos Aires: Carlos Lohle, 1970.

———. *The Liberation of Theology.* Translated by John Drury. Maryknoll, N.Y.: Orbis, 1976.

———. *Masas y minorías en la dialéctica divina de la liberación.* Buenos Aires: La Aurora, 1973.

———. *The Sacraments Today.* His Theology for Artisans of a New Humanity, vol. 4. Translated by John Drury. Maryknoll, N.Y.: Orbis, 1974.

Shaull, Richard. *Encounter with Revolution.* New York: Haddam House, 1955.

———. "Perspectiva teológica de los cambios revolucionarios." In *Hacia una revolución responsable.* Buenos Aires: La Aurora, 1970.

I Simposio sobre teología de la liberación. Bogota: Presencia, 1970.

Sobrino, Jon. *Christology at the Crossroads: A Latin American Approach.* Translated by John Drury. Maryknoll, N.Y.: Orbis, 1978.

———. *Jesús en América Latina.* Santander, Spain: Sal Terrae, 1982.

Steinsleger, José. "La meta comun del cristianismo y el marxismo." *La Hora Dominical* (Guatemala), March 7, 1976.

Torres, Camilo. *Cristianismo y revolución.* Mexico City: Ediciones Era, 1972.

Tschuy, Theo. "El Consejo Mundial de Iglesia y América Latina." In *De la iglesia y la sociedad.* Montevideo: Tierra Nueva, 1971.

Valverde, Carlos. *Los orígenes del marxismo.* Madrid: Biblioteca de Autores Cristianos, 1974.

Volf, Miroslav. "Doing and Interpreting: An Examination of the Relationship Between Theory and Practice in Latin American Liberation Theology." *Themelios,* N. s. 8, 3 (April 1983): 11-19.

The Willowbank Report: Report of a Consultation on Gospel and Culture. Lausanne Occasional Papers, 2. Wheaton, Ill.: Lausanne Committee for World Evangelization, 1978.

Zahrnt, Heinz. *The Question of God: Protestant Theology in the Twentieth Century.* Translated by R. A. Wilson. New York: Harcourt, Brace, Jovanovich, 1969.

General Index

Adam, Karl, 85
Albrecht, Paul, 65
Alves, Rubem, 43, 72-74, 124-25
Assmann, Hugo, 43, 48, 62, 100,
    126, 132, 141, 146-49, 207,
    214, 263-64
Atheism, 87
Authority of Scripture, 142-43,
    150-52, 250-51

Barth, Karl, 37-38
Biblical theology for Latin Amer-
    ica, 280-81
Bloch, Ernst, 42, 47-48, 197, 198
Boff, Leonardo, 207, 217-20, 232,
    245-47, 278
Bonhoeffer, Dietrich, 39, 54
Bonino, Jose Miguez, 45, 48, 49,
    57, 67, 98, 270-71
Brown, Raymond E., 189
Brown, Robert McAfee, 62, 89-90
Bultmann, Rudolph, 38-44

Camara, Helder, 105-9

Capitalism, 56-57, 117, 124-26,
    152
Cardenal, Ernesto, 101-3
Castro, Emilio, 54, 64
Catholicism, Latin American, 19-
    20, 26
    liberalism in, 23-24
    liberation theology in, 11, 30,
      83-112
    revolution ferment in Latin
      America, 100-112
    social involvement, 88-90
CELAM, 97-100, 106, 110-12
Charity, 138
Christ
    as liberator, 201-204
    unity in, 251-54
Christian violence, 267-72
Christology, 149, 217-20, 228,
    235-39
    of liberation theology, 207-40
Church
    conversion to world, 244-45

and liberation, 241-74
mission of, 254-72
political option, 264-67
unity, 248-54
Church and society in Latin America. *See* ISAL
Columbus, Christopher, 18-19
Communism, 105
Contextualized theology for Latin America, 283-86
Council of Chalcedon, 216-17
Creation, 184-86

de Chaponay, Henryanne, 63
de Chardin, Pierre Teilhard, 184, 219
Denunciation, 260
Developmentalism, 29-30, 88, 97, 118-20, 132
Dussel, Enrique, 46, 99-100, 111, 114-18

Ebeling, Gerhard, 39
Ecclesiastical theology for Latin America, 281-82
Ecclesiology of liberation, 241-74
Economic development, 94-96
Economics, 91, 95-96
Ecumenical movement, 63-65, 86
Education, 57-61
Election and creation, 185-86
Ellacuria, Ignacio, 267-69
Enriquez, Jose Ramon, 102
Eschatological salvation, 197-204
Eschatology, 123
Escobar, Samuel, 281
European theology
effect on ISAL, 54-55
influence on liberation theology, 35-52, 115-17
Evangelical theology for Latin America, 277-91
Existentialism, 38-40
Exodus of Israel, 78-79, 186-95

Faith, 155, 193-95, 200-01
Faus, Jose I. Gonzalez, 58, 152, 155
Form criticism, 210
Franco, Leonardo, 67-68
Freire, Paulo, 54, 57-61, 72, 100

Galilea, Segundo, 132, 133, 137, 138-39, 146
Garaudy, Roger, 56
Garland, Alfred, 113
Gera, Lucio, 120
God, 153-54, 157-58
Gogarten, Friedrich, 39
Guevara, Che, 72
Gutiérrez, Gustavo, 43-45, 49, 100, 115-16, 120-24, 126, 139-40, 144-46, 175-206, 224-25, 228-29, 243-44, 248, 255, 258, 263, 264, 269-270

Hermeneutics of liberation theology, 143-59
Hope, 155, 198
Human rights, 25
Humanism, 37, 56
Humanization, 78

Ideology, 193-95
Illich, Ivan, 117, 118
Independence movement in Latin America, 21-22
Inspiration of Scripture. *See* Scripture
Intrahistorical salvation, 183-84
ISAL, 26, 53-82
continental assemblies, 65-77
demise of, 77
European theology and, 54-55
local church needs, 74-77
Marxist influence, 55-57
revolutionary involvement, 69-70

view of Scripture, 78-80

Jesus, 155
  as liberator, 207-40
  death, 229-35
  earthly ministry, 224-29
  political implications, 224-25
Judgment, 154, 157
Justice, 157

King, Martin Luther, 268
Kingdom of God, 204, 226, 262-64
Kirk, J. Andrew, 51, 78-80, 113, 153, 183, 190, 207
Kung, Hans, 181-82

Latin America
  biblical theology for, 277-91
  Catholicism in, 19-20
  Christian praxis, 287-91
  colonization, 18-20
  history of, 18-26
  independence movement, 21-22
  liberalism, 21, 22-26
  oppression in, 18-20
  Protestantism in, 22-23
  revolutionary theology, 64
  socialism in, 23-24
Latin American Episcopal Council (CELAM). *See* CELAM
Lehmann, Karl, 245
Lehmann, Paul, 55, 69
Liberalism, 21, 22-26, 36-37
Liberation and salvation, 175-206
Liberation
  biblical support for, 247-48
  ecclesiology of, 241-74
  goals of, 99
Liberation theology
  acceptance in Latin America, 10-11
  basis of, 134-36

Catholicism and, 11
  christology, 149, 207-40
  economics of, 91
  European influence, 35-52, 115-17
  hermeneutics of, 143-59
  in Latin America, 113-28
  Marxism and, 46-52, 152-53
  natural sciences in, 147-48
  politics and, 12
  Scriptural view, 142-43, 145-46, 150-52, 189-190, 250-251
  seminaries, 115-18
  sociology of, 140-42
  theological response to, 279-80
  theology of, 131-59
Lorscheider, Aloisio, 98
Love, 148, 228-29

Maqueo, Roberto Oliveros, 100
Marcuse, Herbert, 47-48, 72
Marxism, 71, 102-3, 118, 125, 138-39, 150, 156, 197, 215
  and Bible, 156
  effect on ISAL, 55-57
  influence on Biblical interpretation, 158
  liberation theology and, 28, 46-52, 152-53
Mater et Magistra, 89-90
Metz, J. B., 44-45
Miranda, José Porfirio, 50-51, 152-59, 176
Missionary theology for Latin America, 286
Modernism, 36
Moltmann, Jürgen, 41-44, 46-47, 133, 197, 289

Nonviolence, 108-9, 228-29

Odell, Luis E., 64
Oppression, 18-20, 59-60

Pacem in Terris, 89, 91-93
Padilla, C. René, 80-81, 145, 158-
    59, 286
Pastoral theology for Latin Amer-
    ica, 283
Political humanism, 72-74
Political options of church, 264-
    67
Pope John Paul II, 110-11, 278
Pope, John XXIII, 83-84, 89-93
Pope, Leo XIII, 88
Pope Paul VI, 93-97, 109-10
Populorum progressio, 94-99, 202
Positivism, 23
Poverty, 9, 26, 116, 121, 123, 132,
    140, 245-47, 254-58
Praxis, 136-37
Predestination, 186
Prophetic denunciation, 258-62
Protestantism in Latin America,
    22-23

Quiroz, Arana, 78

Rahner, Karl, 180-81, 208, 216
Ratzinger, Joseph, 278
Redaction criticism, 211
Resurrection of Jesus, 150, 223
Revelation, 151, 194
Revolution, 30-31, 96
Roman Catholic Church. *See* Ca-
    tholicism
Ruchs, Ernst, 39
Rycrofft, W. Stanley, 65

Salvation, 123, 124, 126, 197-204,
    254
    creation and, 184-85
    liberation and, 175-206
    universal, 85, 179-182, 242-44
Santa Ana, Julio de, 54, 61-62, 66-
    67

Schaull, Richard, 68-69
Schillebeeckx, Edward, 212-14
Scripture, 142-43, 146-47, 150-
    52
    authority of, 250-51
    inspiration of, 142-43
    ISAL view of, 74, 78-80
    liberation theology view, 145-
      46, 189-90
Secular ecumenism, 249
Segundo, Juan Luis, 120, 124, 159,
    182-83, 192, 195, 200, 289
Seminaries, role in liberation the-
    ology, 115-18
Shaull, Richard, 62, 64
Sin, 154, 176-77
Sobrino, John, 149-52, 210, 214-
    15, 220-24, 226, 228, 229-32
Social justice, 155
Social radicalism, 71-72
Social responsibility, 65, 88-89
Social revolution 121-24
Social salvation, 175-78
Socialism, 23-24, 106-7, 266-67
Stott, John R. W., 62

Textual criticism, 210-14
Theology, 140-42
    of revolution, 80-81
Torres, Camilo, 75, 103-5, 268
Trujillo, Alfonso Lopez, 98, 99, 241
Tschuy, Theo, 63

Underdevelopment, 132, 140
Unity of Christ, 251-54
Unity of church, 248
Universalism, 84-88. *See also* Sal-
    vation, universal
Utopia, 195-97, 200-201

Vatican II, 83-88, 90, 243
Violence, 267-72

World Council of Churches, 61-63

Scripture Index

Genesis
1:28   185
18:17-22   157

Exodus
3:18   192
4:23   192
5:1   192

Deuteronomy
4:34-35   192

Isaiah
43:1   185
44:24   185
53   233
55:4   185

Ezekiel
20:5-9   192

Hosea
12:9   192

13:4   192

Matthew
5:13-16   247
11:27   220
11:28   256
16:16   218
16:17   218
16:24   289
27:42   231
28:18-20   254, 286

Mark
10:35-45   225, 227

Luke
13:32   225
24:45-46   227

John
1:11-13   287
3:16   254
3:36   248

6:37   256
7:17   151
10:30   220
10:36   220
10:38   220
12:8   27
12:32   182
14:6   248
14:15   150
17   247, 252
17:5   253
17:6   252
17:8   252, 253
17:9-10   252
17:11-17   252
17:18   252, 253
17:21   253
17:22   252
17:24   253
18:36   204

Acts
4:12   248

4:27-28	227	2 Corinthians		1 Timothy		
5:37	251	13:4	231	2:5	248	
11	288					
		Galatians		2 Timothy		
Romans		3:6-18	157	1:9	186	
1:15-18	158	3:27-28	253	3:14-17	279	
2:13-15	158	5:11	231			
2:26-29	158	6:14	231	James		
3:9-31	158			2:14-26	151	
3:10	158	Ephesians				
3:10-18	268	1:3-5	185	1 Peter		
3:23	257	1:3-14	186	1:19-20	227	
5:1-11	158	2:14-15	253	1:25	279	
10:8-13	158	3:17-18	150	2:9-10	247, 287	
14:12	262	4:1-16	253			
15:4	256, 261			2 Peter		
		Philippians		1:21	279	
1 Corinthians		3:18	231			
1:18	231, 251	Colossians		Jude		
2:1-2	231	1:13	287	3	286	
2:7	186					
12:13	253	2 Thessalonians		Revelation		
15:3-5	231	1:3-10	248	1:6	287